DEDICATION

To my wife Marsha
for her love, encouragement, and support.

To my children, whom I love,
but especially Blake,
for his wonderful artistic contributions.

To the faithful in Christ,
so that they may be renewed in hope.

To those without Christ,
so that in seeing Him,
they will discover their greatest ally and friend.

REMEMBRANCE

*In loving memory of my father, Emil Vilhauer,
a man whose intelligence far exceeded his education.*

APPRECIATION

Special thanks is extended to the following individuals
for their assistance in the development and
completion of this book:
Rev. Kenneth and Tresa Ewerdt
Rev. Robert Flohrs
Prof. emeritus Dan and Marty Spiro

CONTENTS

- INTRODUCTION -

It became a world rent asunder; a world in chaos; a world filled with hatred and violence in their grossest forms; a world where for that moment in time evil seemed to reign supreme. It was a world that was collapsing, crumbling down around them. What were people thinking as they viewed this spectacle? We know now that some were laughing, some were even rejoicing in the streets, and some were staring blankly, transfixed in horrified unbelief. Yet others were crying and some wept uncontrollably. On that day, the range of emotions displayed was almost as disturbing as the scene itself, so grotesque in its magnitude. It was a day that, like only a few others in world history, would be remembered by so many not because it was such a great day but because of the great evil that was so boldly displayed that day. People would forever speak of it despairingly and regretfully to be sure, but speak of it, nonetheless, also out of necessity. So terrible was it, in fact, that it had to be remembered and dare never be forgotten.

What day was it? No, as evil as that day was, we are not speaking of September 11, 2001, but another day. It was a day lived out in death unlike any other in the history of the world. This world has seen many evil days but none quite like that one. One spring day in the early 1st century, around 30 AD, evil had its day but, thankfully, not the victory. It was the day the redemptive price was offered for the sins of the world. It was the day Jesus, the Son of God and Savior of the world, died

11

brutally by crucifixion at The Place of the Skull on Calvary's holy hill. It was Good Friday.

Why speak of it now? Why speak if it first, before we speak of September 11? It is simply because we cannot even begin to properly understand and deal with the events of Tuesday, 9-11, unless we first understand Good Friday, circa 30 AD. Without a proper understanding of Good Friday and the subsequent events of Easter morning, not only September 11, but every unfortunate occurrence suffered in life will lead us to despair and to a conclusion that life is nothing more than an endless evil. However, nothing could be further from the truth and Good Friday, coupled with Easter Sunday, gives us every reason to think otherwise.

On Tuesday, September 11, 2001, I, like so many citizens of the United States, awoke to a shocking spectacle unlike anything else we had ever seen before. We soon realized this was an event put on display not just for us but also for the citizenship of the whole world. Amazingly, manmade technology had been employed by evil to create the events of 9-11, and now manmade technology was being used to broadcast the events of that day so that the whole world could see. With us, they were destined to witness what evil had befallen the citizens of the most freedom-loving nation this world has ever known. It was pure terror, in the land of the free and the home of the brave, where terror like this had never before shown its ugly face.

We are now no more able to erase the pictures of 9-11 from our minds than we are able to reverse history and alter what happened on that spring-like pre-fall day. It is now a reality we will have to live with, much like the memories we have of Pearl Harbor and the assassination of President Kennedy in Dallas,

Texas. As we recall those days, we tend to ask questions like, "What were you doing the day President Kennedy was shot? Do you remember what you were doing the day Pearl Harbor came under attack?" It pains us to remember though and we don't like that feeling. It hurts. It hurts a great deal. It pains us so much that we may begin again to tear-up inside just like the day when we first heard the report. Remembering in this way almost makes us feel as though it's happening all over again, like a recurring nightmare. It is a pain, an evil, which in some ways never seems to want to go away. But then we remember, that day is no more. God in His love has brought us to a new point in time, a better time. He has seen us through the storm. His strength, His power, and His might have prevailed and we are at peace again.

So it was on 9-11. After the initial shock had worn off and the hours passed, offering time to recover and reflect upon what had happened, I began to think about the evil days this world has known. I kept going back, for some reason, to Good Friday, not Dallas, not Omaha beach, not Pearl Harbor or any other day of evil known in history—of which there are certainly many—but to Good Friday. I thought, "Perhaps now I feel something of what those first disciples felt as they watched Jesus slip away from their grasp and into death as He hung upon that gruesome tree." Then they must have felt great shock, horror, terror, bewilderment, and helplessness. While Jesus hung on the cross these were the senses of dread and the emotions of loss that hung upon their hearts and so weighed them down. What a day of evil that must have been for those first disciples. What a day of sorrow. What a day for weeping and great mourning. What brutal hatred and profound evil they witnessed. What unfathomable evil we have witnessed now.

Interestingly enough, though both events are centuries apart, the one still has so much to do with the other.

At this writing we are 3 months from the events of September 11, yet every time we see those pictures of buildings collapsing and airplanes disappearing into evil's deathtrap, everything returns and we continue to have difficulty believing what we are seeing. For the surviving friends and family of those who lost their lives that day, the shock's aftermath will be even greater, felt for years to come in ways that we can only hope to begin to understand. As a community of Christians, we want to reach out to them and help them in every way we can. There is indeed much work for us to do. It is an opportunity to let the love of Christ shine through us, as a light in a dark place, as we reach out to them with a hope that is certain, strong, and eternal. In great part, that is one of the purposes of this book.

Yet, in the aftermath of September 11, after all the pictures have been viewed over and over again; after so many political analyses have been expressed, then evaluated, then reevaluated, then restated and then expressed all over again; after we have heard from state leaders and religious leaders and entertainment leaders and some people we don't even want to regard as leaders; after we have read all our newspapers and magazines and watched all our television news and visited our web pages; after we have heard from our allies and even heard from our enemies; after all this that we have heard with our ears and seen with our eyes, if we have not yet taken the time to let God speak to us through His life-giving Word, then we have shut out from our lives the one who alone has the ability to give us understanding and meaning to properly deal with the events of 9-11.

May this be the primary purpose of this book: It offers an opportunity to sit down, shut off our TVs and radios, set aside the newspapers and editorial pages, move away from the information provided by the internet, and move closer to the information provided through God's Word for the ages. It is time we let Him speak to us and time for us to open our ears and listen. Take the time and you might be made more thankful than you could ever have imagined. You may just gain more knowledge and insight than you thought was ever possible. In fact, you might just come up with some answers for 9-11 that have tremendous meaning for your life and for the lives of others that have been devastatingly affected by the evil events of that day.

Let God speak to you for a while. Discover the wisdom He imparts and the blessings He has in store for you not just on good days, but the blessings He can impart for you even through the bad days that come. Jesus said, "He who has an ear to hear, let him hear." He invites you to take some time now to do just that and in so doing move from terror to triumph.

- CHAPTER ONE -

INSIGHT #1

The ultimate strategy of evil is to change our focus and redirect our view so that we see God Himself as the enemy, not sin or Satan.

Man Lost in Sin & Unbelief

We heard from a great many people after the September 11 tragedy. It wasn't long after the U.S. and British air strikes began in Afghanistan that we even heard from our enemy himself, Osama bin Laden, the man who will very likely go down in history as the instigator of the greatest terrorist attack the world has ever known. All indications were that his remarks, broadcast worldwide from a taped message, had been prepared even before the September 11 attacks. His words were jubilant yet seething with hatred for America. In part, he said,

> "I bear witness that there is no God but Allah and that Mohammed is his messenger. There is America, hit by God in one of its softest spots. Its greatest buildings were destroyed, thank God for that. There is America, full of fear from its north to its south, from its west to its east. Thank God for that.... They have

followed injustice. They supported the victim, the
oppressor over the innocent child. May God show
them his wrath and give them what they deserve."
- Osama bin Laden

I don't think any of us in America were completely surprised by his remarks. Most expected that such a despicable
act of evil would be matched with words that would not only
defend the dreadful deed, but also rejoice over its accomplish-
ment. It is a living picture of man lost in sin and unbelief. It is
a picture of evil venting through the mouth of man in ways
that we often forget is possible when the love of God in Christ
does not rule in the heart of man. However, we need to take
note of it well and not forget, for it is a picture of what man can
be apart from Christ. It is a picture of what we too could be
under different circumstances.

It may remind you of the bully you knew back in elemen-
tary school, "Yea, I hit him and I hit him good too, and I'm glad
I did." But it's a bit worse than that, isn't it? Perhaps it's more
like the words Cain spoke so arrogantly before his Creator after he had committed the first murder by taking his brother
Abel's life. It too was a despicable act of evil against an innocent victim. Yet, when the Lord came to Cain and asked him,
"Where is your brother Abel?" Cain could still find it in his
heart to proclaim before God Himself, unabashedly and sar-
castically, "I don't know. Am I my brother's keeper?" (Genesis
4:9). Do you hear the anger, the hatred, and the bitterness in
his voice? This is what sin can do when it gains control of a
person's life.

When sin and unbelief exist in tandem, the results can be
terrible and brutal to behold. Yes, for Cain, it was just as the

Lord had warned him, "... sin is crouching at the door; it desires to have you, but you must master it" (Genesis 4:7).

We often forget that it is the power of faith at work within us that holds the sin within us in check. Faith is a great gift from God. It guides us and strengthens us in the most trying and tempting of circumstances so that sin does not rule in our lives. However, Cain chose to ignore God's loving warning and sin did take hold of him. He let it become his master and we see the terrible result. It has happened to Osama bin Laden too and we who live today see once again the dreadful consequences of sin's continued rule in the heart of unbelieving man.

Man Out of Focus & Unprepared

However, sin's effect is much more widespread than just in those who are lost in it. Its strength can even be seen in those who have been found. To be sure, in Christ, we have been delivered from the eternal effects of sin, but we have not been completely freed from its power while we live out our lives in this world. It still threatens us. It still wants to rule over us. It still wants to change us back to what we were before faith came and if it cannot do that, it will try to alter our view, even while we live in faith. Sin can do strange things to us still, even while we live out our lives as God's dear children.

Did you ever stand up real fast after bending over for a while, maybe after working on something that was very low to the ground? You know what happens. Sometimes you get up so quickly that you get dizzy, your eyes are unable to focus, and you feel like you might pass out! Why does this happen? Your eyes are the same. Your body is the same. No one knocked you over the head when you stood up. Certainly, a doctor could provide a detailed medical explanation for this phenomenon, but we all know that it happens with a sudden change in movement. The body reacts unexpectedly as though it was unprepared for the shocking change in motion and position.

Something like that also can happen to us as Christians from time to time, especially in times of stress like on 9-11. On that day, evil seemed to come not just knocking at our door but burst into our own living room without even the slightest warning. It was sudden; it was unexpected; it was shocking; and it caused some in the Christian community to lose focus for a time. Hopefully, that focus has since been restored. If it has not, it needs to be restored, and soon. As ambassadors of Christ, we cannot afford to be going out into the world proclaiming a message of eternal importance, if our spiritual focus has been altered by the sin that still infects us too. If our spiritual focus is lost, the message we share will not be accurately conveyed either. This is something we cannot afford to let happen.

It is, therefore, an unfortunate circumstance, but nonetheless a circumstance to be acknowledged and corrected, that in the aftershock of September 11, even some members of the Christian community lost their focus. They were led, by the sin that is present in us all, to say some things that simply should not have been said. Sin can do that to people, even Christian people. That is why God in His Word so often encourages us to be on the alert and ready for anything in life that might come upon us. We need to understand that when the day of evil comes, if we are not in focus, we will not respond appropriately. We will not be the beacon of light that Christ intended us to be.

So it happened, after the September 11 tragedy, that some in the Christian community reacted entirely inappropriately with words that should have never been uttered. Some found it desirable to point the finger at others in our nation and find in their immoral lifestyles ample reason for the evil that came upon us. Others found it reasonable to blame liberal politicians whom they blamed for having thrown God out of our public institutions with the help of our federal courts. They said God was mocked. They said God is angry and now we have this great tragedy as a just reward. Abortionists were blamed. The ACLU and other organizations like them were found partially responsible. Some passionately declared that feminists, gays, and lesbians had a role to play in this event. Still others implied that God was simply doing the gentlemanly thing and turning His back on us after the many times we had turned our backs on Him.

I believe the majority within the Christian community grieved when these words were spoken after September 11 and rightly so. I know I resented them. Those words were simply not representative of the Christian community as a whole. What's wrong with them? Many things, but most importantly, for our study, they represent an improper focus and mistaken Christian perspective. If there are Christians out there who truly do think this way, they need to carefully review their position and pray the Holy Spirit to implant the rule of Christ's law of love more firmly in their hearts. Responses like these do not flow from the loving spirit of the gospel of our Lord but from a harsh, angry, and bitter misapplication of God's law.

As Christians, we cannot establish harmony when we are speaking dissention. We cannot bring comfort when we are speaking hate and we cannot bring unity in the midst of such tragedy when we employ such divisive rhetoric. We cannot advance the cause of Christ when our words do not reflect the one most basic tenet He has given us to follow in our dealings with all men and women, "Love one another."

For now, let this suffice: sin even affects Christians in strange ways and the sudden reality of dealing with gross unexpected evil can sometimes even send our heads a-spinning. We, however, need to strive to keep our perspective. Only then can we hope to prove ourselves worthy servants of the saving gospel Christ has entrusted to our care. After all, God Himself encourages us through the pen of the Apostle Paul, "But you, keep your head in all situations" (II Timothy 4:5). We need to do that and make sure our words do not ring so much like Osama bin Laden, the enemy who attacked us.

In this case, a similarity exists that is unfortunate. He calls us "infidels" and we call others "pagans." He says, "May God show them his wrath," and we say, "God is mad." He points the finger at us saying, "They have followed injustice," and we point the finger at one another saying, "You helped to make this happen."

How terribly, terribly wrong. As children of a loving Savior, we need to tame our tongue at such times. We need to be guided by the words of James in his epistle, "With the tongue we praise our Lord and Father, and with it we curse men, who have been made in God's likeness. Out of the same mouth come praise and cursing. My brothers, this should not be" (James 3:9, 10).

Man in Confusion
I don't know what I would have done if I had been near ground zero on September 11. What would you have done? What would you have said? Where would you have hidden? Where would you have run? The confusion and hysteria we all witnessed on our television screens that day was very disturbing and unsettling. What an ordeal those present had to suffer.

The confusion, though, didn't end soon. In fact, it lingers

even today. It was not long after the reality of the day's events began to sink in that a new kind of confusion emerged. It often happens at times of personal tragedy like this. It was a mental confusion, an emotional confusion, and a spiritual confusion that began to set in. Those questions we so often hear at times of great and unexpected loss were raised this time too, but now by many more, all at the same time. How could this happen? Where was God? Why do bad things happen to good people? If God is good, how could He permit such a thing to happen? How can I believe in a God who allows such evil? Has God abandoned us? Has God left us? Is God punishing us? Where do we go from here? Should we seek peace? Should we seek revenge? Should we seek justice? Should we retaliate? Should we reconcile? What do we do now? Where is God?

The confusion is obvious in all of these questions and in many more like them that have been asked since that day. However, as I followed the news reports and stories of life and death after 9-11, I came across one statement in the newspaper that defined the confusion and the terror of that Tuesday more than did anything else that I found. It too was one of those defining moments in my life for it struck with such force when I read it, that I will forever remember where I was and what I was doing at that moment in time.

I was sitting in the family room at home, reading the day's newspaper while at the same time watching the news unfold with the television turned on. I came across an article about one New York firefighter who had survived the day but had lost many friends in the attack. He was now left with the seemingly endless and frightful task of rescue and recovery. The problem—and what was so troubling to me—was that this firefighter, though a physical survivor, had not survived 9-11. When

asked to share his thoughts about all that had recently transpired, he was quoted as uttering these chilling words,

> "If this was a test from God, I failed because what-
> ever faith I had before is gone."

When I read that, I let out an audible moan and felt my
heart sink low. If any question or any statement defined the
spiritual confusion and terror of 9-11 it was that one. It disturbed me and I felt deeply saddened as if a dear friend was
now no longer with us. At that moment, he became, for me, the
latest and perhaps the most significant victim of 9-11. Indeed,
he too was a victim, a victim of the most terrible kind. I do not
know for sure what faith this was that he said he lost that day,
but I assumed it was Christian faith, faith in Christ, faith in
the saving God as his protector and Savior. As sure as hundreds had physically died that awful day, his confession now
told a story that he too was now dead, spiritually dead. I had to
fight off tears. It was that sad for me to hear.

If any one story gave me justified reason for writing this
book, it was that one. The story needs to be repeated how God
is still with us in the midst of all the confusion. The story needs
to be told that we dare not abandon the spiritual struggle when
the day of evil comes. The story needs to be shared anew of
how we can move from terror to triumph even now. The story
needs to be uttered confidently so that maybe this man will be
restored to faith again. The story needs to be communicated as
clearly as possible so that others will not suffer the same fate.

God Speaks to Us

Now it is time to let God speak to us. After hearing from so many others, it is time to be quiet for a while, open our ears, and just listen attentively to God's voice. He has told us much that can help us at times like these. We have so much to choose from, but let's start at a place where He gets right to the point.

We are dealing with a great evil on 9-11. What has God said to us about this evil that was exposed with such force and such terror on that frightful day? This is what He said through the pen of the Apostle Paul nearly 2000 years ago. Here is where we will launch our study and where God will begin to lead us to triumph over the terror of 9-11.

> "Finally, be strong in the Lord and in his mighty power. Put on the full armor of God so that you can take your stand against the devil's schemes. For our struggle is not against flesh and blood, but against the rulers, against the authorities, against the powers of this dark world and against the spiritual forces of evil in the heavenly realms. Therefore put on the full armor of God, so that when the day of evil comes, you may be able to stand your ground, and after you have done everything to stand. Stand firm then, with the belt of truth buckled around your waist, with the breastplate of righteousness in place, and with your feet fitted with the readiness that comes from the gospel of peace. In addition to all this, take up the shield of faith, with which you can extinguish all the flaming arrows of the evil one. Take the helmet of salvation and the sword of the Spirit, which is the Word of God. And pray in the Spirit on all occasions with all kinds of prayers and requests. With this in mind, be alert and always keep on praying for all the

saints."

- Ephesians 6:10-18

Oh yes, "when the day of evil comes." If in our lifetimes ever a bell rang out most loudly and most true announcing such a day, it was on September 11, 2001. The problem is, evil does not always come so loudly. Sometimes it comes very quietly, very deceptively, and very cleverly. Its desire, however, is always the same, our ruin in any and every way possible.

The Apostle Paul wrote these words at a time in his life when a great evil had befallen him and many other early Christians. He wrote these words from prison in Rome. You see, in the first century Roman world, Christianity was not a legal religion of the Roman state. Members of *The Way* (as it was referred to then), followers of this crucified Jew by the name of Jesus Christ, could therefore be subject to fines, loss of property, imprisonment, and even death for promoting their religious views. It was for this very reason that Paul was imprisoned in Rome. Tradition has it that this mission activity eventually led to his death by decapitation.

While Paul was in Rome, he grew increasingly concerned with the great struggle many Christians faced in proclaiming the saving gospel of Jesus Christ. Already many from *The Way* had suffered loss of property, had been imprisoned and some had even been put to death for their convictions. However, it almost appears that Paul knew somehow that the worst had not yet come. Indeed, the great persecution of Christians had not yet reached its peak. Very soon, under the reign of Nero, many more Christians would die and evil would feast off the blood of these first century saints. But even if Paul didn't know this to be soon in coming, God knew, and so He led Paul to write these words to fellow Christians at the church in Ephesus. However, they are words for the ages and certainly ring just as true, with tremendous meaning, for us today.

When the day of evil comes, God tells us through His servant Paul, you must do four important things:

- **KNOW THE ENEMY**, get him in focus and be alert to his schemes,
- **FIND STRENGTH** in God's mighty power & stand,
- **ARM YOURSELF** for the struggle with God's gifts,
- **PRAY** in the Spirit for everyone & keep praying!

I cannot help but wonder if that firefighter in New York knew these words of the Apostle Paul. Did he use them to guide him through this great day of evil that came upon him, his family, and his friends? "If this was a test from God, I failed because whatever faith I had before is gone." Does he know who the enemy was who attacked us on 9-11? Is he focused in upon that enemy? Has he looked to God as a source of great strength and comfort at this difficult time, or has he mistakenly looked upon God as weak and God as the enemy? Has he armed himself for the struggle with the armaments God would give him so that he might stand victorious? Is he praying as God would have him pray, for himself, for his family, for his friends, for spouses & children who survive the tragic unexpected death of loved ones, for his nation, for his President, and for the soldiers in battle who now fight bravely to defend our national liberties? Or, are all these people and many more like them, now left without the power of his prayers because they no longer rise up to God as a fragrant offering?

I pray for him, and all other Christians need to pray for

him and others like him, so that God in Christ would lead him
out of this abyss of sorrow, hopelessness, and unbelief; out of
all the tragedy he suffered on September 11, and restore him
to his more meaningful and powerful role as one of Christ's
productive servants. He can be renewed and restored again to
his special place in God's kingdom of believers. If that happens, he will come to know who the enemy actually is. This is
something all of us need to know, if we don't already. That brings
us to our first insight drawn from these words of the Apostle
Paul.

INSIGHT #1

The ultimate strategy of evil is to change our focus
and redirect our view so that we see God Himself as
the enemy, not sin or Satan.

Paul wrote, ". . . take your stand against the devil's schemes.
For our struggle is not against flesh and blood, but against the
rulers, against the authorities, against the powers of this dark
world and against the spiritual forces of evil in the heavenly
realms. . . ." (Ephesians 6:12).

Isn't it interesting that, though Paul was imprisoned by
Romans, he does not write of the Roman people as his enemy!
Isn't it interesting, that even though he suffered at the hands
of his fellow Jews—Paul himself was Jewish—he does not write
of the Jewish people as his enemy! No, Paul was always more
focused than to do something as foolish as that. God had blessed
him with tremendous knowledge, tremendous wisdom, and a
tremendous gift of faith that guided him unswervingly right
straight through even the most troubling of times. In this section of Ephesians, God uses him again to guide us through this

day of evil we are in, just as He used him to guide those first century Christians when their day of evil came.

Who is our enemy today? Who is the source of all this evil? If Paul didn't blame the Romans or his fellow Jews for his troubles then who should we rightly blame today; Osama bin Laden, al-Qaida, all of Islam, part of Islam, pagans, infidels, abortionists, feminists, gays, lesbians, the ACLU, the FFA, the FHA, whom?

If we do not close our ears, and if we do not rant and rave so loudly so that we are unable to hear God speaking to us, then we will know whom the enemy is, for God is telling us. It is not a physical enemy. This fight is "not against flesh and blood." Yet it is against "rulers" and "authorities" and "powers of this dark world." Does it sound spooky? It should. We should all sit up and take notice with eyes burst wide open, for we are warring against an enemy that we cannot even see. We fight against "spiritual forces of evil in the heavenly realms." No, that does not mean in heaven, God's dwelling place, but it does mean here, on earth, above ground, right where we live!

Put away the notion that Satan and his forces of evil are locked up in some fiery hot dungeon somewhere deep inside the earth's core. For too long this enemy has been portrayed in the most comical of terms with his red cape, stubby horns, pointed goatee, and long arrowhead tipped tail. We dressed our kids in his comical likeness for Halloween and treated him as if he were some make-believe comic book figure rather than the Creator's archenemy. It would be wise for us to stop doing this and take him and God's warnings to us about him far more seriously. Satan loves a good joke too and none more than the joke that he doesn't exist. It makes his work so much easier.

Just as September 11 is no joke, this enemy is no joke. Paul experienced his power as he lived out his ministry. We experience his power in our ministries as well and we saw his great strength unleashed on Tuesday, September 11. That day alone shows us how alive, well, and active Satan is. His forces of evil are right here among us.

If we need further evidence, we need not look very far at all. God has revealed to us that He is spirit and not flesh and blood like us, except in the person of His Son, Jesus Christ. We seem to have no trouble accepting this idea, that God is real and exists as spirit, but for some reason many people have trouble accepting the reality that Satan and his army is not flesh and blood, but spirit. Why is that? God has revealed this to us for our good, to aid us in our struggle, so that we might see clearly that we do not fight against "flesh and blood" but against "spiritual forces of evil." If we know that, and believe it to be true, we will then have taken the first step in the triumphant victory that will be ours over the terror of evil.

Know the Enemy: Satan and His Host

Do you remember how our President approached the disaster when it struck? I'm sure there was a period of time when things were quite hectic and chaotic. That's bound to happen under such traumatic circumstances. But in the face of it all our Commander in Chief remained focused, focused on this nation, focused on the welfare of its citizens, focused on their physical, emotional and spiritual well-being, focused upon the safety of their elected leaders. Then he began to focus in upon the enemy. As the Commander in Chief, he knew this event meant our nation was at war but the important question was, with whom? Therefore, he focused next upon identifying that enemy. This is not a profound thing. The point is that it simply is the right thing to do, the next necessary thing to do.

We need to approach the spiritual aspects of this struggle in the same way. The problem, for some strange reason, is that we don't always do that next very right and very necessary thing, and by failing to do so, we commit other even greater spiritual mistakes. We need to do just what President Bush did. We need to get the enemy in focus, know who and what he is, where he is, how he operates, and what his objectives are. How can we expect to defeat him and how can we expect to walk away victorious, if we don't even know against whom the battle must be waged? The good news is that God provides us with what we need to know. He has already identified what kind of enemy he is, a spiritual enemy, but He reveals so much more to us. This is first and foremost. We must KNOW THE ENEMY.

There is much that we can know about our great enemy, the source of all evil, by the names used for him. From the Hebrew comes the name Satan meaning an "enemy, adversary, someone who opposes." He is the one who is our great enemy and God's enemy too. He is our great adversary. He is the one who opposes God and opposes us, especially when our desire to remain in good standing with our Creator is detected by him. Peter described him in his first epistle in this way:

> "Your enemy the devil prowls around like a roaring
> lion looking for someone to devour. Resist him, stand-
> ing firm in the faith because you know that your
> brothers throughout the world are undergoing the
> same kind of sufferings."
> - I Peter 5:8, 9

This enemy would devour us, wholly, completely. He is on the prowl, always watching, always lurking in the shadows, always attentive to find some weakness that he might exploit. When it is found, he pounces, attacks, and destroys.

Just this morning I read an article in the newspaper about a man hiking in the mountains of Arizona. He described his harrowing experience with a mountain lion that was stalking him. He'd ventured unarmed into the wilderness that day scouting for elk. As he walked, something caught his attention out of the corner of his eye but just as suddenly, it was gone. A short time passed and then there it was again but this time closer to his position. Still he could not focus in on what was there. Then suddenly he heard what he described as a growling/hissing sound. He looked, and the lion was there. He said he had to fight a tremendous desire within himself to run back to his truck that was, by this time, about 300 yards in the distance. His only hope was to stand his ground and resist as best he could.

He waved his arms wildly and yelled at the creature in an attempt to make himself appear as formidable an opponent as possible. He saw, not far from his feet, a large decaying tree root exposed above the ground, so he broke it off, swung it in the direction of the 150 pound cat but it only seemed to make the beast more vicious and it growled and hissed even more. Now the temptation to turn and run was almost impossible to resist, but he held his ground. In a low to the ground crouching position, the lion continued to advance ever closer, relentlessly stalking. Now only 20 ft separated them. In desperation, this man bravely lunged forward, swinging his club and yelling as loud as he could. Suddenly, with one last hiss, the huge cat backed down, took a few paces back and then suddenly disappeared into the brush. There was no time lost in making an immediate beeline back to the truck but the whole time this man kept looking about him to see if the cat was still in pursuit. He never saw the animal again.

We are not so fortunate. Do you really think that Satan will ever let a day pass in which you are not watched, stalked, and pursued? Be sure of it, "your enemy, the devil prowls around like a roaring lion looking" for *you* to devour. So "resist him." But how? Certainly not by running, because he's always in pursuit, and when you run, you're no longer facing him. You no longer can see where he is, what he's up to, or where he's going to come from next. You are then vulnerable prey.

No, "resist him," Peter writes by "standing firm." Hold your ground! Keep him in focus! Stand fearless, *firm in faith!* For you know that you are not the only one he pursues. He has pursued others but they stood their ground, they held to their faith, and they triumphed. So too can you, all of us can, even after 9-11. Don't let the enemy destroy and devour you!

From the Greek we know him as devil, meaning "slanderer, liar." To those who rejected Christ and sought his death, Jesus said,

> "You belong to your father, the devil, and you want to carry out your father's desire. He was a murderer from the beginning, not holding to the truth, for there is no truth in him. When he lies, he speaks his native language, for he is a liar and the father of lies."
> - John 8:44

What is Jesus talking about here? How was the devil "a murderer from the beginning?" Go back to the third chapter of

Genesis and the fall of man into sin. The devil was there pursuing, stalking, seeking to devour. His methods employed then are the same methods employed today: deceit, lies, falsehood. "Did God really say?" he asked Eve. "You will not surely die," he lied. "God knows that when you eat of it your eyes will be opened," he falsely asserted. Adam and Eve believed the lie. They fell prey to Satan's attack. Death entered the world. In accomplishing this, the devil, the great liar, had effectively brought about the murder of the entire human race.

He did it by inventing lies. This is native to him, Jesus tells us. Wherever there is great evil, expect to find great lies. The lies of Satan were wholeheartedly accepted in the hearts of ruthless, evil men on 9-11. We see the dreadful result. This was not God's doing. This was the devil, Satan in his most pure form, at his best, employing his host of followers, fellow deceived and fellow liars, to do his bidding. The result was the same as in the beginning: murder, death, and destruction. From day one to September 11, 2001, nothing has changed. Today he remains in pursuit.

How many of Satan and his host are there? We seem to argue amongst ourselves these days as to whether or not there is such a thing as demon possession. I don't know why. We have plenty of accounts where Jesus miraculously cast out evil spirits. For every Christian, that question should be answered in the affirmative and without hesitation. If not, we would have to conclude that Jesus, our Savior, was some kind of lunatic to believe he could actually do such a thing. In one account, from Mark's Gospel, a man suddenly rushed up to Jesus when he saw Him coming in the distance. This man shouted at the top of his voice,

"'What do you want with me, Jesus, Son of the Most High God? Swear to God that you won't torture me!' For Jesus was saying to him, 'Come out of this man you evil spirit!' Then Jesus asked him, 'What is your name?' 'My name is Legion,' he replied, for we are many.'"
- Mark 5:7-9

Indeed, "we are many." Our struggle is not against just one single entity but an army, a host. As Paul wrote in Ephesians, we war against a multitude, "spiritual forces of evil." Paul wrote with this truth in mind. These spiritual forces at work in the world themselves acknowledge that they are many. They are either angels of great power who, with Satan, rebelled against God, or men and women who have fallen to Satan's deceiving trickery, and now work to carry out his evil desires. Either way, they represent the host, the many, that we now face daily.

Satan and His Host: Their Schemes
How do they operate? What are their objectives, their methods, their schemes? First of all, we learn that a primary objective is to **create spiritual blindness**. The Apostle Paul wrote,

"The god of this age has blinded the minds of unbelievers, so that they cannot see the light of the gospel of the glory of Christ, who is the image of God."
- II Corinthians 4:4

Young people today have an expression, "Duh." That's all it is, just, "Duh." You've probably heard them say it. Maybe you say it once and a while too. It is kind of catchy. "Duuuhhh...

helllooo! Is anybody in there?" Or like in, "Duh. What do you think? Get real!" (That one helps if you say it with a little bit of a valley-girl accent.) Or how about this one, "Duuuhhh, dude." It actually fits with a whole bunch of things. But what does it mean?! It means, "Duh. Are you blind?" It means, "Duh. Can't you see that?" It means, "Duh. Don't you get it?"

"The god of this age has blinded the minds of unbelievers so that" duuuhhh! Get it now? For those of you who still—duh—don't get it, that's OK. Putting the colloquial paraphrasing aside, Paul finishes the thought for us in clearer verbiage, "so that they cannot see the light of the gospel of the glory of Christ, who is the image of God."

Light, truth, knowledge, wisdom, understanding, freedom—none of these can be gained where there is spiritual blindness. We are born spiritually blind. It is our enemy's great objective to keep us from seeing Christ as our great healer. It is our enemy's great desire to keep us enslaved to sin by keeping us spiritually blind. He does this also with his many lies and deceitful tricks.

Another objective of the forces of evil is to **entrap us and take us captive**. When Paul wrote to his young brother in Christ, Timothy, he wanted to give him some guidance on how he should conduct himself as a young pastor and minister of God. He told him that it wouldn't always be easy because people would oppose him and the work he would do. Then Paul instructed him,

> "Those who oppose him he must gently instruct, in
> the hope that God will grant them repentance lead-
> ing them to a knowledge of the truth, and that they
> will come to their senses and escape from the trap of

the devil, who has taken them captive to do his will."
- II Timothy 2:25-26

What does this say about the events of 9-11? It tells us that, unfortunately, it is too late for those who piloted their hijacked planes into the Twin Towers, the Pentagon, and the grassy fields of Pennsylvania to "come to their senses." The master of evil had set a trap for them. They followed, did his will, and are now eternally in captive to him—a trap from which they will never escape.

Satan and his host will also attempt to **redirect people's thoughts against their Creator**. In the book of Job, we have a very interesting picture of the ruler of this age coming before God Himself in order to incite God against man. In this case, it was to incite God against His faithful servant Job. He began by challenging the Lord's high opinion of Job.

> "'Does Job fear God for nothing?' Satan replied. 'Have you not put a hedge around him and his household and everything he has? You have blessed the work of his hands, so that his flocks and herds are spread throughout the land. But stretch out your hand and strike everything he has, and he will surely curse you to your face.'"
> - Job 1:9-11

What a treacherous deceiver Satan shows himself to be. He will either incite God to act against man or incite man to act against God. He loves nothing more than to challenge our faithfulness so that we end up cursing God for the gloom and sorrow that, in fact, Satan himself brings to those who live on the earth. Fortunately, God is not victimized by his lies but we too often fall so easily into his trap and blame God for the evil to which Satan alone is party.

It is the desire of Satan and his host to **steal the word from the heart of all people**. In His parable of the sower, Jesus reveals the meaning of the seed that fell along the path.

> "Those along the path are the ones who hear, and then the devil comes and takes away the word from their hearts, so that they cannot believe and be saved."
> - Luke 8:12

"Faith comes by hearing the message" (Romans 10:17). If the message, the seed of the saving gospel, is snatched up and taken away from the lost before it can even take root in them and grow, then there can be no faith. With no faith, there is no life, and no salvation.

Nations that do not live under the freedoms that we treasure here, especially the freedom of religion, are nations that often prohibit the free advance of the Christian gospel. So if we, in such circumstances, see men and women coming from such nations without faith, without the peace that comes from knowing Christ as the resurrected Lord, and without the love that guides those who are servants of Christ, it is to a great extent Satan's doing. It is his will to both steal the word from the heart of man and to **hinder the spread of the gospel**. He did this very thing against the Apostle Paul. This was not God's doing. This was not God putting these great obstacles in Paul's way as he worked to bring a change in people's hearts through the proclamation of the saving gospel. It was Satan's doing.

"For we wanted to come to you—certainly I, Paul, did,
again and again—but Satan stopped us."
- I Thessalonians 2:18

It naturally follows that if Satan and his host will do all
they can to hinder the spread of the gospel, that they will find
something to also take its place. To this end, they **promote
their own lies and false doctrine.** Paul wrote to Timothy,
his brother in Christ,

"The Spirit clearly says that in the later times some
will abandon the faith and follow deceiving spirits
and things taught by demons. Such teachings come
through hypocritical liars, whose consciences have
been seared as with a hot iron."
- I Timothy 3:16

I suppose 9-11 was a wake-up call for us to this truth. We
need to look and see what is being taught in the world today.
There are teachings in some religious circles that are so evil in
their very nature, so far from God's principles of love by which
He would have us live, so removed from everything that in
God's sight is good, pure, and holy, that they can only have
their origin in the evil one. Those who follow such hatred are
not of God, for their consciences bear witness to the sad state
of their lives. As Paul wrote, it appears as though they no longer
have a conscience and that they no longer feel anything for
their neighbor. Their "consciences have been seared as with a
hot iron." Their soul's nerve endings of empathy, love, and compassion have been destroyed. They are now numb to the evil in
which they live.

Such teachings do not come only from that which is of the
occult, or witchcraft, or Satanism. They exist there, to be sure,
but they can be found elsewhere. Whether it is the suicidal
acts of a Jim Jones or the blind obedience from followers of
Osama bin Laden, Satan and his host will implant the seed of
evil destructive teachings wherever they can. To take a position that all the religions of the world are essentially the same,
and that the teachings of one are just as valid as another, is
folly, pure and simple.

As children of God, set free from sin through the truth of
the gospel of Jesus Christ, we can never accept such a position
as that. It cuts at the very core of that which keeps us spiritually whole and right with God. To believe otherwise would be
for us to abandon what we know is right and true in Christ.

So far, we have seen the work of our great enemy primarily
in a spiritual light, but there is a physical side as well. Our
enemy does not hesitate to **bring physical harm to mankind** if it will also serve his purposes, and it often does.

One day, while teaching in the synagogue, Jesus saw a severely crippled woman who suffered immensely from her condition. It was a Sabbath, a day set-aside for worship, study,
and prayer. There were those, particularly from the legalistic
minded scribes and Pharisees, who felt that even to heal someone on the Sabbath was work, and therefore a violation of the
holy day. Nevertheless, when Jesus saw her, He called her forward to Him and immediately healed her. The synagogue ruler
criticized Jesus for healing on the Sabbath. This was work!
How dare He do such a thing! Jesus didn't hesitate to point out
to them their hypocrisy. They would castigate Him for this healing, yet they themselves would, on the Sabbath, untie a don-
key from its stall and lead it out to water. That was work too!

Jesus replied,

> "Then why should not this woman, a daughter of
> Abraham, whom Satan has kept bound for eighteen
> long years, be set free on the Sabbath day from what
> bound her?"
> - Luke 13:16

Setting aside the many other lessons that could be taught from this miracle, note whom Jesus said had held this woman in this state for more than eighteen years. It was Satan, the great enemy of God and all mankind. In Ephesians Paul wrote that our struggle is against the "powers of this dark world." We have a tendency to forget about the great power that is possessed by Satan and his army of demonic spirits. Here, Jesus revealed that Satan's grip had kept this woman physically bound as a cripple for years. This was not God's doing but Satan's. In Job, we find the same root cause.

> "So Satan went out from the presence of the Lord
> and afflicted Job with painful sores from the soles of
> his feet to the top of his head."
> - Job 2:7

Job's great suffering was brought about not by God, but by Satan himself! I suspect that there are often times when we "credit," or perhaps I should say "blame," God for many kinds of misfortunes that come upon us in life, when in fact the "credit"—the "blame"—should be directed at Satan. But he wouldn't want us to think such a nasty thing of him, would he? Then again, would he want us to think such a nasty thing of

God? Ah yes, and there's the rub.

It has always both confounded and amazed me that so often when a "natural" disaster strikes, a tornado sweeps through a community or a sudden flood takes the lives of dozens of innocent souls, that we speak of it as an "act of God." Should we? Do we know that to be accurate? Maybe it isn't "natural" at all. Maybe, just maybe, we should give Satan his due. He is, after all, a fallen archangel. He has power of which we know very little. Do we really think he's just going to relax on the sidelines, having been cast out of heavenly dwellings, and let his power rest? That is unlikely. The reaction of evil is to retaliate, to act, not to lie down listless and belly up like a wounded puppy. Our enemy is no kitty cat. That is evidently clear from what we witnessed in our horror on 9-11.

Then, of course, the great purpose of Satan is **to tempt mankind to sin**. The disciple Peter, also known as Simon, learned that lesson well. At one time, after the disciples had been arguing among themselves as to which of them was the greatest, Jesus turned to Peter and said,

> "Simon, Simon, Satan has asked to sift you as wheat. But I have prayed for you, Simon, that your faith may not fail. And when you have turned back, strengthen your brothers."
> - Luke 22:31, 32

Do you remember how Satan queried God regarding Job's faithfulness? From what Jesus is saying here, Satan was inquiring God about Peter as well. He is a busy one, isn't he? However, in this account, Jesus informed Peter exactly what Satan wanted to do to him, "sift (him) as wheat." It's what Satan wants to do with all of us, sift us, grind us up until there is nothing left but a fine dust, and then cast us to the wind. He wants to do such a number on us so that no matter what the device, no matter what the trick, no matter what the temptation, we're left far from God, either through total rebellion against Him or through total despair and hopelessness. He'll find a way to do it. We'll examine this issue with Peter in more detail in another chapter. It's an astounding story of terror and triumph.

Then there was Judas. How sad and how tragic was Judas' end. The enemy struck him a fatal blow. How did it happen? He didn't even see it coming. He wasn't properly focused.

> "The evening meal was served, and the devil had already prompted Judas Iscariot, son of Simon, to betray Jesus."
> - John 13:2

Of course, what is so sad about Judas is not just that he betrayed his Lord. The saddest part was his total despair that led him to commit suicide, in spite of the fact that forgiveness from Christ was there ready for him too. He didn't believe it. He wouldn't believe it. Satan had not only been successful in tempting him to betray the Son of God, but Satan had also very successfully tempted him to believe that his sin was too great to hope for pardon. Judas believed that his situation was beyond repair.

The fact is, Judas could have been saved too, but Satan, that vicious master of everything evil, led him to believe otherwise. That leads us to our other great enemy, our own sin. It is the enemy within.

Know the Enemy Within

How could anyone be so evil? How could anyone do such a thing and why? These were the kinds of questions people started to ask after it became evident that Tuesday, September 11, was no accident.

I once had a professor who said, "Never ask, 'How can a person commit such a sin?'" Over the years, I've tried as much as possible not to ask that question because I already know the answer, as every Christian should know. My professor spoke those words because the answer always lies within us. Look within.

We all know why sin happens. We feel it daily within our own being. We feel something crawling around inside of us wanting so much to get out, to express itself, to delight in its workings. We feel the desire to hate, to get even, to speak unkindly, to cheat, to curse, and to take advantage of others. We feel the desire to blame God, to blame spouse, to blame son or daughter, mother or father, neighbor or friend, to blame everyone but ourselves. We feel the desire to turn away from those who aren't especially close to us but still very much need us, because that's what sin wants of us. It's the easy thing to do. We may even feel the need to deny something nasty about ourselves, but deep inside we know that it is there, it is real, and it doesn't want to let go.

What is it that makes us feel that way? What is it that is constantly tugging and pulling at us and driving us almost crazy sometimes so that we walk away in shame, shaking our heads and saying, "I don't know why I did that; I don't know why I said that?" Yes we do. We know why. Sin lives within us and daily it tries to gain the upper hand.

"When tempted no one should say, 'God is tempting me.' For God cannot be tempted by evil, nor does he tempt anyone; but each one is tempted when, by his own evil desire, he is dragged away and enticed. Then, after desire has conceived, it gives birth to sin; and sin, when it is full grown, gives birth to death."
- James 1:13-15

We are our worst enemy. The men who flew those planes into the Pentagon and the World Trade Center, the men who failed in their original mission and crashed their plane in the farm fields of Pennsylvania—did Satan make them do that? Did Osama bin Laden make them join his terrorist organization or make them board those planes? For that matter, did Satan or anyone else make Osama bin Laden become the personification of evil that he is today?

No, the fact is, they cannot blame God or even Satan for what they did and what they have become. They were their worst enemy. They were tempted, to be sure, not by God, but by Satan AND by their "own evil desire." Satan saw the opportunity within them and the crafty poisonous serpent that he is, he dragged them away to feed off their feelings of bitterness and hatred and anger within themselves. They were "enticed," filled with an exciting desire to act out their full-grown hatred. Then, when their evil desires had been sufficiently nourished within, those desires gave birth to what we saw on September 11, sin, destruction, and death. Their sin led to physical death for thousands of innocent victims, but for them, the instigators of such ruthless overwhelming violence, spiritual death. They are now forever lost and forever separated from God's love. Those who physically died that day in Christ gained the final victory. They live forever in God's presence, eternally sheltered under the wing of their Savior's love.

The question we need to ask in times like this is not, "How can people commit such sins?" but rather, "How can we be triumphant over this terrible curse of sin that lives within us?" We will explore the answer to that question in chapters to come, but for now, we first need to see clearly the enemy. We also need to focus in upon ourselves and acknowledge unflinchingly that man's corrupt nature is real in each of us and confirmed by our Creator throughout Holy Scripture.

> "For out of the heart come evil thoughts, murder, adultery, sexual immorality, theft, false testimony, slander."
> - Matthew 14:25

> "For the sinful nature desires what is contrary to the Spirit, and the Spirit what is contrary to the sinful nature. They are in conflict with each other, so that you do not do what you want.... The acts of the sinful nature are obvious: sexual immorality, impurity and debauchery; idolatry and witchcraft; hatred, discord, jealousy, fits of rage, selfish ambition, dissentions, factions and envy; drunkenness, orgies and the like."
> - Galatians 5:17, 19-21

Quite a list, isn't it? The list of sins is long because the sinful condition of our hearts is so great. It is what gives birth to "sins," acts of rebellion against God. They are realized because a sinful condition exists within us, giving rise to a whole host of sins, some of them more grievous to us than others are, but in God's eyes, all are equal in their ability to separate us from Him eternally. The first step on the road to triumph is to recognize this enemy within ourselves and then look to God for help.

Oh, there is one more thing, one more very important truth that we must note before we move on to our next subject. The sin that lives within us will work at times, with the prompting and/or encouragement of Satan, to wage a war, a war against God as the enemy. The enemy, which is sin within us, and the enemy, which is Satan and his host outside of us, will at every opportune moment spur us on to believe the lie that God Himself is our enemy. Does this sound preposterous? It is not, for if Satan can redirect our focus as to whom the enemy is, and ultimately redirect the battle so that the forces are turned against their Creator, not only does he avoid the war altogether, but he will win without firing a shot. Consider the following examples drawn from Scripture. Some of these wars waged against God might surprise you. They represent only a few. There are many more.

- **Adam vs. God**, Genesis 3:12. "The woman you put here with me—she gave me some fruit from the tree, and I ate it." Adam blamed God for his sin! This was the first challenge ever entered by man to God's goodness.
- **Pharaoh vs. God**, Exodus 4-14. One of the first world rulers we know of who had openly acknowledged God's power at work, but still sinfully and foolishly waged war against Him.
- **The Nation of Israel vs. God**, Numbers 14. Even after they had been delivered so miraculously from their bondage in Egypt, they blamed God for their struggles in the

wilderness of Sinai and wanted to stone to death His servant Moses.

- **The Children of Abraham vs. God**, John 8:31-59. Jesus, their Messiah, told them, "Everyone who sins is a slave to sin." They looked upon the Son of God as their enemy and picked up stones to stone Him.
- **Peter vs. God**, Matthew 16:23. Peter argued with Jesus, rejecting His notion that it would be necessary for Him to suffer death and then to be raised back to life. Jesus' response to Peter's bold and foolish rebuke is very direct and entirely fitting. He said to Peter, "Out of my sight, Satan! You are a stumbling block to me; you do not have in mind the things of God, but the things of men."
- **Judas vs. God**, Luke 22:1-6. Satan entered Judas. He "went to the chief priests and officers of the temple guard and discussed with them how he might betray Jesus." He entered battle against his Lord, a battle he would ultimately and tragically lose. It would result in Judas taking his own life.
- **Paul (Saul) vs. God**, Acts 9:1-6; I Corinthians 15:7-10. Paul, first a devout Pharisee, an enemy of Christ and persecutor of Christians, found his life changed forever when he was confronted directly by his enemy and, remarkably enough, his friend Jesus, while on the road to Damascus. The incident would later cause Paul to write humbly of himself, "For I am the least of the apostles and do not even deserve to be called an apostle, because I persecuted the church of God. But by the grace of God I am what I am. . . ."

Can you see now how true it is? Can you see times in your life when you might have been tempted or may have even fallen to the temptation to lose your focus and war against God as your enemy? We need to learn this lesson well:

> The ultimate strategy of evil is to change our focus and redirect our view so that we see God Himself as the enemy, not sin or Satan.

What God Hates & What God Loves

God must be true to Himself and through the Scriptures we learn that He is "the same, yesterday, today and forever" (Hebrews 13:8). When good things happen to us, He is the same. When sad things happened to us, He is the same. Concerning evil, this is what He reveals to us and this is what will stand forever:

> "There are six things the Lord hates, seven that are detestable to him: haughty eyes, a lying tongue, hands that shed innocent blood, a heart that devises wicked schemes, feet that are quick to rush into evil, a false witness who pours out lies and a man who stirs up dissention among brothers."
>
> - Proverbs 6:16-19

No further explanation is needed. You see for yourself how God feels about the events of September 11. I hope you can also see, clearly and unequivocally, that He is not the enemy and not the author of that day's transgressions. Perhaps you can also see how He feels about Osama bin Laden and the others who collaborated with him to execute these tragic acts of evil in our sin-sick world. Look closely to see even more. See how great His love is for the lost, for this too is His great desire for all of them:

> "As surely as I live, declares the Lord, I take no pleasure in the death of the wicked, but rather that they turn from their ways and live."
> - Ezekiel 33:11

Our God's love is so great that He desires a turn in heart from even the most wicked, evil, and violent of men, like Osama bin Laden and like the Apostle Paul, who turned from his wicked ways in response to God's loving invitation. We have a God who is the personification of love in the person of His Son, Jesus Christ. All of us, from the most evil, to the most pure, can find ultimate eternal peace and rest in this God of all grace. He invites us—everyone—to find in Him that peace and look to Him as our great Savior-God and friend. This is His voice. Listen to the love, and listen to the tenderness that is there. Listen to its softness. There you find no trace of evil but the purest good:

> "Come to me, all you who are weary and burdened, and I will give you rest. Take my yoke upon you and learn from me, for I am gentle and humble in heart, and you will find rest for your souls."
> - Matthew 11:28-29

This yearning invitation from Christ comes to all, whether you are the guiltiest or the most innocent. It comes to Osama bin Laden himself, still, in the hope that even he might turn from his evil ways. It comes to our nation's religious leaders so that the words they speak will be increasingly more like Christ's words of tolerance, forgiveness, and peace. It comes to our nation's civil leaders so that they might carry out their God given responsibilities in a way that reflects the justice and goodness of the Creator. It comes to all of us so that in this period of war and tragedy we might find rest in the arms of a kind and merciful God. Most importantly, this loving invitation comes to the survivors of those who lost their lives so sadly on September 11.

Jesus invites you to come to Him and find peace. It is there for you. It is rich. It is full. It is powerfully strong for healing and it is yours for the having. It will lead you through the terror of 9-11 to the triumph of a peace that is known only in our Savior Jesus Christ.

CHAPTER TWO

INSIGHT #2

The ultimate deceptive purpose of evil is to blind us to the loving providence of God and His ability to thwart evil's destructive intent, so much so, that we become unable to see and unwilling to yield to His saving plan for a world lost in sin as that plan unfolds before our very eyes.

FIND STRENGTH in God's Mighty Power

When the day of evil comes, it is certainly important to know who the enemy is. That enemy has been identified for us but that enemy is vastly superior in power to our feeble abilities to fend him off all by ourselves. Even that old enemy sin, which lives within us all, wins out far too often. If we cannot even win the war against our own sinful nature by ourselves, how can we ever hope to fight off Satan with his great army? The Apostle Paul wrote,

> "Finally, be strong in the Lord and in his mighty power. Put on the full armor of God so that you can take your stand against the devil's schemes."
> - Ephesians 6:10-11

Be "strong in the Lord." Find strength for the task "in his mighty power." Paul is inviting us to trust in God's omnipotence and providence.

Another of my college professors once asserted that the greatest challenge to Christianity is the problem of evil. He may very well have been correct. Why? Because evil challenges repeatedly these very propositions: 1) that God is stronger than evil, 2) that God is always in control, and 3) that God ultimately wins over evil. All teachings related to God's loving providence exist to comfort us in the knowledge that God is active in our lives, watching over all things, lovingly protecting and caring for us. It's a nice thought. We go to bed at night thinking that. We assure our children that God is watching over them as they sleep. We want them to know a loving and powerful God protects them. It's a restful, peaceful idea, and quite comforting.

The problem, however, is this: we woke up one morning and saw people jumping to their deaths from 100 stories up to escape smoke and flames. We woke up to buildings collapsing and death in the thousands. That's when people, Christians and non-Christians alike, start to wonder about God's providence. It shakes us up, those days when evil comes. It can shake people's confidence in God too. Perhaps my college professor was right. Maybe the greatest challenge to Christianity is the problem of evil. We need to examine that.

Do you remember the "God is dead" theory promoted in the late 1960s and early 1970s? It created quite a stir in its day. As outrageous as the whole episode was, it did prompt quite a bit of discussion on the subject of God's providence, some of it good, some of it bad. I'm a little surprised that those irreverent ghosts from the past haven't materialized again since 9-11. You see, the questions are being asked again: How could this happen?

Where was God? Is God asleep? Has God abandoned us? Is God even there? If God is so powerful, how could he allow such evil?

If evil does present a powerful challenge to Christianity, and I believe we are foolish if we think it does not, then we need to examine carefully how this challenge manifests itself and how the enemy is using evil to undermine this basic trust in God's providential care of all things. We need to see clearly how significant this challenge is to our faith. Perhaps if we are in tune to Satan's clever scheming on such matters, we will be less likely to fall to his scheming.

Satan Would Have Us Believe, GOD IS WEAK

Did God ever lie to you? By contrast, did you ever lie to anyone? How did you feel after you did? It's a very sick feeling isn't it? Did anyone ever catch you in a lie? How does that feel? It's even worse, isn't it? Now turn the circumstances around. Did you ever catch anyone lying to you? When you caught them in their lie, who was the more powerful, you or them?

You see, there is power in truth and there is weakness in falsehood. We feel the power of truth whenever we are on the side of truth and we can find, within our very souls, the weakness of falsehood whenever we are lying. It's not only embarrassing, it's a very shaming kind of thing. We are truly rendered practically powerless when we are caught in a lie.

The reason I first asked if God had ever lied to you is because we all know the answer to that question. God has never lied to anyone. Simply knowing that truth is to experience the power of God around us and even inside of us. It's an experience drawn from a basic premise that "God is truth," for in truth there is power. Then, to ask, "Did you ever lie to anyone?"

is to set in contrast to God's power, your weakness, because we have all lied at one time or another, in one way or another.

Satan will come and tempt you to think that God is weak and not in control. When Satan challenges your thinking on God's providence, you are left with a choice. The first is to trust that God never lies, and therefore, everything He says about His providence is reliable and true. The second choice is to trust your own self. So, when the day of evil comes, you can either rely upon doubts, that are based upon Satan's lies to you, and conclude that God is not in control, or you can take God at his word and trust that in spite of what may seem to the contrary, by your weak understanding of all things, God remains in control as our loving, providential ruler in heaven. As we examine this issue more closely, we begin to see that God's providence is never forfeited—that is, He never neglects us—but it is often challenged by outside forces. The question is, why is God's providence challenged and by whom?

Look once again at what Jesus said about Satan, the great liar.

> "You belong to your father, the devil, and you want to
> carry out your father's desire. He was a murderer
> from the beginning, not holding to the truth, for there
> is no truth in him. When he lies, he speaks his native
> language, for he is a liar and the father of lies."
> - John 8:44

The devil is the liar of the ages. In fact, Jesus said, lying is so much a part of his nature that no truth even exists in him. As this great liar, do you suppose Satan ever measures himself against the standard of God's truthfulness? What do you suppose he sees? Does he see himself equal to God in power or does he realize that his lies and deceitfulness have dramatically weakened him in comparison to his Creator? The rebel that he is, does that knowledge please him, make him happy, or could it be that it fills him with a burning desire to go out from God's presence like a jealous, angry, bitter child, and destroy every good thing that God, in His power, has created?

Rest assured, Satan's goal is to use his cunning and his lies to alter how God's children view their Creator. He cannot take His power from Him but he can destroy, in the hearts of God's children, their trust in the loving providence of their heavenly Father. He can lie, and make them think God is not strong but weak, and then they may just turn from Him.

Satan would have us believe, amazingly enough, that God is weak. Unfortunately, he is often successful in this effort. First, he wants us to think that God is,

- "weak" in being honest with us.

He's been employing that strategy from the very beginning of time.

> "'You will not surely die,' the serpent said to the woman. 'For God knows that when you eat of it your eyes will be opened and you will be like God, knowing good and evil.'"
> - Genesis 3:4, 5

"You will not die... your eyes will be opened." What a lie! Satan wanted Adam and Eve to believe that God was not being honest with them. In fact, Satan wanted them to believe that

God was lying to them. He wanted them to think that God knew something they didn't know. He wanted them to trust that if they listened to him and his lies, and ate of the fruit of the tree, they would gain some greater knowledge that God had been holding back from them. He wanted them to think that nothing bad was going to happen to them, only good things, better things. Satan said, "Look how weak God is in holding all this back from you! He must not want you to have what He has or you'll be too much like Him! Do you see how weak He is in being truly honest with you? See how jealous He is of you?"

The trap had been set. You wonder what must have been going through their minds, first Eve, and then Adam. Satan had just flat out contradicted what God had told them. He just flat out promised them a gain in knowledge that they would never have. In truth, they were already like God, created in His image, in perfect righteousness and holiness. The fact was, they would not gain knowledge but lose knowledge. They would also lose much in their perfect relationship with their loving Creator. They fell into the trap and brought down all of humanity with them. All this happened because they believed the lie.

When the day of evil comes, Satan still wants us to believe that God is not being honest with us. He does this to destroy trust in his providential care. Satan does this so that we will no longer place our confidence in the truth of His life-giving Word.

Satan would have us believe that God is,

• "weak" in His power to help us.

Satan knows of God's power. He experienced it himself and

in a very personal way when God cast him out of heaven. Yet, Satan continues to challenge God's omnipotence. He often uses a two-pronged approach. He will challenge God to use His power in a way different from God's intended purposes, and then, when God refrains from exercising His might, he challenges our faith in the hope that we begin to question God's strength and His purposes for our lives.

It must have been a great amusement to Satan to see the Son of God humiliate Himself in becoming so human like us that He would be subject to all the weaknesses of our frail physical nature. When he tempted Jesus in the wilderness, he seemed to find great delight in zeroing in on this part of Jesus' nature. Did he truly believe that this was a weakness he would be able to exploit in God's Son? If nothing else, he thought he might at least give it a try.

"Then Jesus was led by the Spirit into the desert to be tempted by the devil. After fasting forty days and forty nights, he was hungry. The tempter came to him and said, 'If you are the Son of God, tell these stones to become bread.' Jesus answered, 'It is written: Man does not live on bread alone, but on every word that comes from the mouth of God.'"
- Matthew 4:1-4

The Spirit had led Jesus into the wilderness. His obedience to His heavenly Father's will for Him would be put to the test, just as man's obedience had been put to the test by Satan in Eden. Then, the man and woman God had created failed, miserably. Now, Jesus could not fail. He could not if He was to complete His mission as the perfect Savior for a world lost in sin. Jesus had come to this world to use His power to save, and for no other purpose than that. Satan was tempting Jesus to use His divine power in a way that His heavenly Father had not intended. Jesus was not fooled. He obeyed His Father's will perfectly, and thus paved the way, to become our perfect Redeemer.

That was, of course, a very direct temptation from Satan to Jesus Himself. Today he will use a little different approach. You've heard his challenges to God's power often. Maybe sometimes they have come from your own lips. "Jesus, I promise I will go to church every day of my life, if you just do this one thing for me now." "God, I know you are so busy with many things, but if you just heal my child of this cancer that is eating away at his body, I will follow you the rest of my life." "Jesus, you have said you are always with us, then come to me now, and deliver me from this tremendous debt I now find myself in. If you do, I promise that I will tithe of everything I receive from this day forward." Do any of these promises sound familiar to you? Are there others like them?

When Satan challenges God's power today, it's often through us and we don't even realize how he's using us. Those requests are rarely answered, and when they are not, Satan uses them against us and says, "See, God isn't as powerful as you thought He was, is He? If He was, then why not heal your child; then why not help you out of financial misery; then why not just do something that will enable you to trust Him and believe Him?"

Jesus has encouraged us to come to Him and ask anything of Him but He has also instructed us that when we ask, we need to remember to qualify our request according to God's will for us. That qualification to prayer is important. It's certainly not because God is unable to grant our any and every request, but because God does not want us to have that which would harm us. Praying according to God's will doesn't let God off the hook; it keeps us from grabbing on to Satan's hook. The devil can't reel us in if our satisfaction in life is God's good will for our lives.

Not everything we ask for is good for us or for others around us, even some things that may seem so right in our own eyes. We need to believe that, as firmly as God knows it to be true about us. If we do, we will not fall to Satan's scheming when he works to have us believe that God is weak in His power to help us. The best parent is many times the parent who has the strength to say no to a child's request. As it is true for us as parents, it is also true in our relationship with our Father in heaven.

However, more than anything else, Satan would have us believe that God is

• "weak" in His love for us.

Listen to what happened to Job. No, I'm not referring to his loss of family, wealth, or health. I'm referring to his wife. Listen to what his wife said when she came to him at his bed of suffering.

> "So Satan went out from the presence of the Lord and afflicted Job with painful sores from the soles of his feet to the top of his head. Then Job took a piece of broken pottery and scraped himself with it as he sat among the ashes. His wife said to him, 'Are you still holding on to your integrity? Curse God and die!'"
> - Job 2:7-9

What a wonderful bedside manner: "Curse God and die!" What amazes me about the story of Job is not that he survived such great physical suffering and loss of life. What amazes me is that he survived his wife! Satan no sooner exits Job's life stage left, and then enters, stage right, Job's wife!

In my lifetime, I have lost my grandparents in their old age, my father to cancer, an aunt to cancer, a cousin to cancer, an uncle to heart disease, another uncle who died in a harrowing accident in his youth, one cousin lost at sea in a commercial fishing accident, another lost at sea in a private airplane crash, not to mention many others who have now parted from this world and have taken their place in heaven with Christ. I mention this, not because these losses are greater than anyone else's loss may be. Indeed, many others have lost more in their lifetimes. The sudden loss of innocent lives on 9-11 leaves mine to pale in comparison.

The point is this: we live in a world filled with death, filled with suffering of all kinds, filled with sadness and sorrow. Satan wants nothing more than for us to look at it all, throw up our hands in despair, view it all as an endless circle of evil and hopelessness, and then curse God for everything. He would have us believe that God really doesn't love as much as He says He does. Questions like, "Where was God? How could this happen? Has God abandoned us? How could God allow such evil?" are all signs that Satan is working hard. He's planting seeds of doubt in the hearts and minds of people everywhere. He wants you to believe that God doesn't really care about you all that much. Satan would have you reason, "If God does love me, why doesn't He just prevent all these tragedies from happening? Why doesn't He just make them go away? Why doesn't He just let good things come to us as we live out our lives in this world?"

There are answers to all these questions, and it is important that we address them, but for now, we first need to know the one who enjoys raising those doubts in our minds. Know that it is our enemy, the devil, who is at work. In truth, HE IS THE ONE WHO DOES NOT LOVE YOU! So don't fall to the lie. Don't turn from Him whose love for you is eternal!

Terror enters our hearts when we believe these lies. Terror enters our hearts when we begin to think God is not being totally honest with us. Terror enters our hearts when we begin to think that God does not have the power needed to protect us completely. Terror enters our hearts when we begin to reason that God does not love us or care about us as much as He wants us to believe He does. Terror enters our hearts because we feel we are so very vulnerable to every malady, so open to every misfortune, and so easily victimized by the many dangers that lurk about.

What happens to a child when he is in his bed alone at night and suddenly the lightning strikes with its thunderous crash? You'll often find him in bed with mom and dad in a split second.

That also is where God wants us to flee when tragedy strikes in our lives. He wants us to flee to Him where we will find comfort, strength, and protection in His arms. But Satan does not want us to go there, and he will do everything in his power to keep us from fleeing to the loving, open arms of our great protector and friend. We come to our second insight.

INSIGHT #2
The ultimate deceptive purpose of evil is to blind us
to the loving providence of God and His ability to

thwart evil's destructive intent, so much so, that we become unable to see and unwilling to yield to His saving plan for a world lost in sin as that plan unfolds before our very eyes.

In Mark's Gospel, we find an amazing example of how man so often responds when life's dark clouds come to rest over us. It is the account of The Storm.

"That day when evening came, he said to his disciples, 'Let us go over to the other side.' Leaving the crowd behind, they took him along, just as he was, in a boat. There were also other boats with him. A furious squall came up, and the waves broke over the boat, so that it was nearly swamped. Jesus was in the stern, sleeping on a cushion. The disciples woke him and said to him, 'Teacher, don't you care if we drown?' He got up, rebuked the wind and said to the waves, 'Quiet! Be still!' Then the wind died down and it was completely calm. He said to his disciples, 'Why are you so afraid? Do you still have no faith?' They were terrified and asked each other, 'Who is this? Even the wind and the waves obey him?'"
- Mark 4:35-41

What an amazing story in the life of our Lord, and what a blessing for us that it has been recorded for all time in Holy Scripture. When life's storms come upon us, it can seem like Jesus is away, sleeping on His cushioned pillow in heaven, oblivious to our desperate condition and needs. We respond much as the disciples who must have gone to Jesus in the boat, shook

Him violently to wake Him up, and then exclaimed, "Teacher, don't you care if we drown?"

"God, don't you care?" Down through the ages, that question has often been leveled squarely at God in times of suffering. It continues to be asked to this day. We never seem to learn the answer. Before Jesus intervened, the disciples were terrified. Also note, that even after Jesus intervened, the disciples were terrified, but for a different reason.

Of what were they afraid? Initially, I suppose they were afraid of the storm itself. They were afraid they might drown. However, what also made them afraid was that Jesus was sound asleep while all this was going on. They had seen Him in action. This man could perform miracles! He had saved others. By this time, they had seen Him perform numerous miracles. He had been attentive to the needs of others. Why was He sleeping now? They interpreted His sound sleep as a lack of concern for them and so after waking Him, they said to Him, "Don't you care if we drown?" They were terrified because Jesus didn't seem to care about them.

When Jesus finally did do something, it must have brought them a great sigh of relief. At His word, the winds died down, the sea became perfectly calm, and Jesus asked them why they were so afraid. "Do you still have no faith?" He asked, and they were still terrified! Why? Was it because they were now the ones who had been awakened, awakened to who Jesus really was, and the great power of God He now displayed in their midst? Or were they awakened to their lack of faith, evident now for Christ to see so clearly? Perhaps it made them ashamed and even terrified to stand in such greatness, such power, with so little faith, and so little trust.

When the storms of life come we too might ask, "God, don't

you care?" Sometimes it seems to us that God doesn't care. This is what Satan wants us to think. We too will often exhibit a lack of faith. We too are terrified. The storm and what it might do to us may terrify us, but it's not just the storm that causes alarm. Sometimes we are terrified because God doesn't seem to care about us, and it makes us very afraid. We know we need Him. When God does finally act, in His good hour, we may still be terrified, because after everything is done, we have our lack of faith staring back at us and we are terrified over what God must think of us.

At that very moment, we need to ask what those disciples asked on that frightful day at sea, "Who is this?" because in that question is the answer. This is your God, who loves you, who has come to help you, in spite of your weakness, in spite of your faithlessness, in spite of your lack of trust, in spite of your doubts and fears. This is your saving God, your living and all-powerful God, your hope for the present and your certainty for the future. He is here to calm the storm and take away your fears.

The Providence of God

From Genesis and the deliverance of God's chosen people Israel, to the beauty of the Psalms and God's protective acts on behalf of His prophets, the Scriptures are filled with examples of God's providence. However, of them all, the most kind and loving expression of God's providence, other than perhaps the 23rd Psalm, is arguably found in Jesus' Sermon on the Mount. Down through the ages these words of our Lord have brought unending comfort and peace to people weighed down by life's sorrows and tragedies. We need to heed them well for the strengthening of our faith.

"Therefore I tell you, do not worry about your life, what you will eat or drink; or about your body, what you will wear. Is not life more important than food, and the body more important than clothes? Look at the birds of the air; they do not sow or reap or store away in barns, and yet your heavenly Father feeds them. Are you not much more valuable than they? Who of you by worrying can add a single hour to his life? And why do you worry about clothes? See how the lilies of the field grow. They do not labor or spin. Yet I tell you that not even Solomon in all his splendor was dressed like one of these. If this is how God clothes the grass of the field, which is here today and tomorrow is thrown into the fire, will he not much more clothe you, O you of little faith? So do not worry, saying, 'What shall we eat?' or 'What shall we wear?' For the pagans run after all these things, and your heavenly Father knows that you need them."
- Matthew 6:25-32

"Don't worry," Jesus said. Our heavenly Father is there, always, preserving all things (Psalm 36:6). He is there sustaining and working in all things (Acts 17:28). He is there directing and governing all things according to His good pleasure for the good of His children (Psalm 33:143, 14). God knows our situation. He knows our needs and will continue to provide.

It is an amazing thing, to be sure, that God is daily at work doing all these things for the least and for the greatest of His creation. It is a wondrous testament to His wisdom and power at work daily in our world.

However, to Satan's delight, there is an element to this providential activity of God that is often overlooked. This is unfortunate, for it holds the key to a deeper and richer understanding of all that goes on in this world, the good with the bad.

It has often been said, when days of evil have come upon us, that we cannot explain why the evil is happening. That is true only in part. The fact is, there is much that can be said. We need to explore that now, though Satan would just as soon we did not. We need to explore that now, because the light of God's truth will illuminate our situation and weaken Satan's ability to terrorize us and turn us from our Creator.

To begin, churn over in your mind this thought: Without the reality of sin and evil in the world, how easy would it be for God, in His providence, to care for and protect all things? Imagine it: no greed, no theft, no murder, no plundering, no hatred, no bitterness, no anger, no strife, no drunkenness, no drug abuse, no unfaithfulness, no war, no divorce, no unkind words, no slander, no cursing, no faithlessness, no vanity, no pride, no disobedience, etc., etc., etc.—no sin, no evil of any kind. But that's not the kind of world we live in, is it? That's not what's real today.

When God wakes up every morning, puts on His suit and tie and heads off to work, what He finds is trouble everywhere. Did He cause the trouble? Did He invite it? Did He desire it? No, He's just left with it. This is what He has to work with. Yet, in His magnificence, grace, wisdom, and goodness, He finds ways to keep everything running, and has even promised us that some day, when the time is right, He will make all things new again. He will restore us and restore everything in this world to what it was at the beginning of time. What a great and glorious day that will be! Nevertheless, for now, He does for us what He must. He is patient, and lovingly deals with everything, in a world that we have corrupted to the core through the dreadful effects of our sin.

So, the way it is now, with sin and evil in the world, what must it be like for Him? Does the evil that is so prevalent in this world please Him? Is the Holy Spirit filled with joy or deeply grieved by our many sins? We know the answers to these questions. However, we may not think upon them often enough or seriously enough.

You see, when the day of evil comes, we too often look up to God with this questioning expression of "why" on our wrinkled brows. What we should be doing is bowing our heads before Him and confessing, "God, I'm sorry that we have made such a mess of this world. I'm sorry that my sin too has often made it such a dark place to live and that my sin has even sought to frustrate your saving purposes for this world and everyone in it." To make such a confession shows that we are beginning to understand everything we have dumped onto God's lap. To make such a confession also shows that we are beginning to appreciate His great power to save.

The Providence of God in the Wake of Sin

How everything changed with the advent of sin, for with sin some hard choices had to be made. What we don't realize is that those same choices continue being made to this very day. When sin entered the world, God was left with a world that had become imperfect. What should he do? Yes, that decision had been made from eternity and He had already determined what He was going to do, but what would you have done? In time and eternity, He had, basically, four choices:

- Destroy Adam & Eve,
- Destroy everything He had created,
- Leave the world to continue on its own in its corrupt state, or
- Save and restore what was lost through sin.

Two short yet very key verses of Scripture guide us into a richer understanding of why God made the choice He did, and why He continues along that same path to this very day. In these verses of Scripture, two key attributes of God are identified.

"God is just."
- II Thessalonians 1:6
and
"God is love."
- I John 4:16

God's justice requires satisfaction for every transgression. Because God is perfect, sin cannot remain with Him, in Him, or even around Him. Heaven is a place of perfection. Sin is by its very nature an imperfection and, therefore, cannot dwell where God is. Justice demands that anything that is sin or of sin must be removed from God's presence. That includes us. Otherwise, heaven is no longer heaven and that which was perfect is no longer perfect. God's justice requires it and "God is just."

Yet, we also read, "God is love." His love demanded something else of Him. It demanded compassion, mercy, forbearance, and patience. Maybe we go too far to say that it was required of God to act with love. But if it was not required, then it was most certainly desired by God to be loving toward man, even after sin entered the world, for "God so loved the world that he gave His one and only Son... " (John 3:16). To be true to Himself, God had to show love.

As we examine God's choices in the light of these two attributes, we see much more. He could not just destroy Adam and Eve. It would have been just. They deserved to be separated forever from God's Holy presence but it was not, for God, who is rich in mercy, a loving thing to do. He could not, He would not, and He did not do that.

God could not just destroy everything as if He might start all over again. Once again, God's justice may have been served by such an approach, but not His love.

The third choice, to leave the world to continue on its own chosen course, might have been something we deserved, but would have also been very unmerciful. Can you imagine actually having to live forever in this world with never a hope for improvement in our condition? We have every reason to be daily thankful that our Creator is who He is and what He is, a just God, yet a loving and merciful God at one and the same time. It led Him to make the only choice His justice and His love would accept. Our Lord God worked His eternal plan to save and restore what was lost as a result of sin.

God's Choice for Us

Most of the time, the choices we make in life are very self-serving, from the food we eat to the careers we choose for ourselves. We choose food that is palatable to us, and we try to select careers that are attractive to our tastes as well, and our pocket books. Rarely do we choose anything that would be painful for us or distasteful to our personal preferences. If you can choose between having a tooth pulled with or without Novocaine, you will choose the Novocaine.

How easy it would have been for God to choose destruction for Adam and Eve, but He loved them too much. How easy it would have been for God to just give up on the whole of His creation and destroy everything in it, but His love was too great to do that. How easy it would have been for God to just give up on us and let us go forever trudging along that sad and weary sin-filled path we had chosen for ourselves, but God loved us too much to let that happen.

What we desperately need to see, if we ever hope to understand why evil still exists in this world, is that the path God chose, to save and rescue us, was the hardest of the four choices that were before Him. It was not a self-serving choice like the choices we make in life. It was fully and completely, a self-sacrificing choice, a painful choice. It would cost Him His one and only Son and the painful price of divine justice would fall fully upon Him, culminating at Calvary.

Furthermore, God's choice would require great pain and heartache for centuries to come in the form of patience, a heart-wrenching patience that is still at work in the world today as He continues to bring His message to a world lost in sin. He does this in the hope of saving many more. He does it all the while knowing that He must let evil have its day, for now. He knows that to snuff evil out completely would be to snuff mankind out as well, for all humanity is a guilty partner in evil's stranglehold on this world. It grieves the Holy Spirit daily to witness man's sin repeating its deadly cycle over and over again, but God in His great love bears that price today and every day, just as He bore the sins of the world 2000 years ago in the person of His Son and our Savior, Jesus Christ.

That choice of God was first made known to Adam and Eve in Eden.

> "God said to the serpent, 'Because you have done this, cursed are you above all the livestock and all the wild animals! You will crawl on your belly and you will eat dust all the days of your life. And I will put enmity between you and the woman, and between your offspring and hers; he will crush your head, and you will strike his heel.'"
> - Genesis 3:14, 15

Satan had struck quite a blow to man, the crown of God's creation, but now God was determined to strike a crushing blow to Satan, that crafty serpent of old. God would send an "offspring" of the woman whom Satan had led into corruption. This offspring would "crush" the serpent's head, destroying his power forever. However, Satan, the serpent, would strike the heel of the woman's offspring.

When a serpent strikes, its sharp teeth penetrate to inject its venomous poison, poison that can be deadly. Satan struck hard, inflicting the poison of sin and death when Jesus, the long-awaited offspring of the woman, came to fulfill His God-given task. Yet, death could not hold Him. Satan had his day, but God had the greater day on Easter morning and there the victory was won. It was a promise given centuries earlier. It was a promise that reached fruition in the fullness of time—God's chosen time.

It was a promise that would still be in effect after years of suffering and evil on this planet. It was repeated in words spoken by God to King David, through the prophet Nathan.

"When your days are over and you rest with your fathers, I will raise up your offspring to succeed you, who will come from your own body, and I will establish his kingdom. He is the one who will build a house for my Name, and I will establish the throne of his kingdom forever. I will be his father, and he will be my son. When he does wrong, I will punish him with the rod of men, with floggings inflicted by men. But my love will never be taken away from him."
- II Samuel 7:12-15

A son was promised, from the line of a king, King David. To this son would be given a kingdom and a house would be built by Him, built to the glory of God. He would rule on a new throne and His rule and His kingdom would never end. But He would be more than a king; He would also be the Son of God. Yet, God would punish Him with the rod of men, "with floggings inflicted by men."

Does this strike a familiar picture? It certainly should. When Jesus bore the weight of our sins upon the cross, when He became sin for us, when He became the sinner, God's divine justice came down heavy upon Him. The scourging and flogging at the hands of the Roman soldiers—the crown of thorns and the kingly robe placed upon His shoulders—the nails that pierced His hands from which He hung to the cross and the spear that pierced His side—all this was the punishment that came from the righteous arm of God's justice when He took our place to pay the dreadful price for sin and usher in a new kingdom. He died that day but death could not hold Him. His Father's love for Him remained and on the third day, Easter morning, He rose to life to begin His reign as the King of kings and

Lord of lords forevermore. He has now established a new kingdom of God, a kingdom of believers, a Holy Christian Church and we are that house—built by God's own Son—if we hold to the faith we profess in every time of prosperity and in every time of suffering, like on 9-11.

As I write this, we are only six days from Christmas. What a wondrous time and what a glorious time. How fitting that we have this great blessing to think about now in the wake of September 11. What comfort it brings to be reminded that God has not abandoned us but that, in fact, God has visited us in the person of this dear child who came to us at Bethlehem in a manger so small. This was God's choice for us, made known through the word of the prophets,

> "For to us a child is born, to us a son is given, and the government will be on his shoulders. And he will be called Wonderful Counselor, Mighty God, Everlasting Father, Prince of Peace."
>
> - Isaiah 9:6

Many more years passed after that prophecy was given to David through the prophet Nathan. So much more suffering was endured. Evil continued its God-defying march across our sin-infected world but God remained strong in His resolve to remain true to His promise. His choice, to restore and to save mankind through the gift of His Son would be accomplished. As promised, God's choice for us was made known at the appointed time.

> "But when the time had fully come, God sent his Son, born of a woman, born under law, to redeem those

under law, that we might receive the full rights of sons. Because you are sons, God sent the Spirit of his Son into our hearts, the Spirit who calls out, '*Abba*, Father.' So you are no longer a slave, but a son; and since you are a son, God has made you also an heir."
- Galatians 4:4-7

Look what God has done! Look at His grace! Look at His faithfulness! Look at His patience! Look at His sacrifice! Look at His love!

Through all these years, God has remained focused on His plan to save us. The question is, have *we* remained focused on His plan to save us? When God's Son, our Savior, came, the world was not very focused. God had made known His choice for us. His choice was the saving gift of His Son, but this gift of flesh and blood was, remarkably, unknown to us when He came into our world.

"In the beginning was the Word, and the Word was with God, and the Word was God. He was with God in the beginning. Through him all things were made; without him nothing was made that has been made. In him was life, and that life was the light of men. The light shines in the darkness, but the darkness has not understood it.... The true light that gives light to every man was coming into the world. He was in the world, and though the world was made through him, the world did not recognize him. He came to that which was his own, but his own did not receive him... Yet to all who did receive him, to those who believed in his name, he gave the right to become

children of God—children born not of natural descent,
nor of human decision or a husband's will, but born
of God. The Word became flesh and lived for a while
among us. We have seen his glory, the glory of the
one and only Son, who came from the Father, full of
grace and truth."
- John 1:1-5, 9-14

Yes, God's plan for us was completed in the midst of evil
and of suffering. It was completed in the midst of tremendous
sacrifice, in the midst of betrayal and in the midst of torture,
death, abandonment, and unbelief. When this great good came
to earth, He came as an unknown. In fact, when He came, evil
remained intent on snuffing out His life. From infancy through
adulthood, Jesus was in constant danger. When this great good
came of age and suffered the evils of sin for us, none saw in
Him, as He hung upon that tree, a great gift of God in the
midst of tremendous evil. Why was this marvelous gift not recognized? Why do we have such trouble seeing God's hand at
work through the evil that goes on all around us? To a great
extent, it is for this reason:

> The ultimate deceptive purpose of evil is
> to blind us to the loving providence of
> God and His ability to thwart evil's de-
> structive intent, so much so, that we be-
> come unable to see and unwilling to yield
> to His saving plan for a world lost in sin
> as that plan unfolds before our very eyes.

The Strength of God Revealed

In the past, God's plan of salvation for us was foremost. He would work through all the evil of the centuries and all the sorrows brought on by sin, in order to complete His plan of redemption for the world. As that was true in the past, it remains true for us today, in our present time, and true for us tomorrow, even well into the future. Why would we dare think that God would do otherwise?

God is on a mission of life and salvation. It did not end at Calvary. It started there. Even today, it continues. He asks us to join Him in that mission, not to change it.

It is more understandable, I suppose, that those who do not yet know Christ as their personal Savior will have more difficulty understanding the interrelationship between God's mission of life for the world and Satan's mission of evil. They will have more trouble understanding that, for now, we must have both and that in God's plan for the present we can't have one without the other.

It also becomes understandable that as professing Christians are tempted by Satan to abandon this spiritual, evangelical mission God has set before them, in favor of more politically correct or socially acceptable endeavors, they too will experience a growing difficulty in understanding why evil continues to exist in the world. They will continue to have difficulty explaining why the existence of God's love and the reality of evil are interrelated in God's great plan for the world. Consequently, they will also have difficulty defending God, His claim of love for us, and His seeming inactivity in the face of continued and increasing evil in this world.

I fear that this is becoming far too common a problem in many Christian circles. The proper answers are not being given when questions arise as to the prevalence of so much evil in the world, while we continue to stress, at the same time, God's loving providence. Christians and non-Christians alike deserve solid, foundational answers to those questions. God-given answers are available, but if we try to answer those questions, having separated ourselves from the very mission Jesus Christ has set before us, for another mission of our own making, then the answers God would have us give will not be forthcoming. Then the answers we give will be both flat and true only in part, incomplete, outright wrong, or we will find it necessary to plead ignorance.

Understanding God's mission for the world is that important and that key to properly understanding why evil continues to exist. Unfortunately, Satan knows this better than even many children of God know this today. Therefore, we see the mission of evangelical Christianity, God's mission for mankind, under continued and increasing attack. This is Satan's ongoing plan for the ages. Today, when evangelical Christians are made to feel guilty for desiring the conversion of unbelievers to faith in Christ; when Christians are ridiculed for their desire to send not just humanitarian aid workers into foreign lands but missionaries to proclaim the gospel of Jesus Christ; when Christians are asked to treat the missions of all other world religions as equally valid to the mission of bringing the message of Christ's love to the nations; when Christians are asked to compromise the fundamental principles of their faith in ways like this, you can be sure Satan is there stirring the pot.

For us, therefore, to change our spiritual mission in life would be to cripple ourselves. It is at the heart of everything we do. It is the inevitable result of every truth the Holy Spirit has led us to embrace.

It might be helpful to note that when Jesus came to this world, He came, sent by His heavenly Father on a very specific mission. He did not deviate from it. In the garden of Gethsemane, though He prayed that if possible it might be altered, it wasn't. He accepted that and went the way of the cross. He endured the evil to accomplish a far greater good.

At the beginning of His ministry, when Satan tempted him in the desert, every trick employed by the father of lies, was meant to lead Jesus away from His mission to this world, His very reason for being here. However, He wasn't here to use His power to turn stones into bread, but to use His power as God to become the bread of life for the world. He wasn't here to gain a following by showing off His power over the forces of nature, but by exercising His power over sin, death and Satan himself, on Good Friday and Easter morning. He wasn't here to worship Satan as a false god and thus gain kingdoms to rule, He was here to glorify His heavenly Father, the one true God in the world, and in glorifying Him—remaining true to His mission—to rule forevermore as the King of kings.

So now, Jesus Christ, having completed that mission, rules over all things and He does so with a specific good purpose in mind. He rules for the good of His Church. He rules in such a way, that the mission of spreading the gospel throughout the world, where evil continues to reign, might result in more faith, stronger faith, and growth of His Church, the body of believers.

"And God placed all things under his feet and appointed him to be head over everything for the church, which is his body, the fullness of him who fills every-

thing in every way."
- Ephesians 1:22, 23

When the day of evil comes, we will find great peace, even in the midst of tremendous suffering and evil, if we know we are on the side of Christ and in tune with His mission for this world. We have these comforting words from Jesus Himself,

"I have told you these things, so that in me you may have peace. In this world you will have trouble. But take heart! I have overcome the world."
- John 16:33

We are, as Jesus said, in the world but not of the world. We have peace knowing that His providence has a greater good as its goal. However, the peace He gives us is different from what the world gives. It is not a peace that will bring to us immunity from the evil that is so prevalent in this world. In fact, we can expect just the opposite, ever more trouble until this world comes to an end. The evil one will have his day. Nevertheless, while we have trouble, we can still have the peace that Christ gives.

Christ's peace enables us to know that through Him, God has dealt honestly with us in our sinful condition. Now we know who and what we are. We are at peace admitting this because we know that in Jesus Christ we have a Redeemer who has paid the price for all our sins. Forgiveness is ours!

We are at peace because His power is there to heal us of our most serious disease, the malady of sin, which when left untreated, separates from God eternally. We are at peace knowing that we have a different future than that. We have an eternity of being with God who has healed us of every affliction through the sacrifice of His Son.

We are at peace because we know that we are recipients of His love. In spite of our failures, God continues to care for us in those ways that are for our ultimate eternal good. This is the peace that is ready for everyone. It is a peace found in the person and in the life-giving message of Jesus Christ.

God's will for us today is this: STAND FIRM IN YOUR FAITH BY SEEKING THAT WHICH MATTERS THE MOST. Do you remember that beautiful section from Jesus' Sermon on the Mount, found in Matthew's Gospel? "Don't worry," Jesus encouraged us. He asked rhetorically, "Is not life more important than food, and the body more important than clothes?" He ended that section of His sermon with these words,

> "But seek first his kingdom and his righteousness, and all these things will be given to you as well. Therefore do not worry about tomorrow, for tomorrow will worry about itself. Each day has enough trouble of its own."
> - Matthew 7:33, 34

Now that's peace! That's the peace Jesus alone gives. That's the peace Jesus still gives. Don't be blinded to God's saving plan as it unfolds before your very eyes. Let God, through His Son Jesus Christ, turn the evil events of 9-11 upside-down so that a greater good is accomplished. Let His providence rule over the forces of evil, as it always has in the past. He will guide us into the future in those ways that are best for His Church if we but wait upon Him to lead us out of this terror, to our triumph which is found in our Lord and Savior Jesus Christ.

- CHAPTER THREE -

INSIGHT #3

The ultimate goal of evil is spiritual death, to rob us of the victory that is ours through faith . . . *and*

. . . the ultimate meaning of evil is not that it is a test from God of our faith, but a challenge from Satan to our faith.

ARM YOURSELF for the Struggle
The Apostle Paul wrote,

> "Therefore put on the full armor of God, so that when the day of evil comes, you may be able to stand your ground, and after you have done everything, to stand. Stand firm then, with the belt of truth buckled around your waist, with the breastplate of righteousness in place, and with your feet fitted with the readiness that comes from the gospel of peace. In addition to all this, take up the shield of faith, with which you can extinguish all the flaming arrows of the evil one. Take the helmet of salvation and the sword of the Spirit, which is the Word of God."
> - Ephesians 6:13-17

What an amazing world we live in. It's changing so rapidly. Technology and the age of the microchip will be for our time what the harnessing of electricity was for the 19th and 20th centuries.

These thoughts came to mind when the "first war of the 21st century" began, the war on terrorism. President Bush pressed ahead with his campaign to rid our world of this evil threat. That's his God-given role as our President and Commander in Chief. Therefore, he conferred with his cabinet and with Congress. He drew allied forces together and assembled a coalition of nations who, with the United States, were intent in seeing our world rid of this great threat to peace and freedom. Once the enemy was identified, the army was deployed and the task began. We saw those efforts unfold first in the impoverished nation of Afghanistan.

One day as I was reading the newspaper and following the war's progress, I was a little disheartened to read that the Taliban was claiming to have shot down an American plane. However, a day or two later, our military released information that this wasn't a manned fighter plane or bomber that was shot down but a "drone," an unmanned aircraft on a reconnaissance mission over the mountains of Afghanistan. When I heard that, I didn't feel so bad. I even thought it quite remarkable that we now had the capability to send unmanned aircraft into war zones without risking the life of American or Allied troops. It almost seemed like a futuristic tale out of an Arnold Schwarzenegger "Terminator" movie. I learned that they could even be used to deliver bombs and guided missiles. I never knew we had such capability. How times have changed.

Different times call for different methods. Different wars call for different armaments. Fortunately, drones will work for our troops in some situations as we wage this war on terrorism but for the war against the enemy God has identified for us, drones will not do much good. We need a different kind of weapon because it is a different kind of war and a different kind of enemy.

When the Apostle Paul wrote these words, he was drawing from the picture of what a foot soldier in the first century might look like. Actually, it was a picture that existed centuries before Paul's time, but not that much had changed with the passage of time. In certain respects, Roman soldiers still dressed for battle in much the same way as soldiers had done centuries earlier. They had a helmet, a breastplate, a belt to hold everything together, appropriate footwear for battle, their shield, and, of course, their sword.

Like that soldier going out to battle, when the day of evil comes upon us, we need to arm ourselves. After we have identified the enemy and looked to God for strength, we next need to arm ourselves appropriately before we step onto the battlefield to face the enemy.

For this battle against the forces of evil that stand opposing us—Satan and his host—simple earthly armor will never do. God must arm us if we hope to stand our ground victorious. Our arsenal of defense and our weapons of offense must find their origin and effectiveness in the power and richness of God's spiritual gifts to mankind. Paul likens these gifts of God to the armor worn by a common soldier of his day, but these are gifts for the soldiers of God throughout time. They are the gifts we still need today to wage war effectively against our great enemy. In that regard, nothing for us has changed. There are six elements to our armor, as Paul describes our dress for battle:

- TRUTH—as our belt,
- RIGHTEOUSNESS—as our breastplate,
- GOSPEL OF PEACE—as our footwear,
- FAITH—as our shield,
- SALVATION—as our helmet,
- GOD'S WORD—as our sword.

Each of these gifts from God has individual importance in our struggle with the forces of evil. Of equal importance, is the relationship of these gifts one to the other. We also need to be aware of Satan's strategy to strip us of our spiritual armor and thus render us defenseless to his attacks.

God's Great Gifts

So, here they are. Here are the gifts God has provided for you by which you might arm yourself for battle when the day of evil comes. However, pretend for a moment, that you cannot take all of these tools into battle with you. Imagine you have to make a choice the way soldiers sometimes do. Do you choose an automatic rifle over a handgun or a bulletproof vest over a lightweight camouflaged covering? What kind of situation will you be in? Do you choose a tank or a fighter jet, a backpack filled with food and survival equipment or a heavy RPG launcher strapped over your back?

Pretend you have to make a choice. Which would you choose? Would it be God's gift of SALVATION—the life that is now yours in Christ? Would you choose the belt of TRUTH? This gift, Jesus said, brings freedom and deliverance from all the scheming lies of the evil one. How about the breastplate of RIGHTEOUSNESS? Isn't that important? Through it, your relationship with God is right and everything with Him is as it should

be. He is now fighting with you at your side. With righteousness, you bring in the strength of allied forces—God Himself!
Then again, the GOSPEL OF PEACE surely is important. How
can Satan defeat you if the saving gospel has already assured
you that peace with God and forgiveness are both yours? The
battle is won! What about FAITH? Faith sure is nice to have
when you enter into battle with Satan and his army. It provides you with courage, confidence, hope and so much more. It
never quits. It will see you through to the very end. GOD'S
WORD—the Sword of the Spirit—the one offensive weapon in
the whole arsenal, would sure be nice to carry with you into
battle. With it, you can split the enemy in two and defeat them
decisively. It is a hard choice, isn't it? Which would you choose?

Don't feel bad if you can't make a choice. These gifts from
God are all valuable. They're all important. It's hard to choose.
Do you know what else? You never have to make a choice. God
sends you out with all of them! Wherever the battle, whatever
the conditions, whenever the attack comes, God provides you
with gifts that make up the full arsenal of everything you need
to defeat the enemy and win the day!

This is not make-believe. This is quite real. There is one
other important fact you need to know. Even though all these
great gifts are yours, there is one in particular that could render
all the others personally useless if it is lost or forfeited in battle. That is the one Satan is going to attack most fervently. He
will try to disarm you. He will try to steal it from you. You
must know which of God's gifts this is. Do you know which one
it is? Do you know how to protect it?

Look closely at these great gifts God imparts to us so that
we are prepared to fight when the day of evil comes. Here they
are again: TRUTH—RIGHTEOUSNESS—GOSPEL OF

PEACE—FAITH—SALVATION—GOD'S WORD. Do you notice anything interesting about them as they relate one to the other? One stands out in a unique way from the rest. It's different from the others. Which one do you think it is and why? Do you see what God wants you to see?

If you're having some difficulty coming to a conclusion on this matter, then consider these questions as you make your choice. Which gifts stand on their own and are now unalterable God-established realities, in and of themselves? On the other hand, which gift is alterable and subject to change? Also, consider this, which gift makes all the other gifts personally yours? Do you know the answer now? If you do, you now know which gift Satan is going to zero in upon. You know where your ground zero is.

The Christian's ground zero is FAITH. Through faith, all these other great gifts of God, established to be certain and sure through the atoning death and victorious resurrection of Jesus Christ, become our personal possession.

Oh yes, TRUTH is critically important to our spiritual well-being but God's truth stands forever. God's truth is a reality that stands by itself even when unbelieving men and women deny it.

Likewise, RIGHTEOUSNESS is a gift that is now a sure and certain reality. It exists apart from us. There is a righteousness that will avail before God whether it is accepted or rejected. A right and perfect relationship with God is available for us to tap into because of all Jesus has accomplished for us.

Angels sang the GOSPEL OF PEACE on that first Christmas night as an established gift for the world. The Prince of Peace had come into the world. It is still, and always will be, a message of peace and good news for the world in spite of the fact that some people will not believe the report. SALVATION is also now an established fact. It is done. Jesus died and rose again. The gift of life eternal and deliverance from bondage to sin and death was accomplished on Easter morning. It is available for everyone.

So also, the gift of GOD'S WORD remains in the world, now translated in languages almost too numerous to count, so that all people might know about this grace of God that exists in Jesus Christ. Jesus said, "Heaven and earth will pass away, but my words will never pass away" (Matthew 24:35). The Holy Bible, the divinely inspired Word of God, exists for the benefit of all whether a person ever picks up a Bible or not.

These great treasures are always there but, unfortunately, as we know all too well, they are not always treasured. These gifts are often rejected. When they are rejected, they become of no benefit to the person God would have enriched. When they are rejected, there is no nourishment gained, no healing, no spiritual freedom won, no life, and no right relationship with God. When they are rejected, for that person, it is as if they did not exist.

FAITH, on the other hand, makes them all our own. Through FAITH, the TRUTH of God in Christ sets us free from the curse of sin. Through FAITH, the RIGHTEOUSNESS that is available for us through the gift of God's Son to the world becomes a living blessing to us personally, as we enjoy a right relationship with God under the canopy of His mercy and forgiveness. Through FAITH, the GOSPEL OF PEACE is believed wholeheartedly and it brings to us a peace with God that not only calms us in the most unspeakable of circumstances but also fills us with an inexpressible and glorious joy. Through FAITH, the gift of SALVATION now imparts such a measure of new life to us that we no longer even fear death. We confidently say with the faithful of old, "I fear no evil, for what can man, even together with all the powers of darkness, do to me?" Through FAITH, the WORD OF GOD becomes our greatest offensive weapon not because it has the power to condemn—sin has already done that—but because it has the power to save, to turn men's hearts back to God, and impart life to us as a powerful means of God's grace. God's great gift of FAITH brings all these other marvelous gifts into our arsenal, so that we become fully armed when the day of evil comes.

Imagine now, how you would fare, in the great battle with "the powers of this dark world," without the shield of FAITH! It is truly a shield, not only because it shields us from "all the flaming arrows of the evil one" but because it also shields all these other great gifts of God from loss. In this vein, picturing faith as a shield is very appropriate indeed.

The Roman soldier would have been quick to understand the metaphor. Numerous types of shields could be used in battle but one in particular comes to mind. It was slightly curved and rectangular in structure, nearly the height of the soldier himself. On the front lines, when the enemy attacked, this shield would be held directly in front of the soldier as he rested it on the ground. In this way, he would be able to protect his entire body from a variety of onslaughts. Furthermore, an entire battalion could be protected when these shields were raised to form a canopy over the heads of soldiers to protect from aerial attack. Every soldier would raise his shield above his head, except for the front line, and instantly a protective shell was formed above the entire fighting force. They were protected from virtually anything the enemy might choose to fire at them.

In the same way, faith is our shield. It protects us, individually, and all these other great gifts by which we are blessed of God. It can also serve to help protect other brothers and sisters in Christ who come under attack from the evil one. We can raise its shield with works of love and encouragement to try to protect other fellow-Christians from Satan's devices. It truly is a shield with which we can "extinguish all the flaming arrows of the evil one."

Without FAITH, every other blessing of God is suddenly in jeopardy. Without FAITH, there is also no longer a holding to TRUTH. Without FAITH, we forfeit our RIGHTEOUSNESS in Christ that avails before God. Without FAITH, there is no longer any trusting in Christ's GOSPEL OF PEACE. Instead, the world is viewed from the side of death, war, and destruction. Without FAITH, there is no life, no SALVATION. Without FAITH, there is no holding to the "sword of the Spirit, which is the Word of God," for unbelief relinquished the sword and surrendered to the enemy! Without FAITH, all is lost!

In the last chapter, we noted that God's plan for us today is the same as it has always been. He wants us to stand firm by seeking that which matters the most. That is why Jesus said, "But seek first his kingdom and his righteousness, and all these things will be given to you as well."

God now governs all the affairs of the world in such a way that His greatest desire for mankind is served. His desire is that an ever-increasing number of lost souls might have that which is most important. This consists of two things: first, the kingdom of God and second, the righteousness of God.

Remember what Jesus said about the kingdom of God.

"The kingdom of God does not come visibly, nor will people say, 'Here it is,' or 'There it is,' because the

kingdom of God is within you."
- Luke 17:20, 21

God's kingdom does not come visibly. It is invisible. It is within. What does that mean? When Jesus describes the kingdom of God as being "within you," he is speaking of the rule of God in the heart of man. When God rules there, when Christ lives as King within us, we are part of God's kingdom, His kingdom of believers. God commended Abraham, the great man of faith, not because he was without sin. He was commended by God not because he always did everything God told him to do. Here is why Abraham was commended by God:

> "Abraham believed God, and it was credited to him
> as righteousness."
> - Romans 4:3

Abraham had that which God most wanted him to have. He had that which was most important. He had the righteousness of God. He had a right relationship with God and was sinless now in the sight of God because God had credited his faith to him as righteousness. Through faith, he was a child of God.

Through faith, the kingdom of God becomes ours. Through faith, God's righteousness becomes our own. God's will for us is that we be His children. God's plan for us is that we might have the gift of FAITH! In summary, this is *God's will* and *God's plan* for our lives. It is also *God's work* in our lives. It is not a work of man. If faith is ours, it is God's doing and to His glory.

"The work of God is this: to believe in the one he has sent.... For my Father's will is that everyone who looks to the Son and believes in him shall have eternal life . . ."
- John 6:29, 40

Satan too has a plan for us: NO FAITH!

"The god of this age has blinded the minds of unbelievers, so that they cannot see the light of the gospel of the glory of Christ, who is the image of God."
- II Corinthians 4:4

Faith always takes an object. Christian faith takes as its object Jesus Christ, who lives within the heart of every believer. What is important for us to realize is that the spiritual forces of evil in this world—Satan being chief among them—also take an object. In fact, they also take Jesus Christ as their object. But their goal is to take Jesus out of our hearts and out of our lives. Their goal is to rob us of our faith in Christ. This brings us to our third insight.

INSIGHT #3
The ultimate goal of evil is spiritual death, to rob us of the victory that is ours through faith . . . *and*

. . . the ultimate meaning of evil is not that it is a test from God of our faith, but a challenge from Satan to our faith.

The words of that New York firefighter now become even more haunting and troublesome.

> "If this was a test from God, I failed because whatever faith I had before is gone."

When the day of evil came on September 11, 2001, we saw evil at its most grotesque. I, along with you and millions of others, watched, in absolute horror, those Twin Towers crumble into rubble. It is still hard to believe. We actually watched, with our own eyes, those great buildings implode upon themselves. We still feel the ache from this great loss of human life.

When I read the words of that stricken firefighter, I saw that implosion all over again, only this time it was not the World Trade Center, it was a man, under attack by the forces of evil. This was an implosion of spiritual magnitude. His words brought a spiritual picture to mind of faith collapsing, vanishing into evil's dark maze of hopelessness and despair. His words spoke everything Satan wanted to hear. "I failed." Does that mean Satan won? "Whatever faith I had before is gone." Sadly enough, it would appear so. "If this was a test from God . . ." But was it from God? Could it possibly be that it was, in truth, a powerful, forceful, life altering challenge of Satan to God's gift of faith?

FAITH: *The Most Precious of God's Gifts*
FAITH is the most precious of God's gifts not because all the other gifts of God are less valuable. That has nothing to do with it. It is because all the other great gifts of God are lost when there is no faith. Peter wrote magnificently about this glorious gift of faith in his first epistle.

"Praise be to the God and Father of our Lord Jesus Christ! In his great mercy he has given us new birth into a living hope through the resurrection of Jesus Christ from the dead, and into an inheritance that can never perish, spoil or fade—kept in heaven for you, who through faith are shielded by God's power until the coming of the salvation that is ready to be revealed in the last time. In this you greatly rejoice, though now for a little while you may have had to suffer grief in all kinds of trials. These have come so that your faith—of greater worth than gold, which perishes though refined by fire—may prove genuine and may result in praise, glory and honor when Jesus Christ is revealed. Though you have not seen him, you love him; and even though you do not see him now, you believe in him and are filled with an inexpressible and glorious joy, for you are receiving the goal of your faith, the salvation of your souls."
- I Peter 1:3-9

If there was anyone who ever appreciated the great gift of FAITH, it had to be Peter and look at how he speaks of it. He describes it as "new birth." We think of the life, the SALVATION, and the deliverance from death that faith brings to us.

He describes it as a "living hope." Isn't this what the GOSPEL OF PEACE brings to us: peace with God and a sure and certain hope for our future?

He describes God's gift to us as "an inheritance" that can never be taken away. Isn't this what faith does for us? Through it, we cling to the RIGHTEOUSNESS that God has won for us in Christ. Through faith in Him, we become children of God and heirs of heaven.

He speaks of being shielded by "God's power." It was by the power of GOD'S WORD that Jesus fought off Satan's temptations. Through faith we too take up the sword of the Spirit—God's Word—to fight off Satan's attacks.

"Though you do not see him, you love him." The TRUTH of Jesus' resurrection, His love for us, and our love for Him, is that which keeps us going from one day to the next. Jesus said, "Blessed are those who have not seen and yet have believed" (John 20:29). In TRUTH, Jesus is our risen Lord and therefore His comforting assurances of life and salvation are true!

FAITH, Peter also writes, is our great shield. Through faith, we are shielded, so that we do not lose all these great gifts of God.

However, while faith is the most precious of God's gifts, it is also the most vulnerable. Therefore, it will be the primary target of Satan's attacks. It is of eternal, critical importance that we be aware of this. For without faith, there is:

- No hope, only despair (Ephesians 2:12),
- No truth, only deception (II Thessalonians 2:11,12),
- No inheritance, only disavowal (Matthew 25:41),
- No life, only death (Ephesians 2:1,2),
- No rejoicing, only sorrow (I Thessalonians 4:13),
- No peace, only unrest (Ephesians 2:14),
- No purpose, only meaninglessness (Ecclesiastes 1:17),
- No glory, only dishonor (I Corinthians 15:43),
- No freedom, only slavery (John 8:34).

Evil, Temptation & Faith

As important as faith is then, how do we deal properly with

challenges to faith when they come into our lives? This is a very important question. It is multifaceted.

We must first remember that faith is not only *a gift from God;* it is the *will of God* for man. Just as importantly, it is a *work of God* within man. If God is to be true to Himself, He cannot work to destroy, frustrate or undo that which is His own will and work for man. He will not do this. It is preposterous, therefore, and certainly a leap in logic, to blame God not only for the problem of evil in the world, but to accuse God, and fault Him, when faith is assaulted and subsequently relinquished by man. God is not to blame for the loss of faith.

Secondly, it is just as foolhardy and perhaps even sadly laughable, to turn on God when evil rears its ugly head in our lives, blame Him for it, and threaten Him with rejection and unbelief unless somehow He remove the suffering from us. Unfortunately, there are times when this is exactly what happens. It is akin to an immature child throwing a temper tantrum. Unfortunately, it is much more serious. Though God is kind, and in His goodness is patient with us when such childlike anger is exhibited against its Creator, nonetheless, we need to repent of it with deep sorrow, for such anger toward God is entirely out of place. This grievous posturing before God is not only improper, but on our part, it is pompously proud and sinful. Remember, we do not favor God because we have faith, as if faith were some kind of great offering we extend to Him. It is quite the opposite: God favors us, and very graciously, I might add, with faith as a gift. We would be totally lost in this world without it. Furthermore, to blame God for the problem of evil in the world is to ignore completely, with impunity, our own guilt.

When such questions arise in our minds, that would challenge our faith and challenge our trust in God's love for us, it would be far better to recognize that Satan is merely trying to stick his ugly foot in the door, and drive a wedge between the God of our salvation and us. He wants to destroy your relationship with Him. He wants to render everything you believe about God useless and meaningless. He wants to convince you that your faith is accomplishing nothing for you. He wants to steal it away and literally rip it from your heart.

Know then, that the day of evil has come. As sure as those Twin Towers came crashing down, your faith is in danger of extinction too. It is time to draw your sword and attack. We will do that now.

Drawing the sword of the Spirit, we read a rather chilling, yet revealing passage from the Word of God.

> "Then Jesus was led by the Spirit into the desert to
> be tempted by the devil."
> - Matthew 4:1

What's this? Jesus, the Son of God, the Messiah, the chosen servant of the Lord, being tempted by the devil? Why? Look even closer. He's not in the desert by accident. Jesus was "led by the Spirit" to be there! The Spirit of God is there too. The Spirit led Him there. There is good reason for this, an eternally good reason, for when this day of evil would end, Jesus would be one-step closer in securing our salvation. Yes, God allowed this evil day, to accomplish a greater good.

Notice, ". . . led by the Spirit"—yes, but tempted by the Spirit—no. Jesus was facing a challenge. It was a challenge that was necessary if He was to be the true, perfect, sinless Savior for all of mankind, past, present and future. It was a challenge to His faithfulness as the one chosen by God from eternity to do for us what we had been unable to do for ourselves. As true man, He needed to do what Adam and Eve, and all their descendants had failed to do: reject Satan's scheming, remain obedient and faithful to His heavenly Father, and thus retain His sinless state. The Holy Spirit led Him there because it was as necessary a part of our redemption as was His death on the cross. If He failed in the desert, He need not even attempt the other, for sin would hold Him in its death grip too. Led by the Spirit, but tempted by the devil. The challenge came, but not from God. God led Him there only because it was so necessary, because of our sin. The challenge came from Satan. The evil of that day was the devil's and his alone.

However, we also remember that there is an enemy within. Satan will tempt us too, but just as often we are our worst enemy.

> "When tempted, no one should say, 'God is tempting me.' For God cannot be tempted by evil, nor does he tempt anyone; but each one is tempted when, by his own evil desire, he is dragged away and enticed."
> - James 1:13, 14

September 11 has indeed given Satan, and the evil within each of us, an opportunity to try again to find some reason in God for what happened that day. We will not find that reason in Him, at least, not the reason for the evil of that day. When the day of evil comes, as it did on 9-11, does God "tempt" us to fall away from him? Is God active in this sense, testing our faith? Is He, who so much desires faith in our hearts, so toying with us that evil may win the day?

God does not play games with your spiritual well-being. You are much more precious to Him than that. He also knows how fragile we can all be. He takes your life and your relationship with Him most seriously.

God does not tempt anyone. The terrorists were tempted by their own "evil desire" that ugly Tuesday. They gave in to the enemy within themselves. They were their worst enemy. Satan now will use the events of 9-11 to tempt us to blame God for their reality. In this very active sense, evil tempts us to turn away from God. In a passive sense, yes, the day of evil becomes a test of our faith, but only because Satan is very actively tempting us to believe his lies. God tempts no one.

We noted in our first insight, how easy it can be for people to lose their focus in times of tremendous tragedy and trial. Even Christians, whom we would expect to hold steady, can get derailed. Peter, I think, understood so much about the treasure that faith is, because his faith was so often challenged. When those challenges came, he often failed, not because God failed him, but because he failed God. He lost focus, in one way or another. He always found himself focusing on something other than what Jesus wanted him to zero in upon. Therefore, he repeatedly found himself in trouble, not as strong as he supposed himself to be, and not as spiritually healthy as he imagined he was.

One of the first great eye-openers for Peter came immediately after Jesus' miraculous feeding of the 5,000. Jesus had dismissed the crowds and then went up into the hills to be alone in prayer. In the meantime, the disciples had stepped into a boat and gone on ahead of Jesus across the lake. Evening came and the boat, far from land, was being buffeted by winds that had suddenly come up. Somewhere between three and six in the morning, Jesus started to make His way out to them from the shore, but He didn't take a boat. He began to walk out to them on the water! When they saw this apparition approaching them, they were so terrified that they thought it was a ghost. You can well imagine their fright. Have you ever been scared? Did you ever think you saw a ghost? It is not a pleasant experience.

I once had a high-school friend who played a practical joke on me in the dark of night. It almost backfired on him when I nearly took his head off! After catching our breath, we both had a good laugh over the whole thing.

In this instance, the disciples were not laughing. They were terrified. Yet, Jesus was keen to their fear, and so as He walked to them He yelled out, "Take courage! It is I! Don't be afraid." That's when Peter spoke up. It seems like he was always the first to speak. Maybe he spoke too soon. Even so, what he said was bold. These were words driven by faith. What he said, he said with clear focus. "Lord, if it's you, tell me to come to you on the water." If it truly was Jesus, he, Peter, would walk on water too! Such confidence! Such faith! "Come," Jesus said to him. This is what happened next.

> "Then Peter got down out of the boat and walked on the water to Jesus. But when he saw the wind, he was afraid and, beginning to sink, cried out, 'Lord, save me!' Immediately Jesus reached out his hand and caught him. 'You of little faith,' he said, 'why did you doubt?'"
> - Matthew 14:29-31

Someone once said that if God were to extend a long iron

cable across the breadth of the Grand Canyon and then ask, "Do you think I can walk this cable and push this wheel-barrow across to the other side?" faith would not just answer affirmatively; the person of faith would jump into the wheelbarrow and confidently say, "Yes, Lord. I believe you can. Let's roll!"

When Jesus said, "Come," Peter's faith kicked in. He said, "Let's roll," and he went. For a while, he was fine. He was actually walking on water just like Jesus! His eyes looked to his Lord. He could see Him in the distance and He was getting closer and closer to his goal. Then something happened. Peter looked off to the side, to the right, to the left. He looked above him, he looked below, and suddenly he noticed that he was beginning to sink! Then he cried out, "Lord, save me!"

What went wrong? Why did Peter start out so well with such great confidence and end up so terrified and soaked to the brim? Isn't it clear? When he took his eyes off Jesus—when he no longer focused on Christ, his Lord and his God—he faltered. His faith failed him because for that moment he lost faith. He lost faith because he lost focus on Christ. What Peter began to focus upon was the wind and the waves, and when he saw the wind and the waves as greater than Jesus, he sank.

If we see the events of 9-11 as greater than the God of our salvation, we will sink. The fact is, they are not. The fact is, nothing ever is. The fact is, if we remain focused on Christ we will "walk through the valley of the shadow of death and fear no evil, for you are with me."

When the day of evil comes, Satan is going to use anything in his arsenal that will lead us to take our eyes off Christ so that we lose focus, look at everything else he wants us to see, and then, stumble and fall, just like Peter. Why do doubts arise in our hearts and minds? Why do we question God's love for us? Why do we question God's power? Why do we question His will for our lives? Why do we wonder if God's ways are the best? Why? We do so because the primary goal of Satan is to challenge our faith. He does it relentlessly. He does it daily. He did it to us big time on September 11. He's still working at it to this day. He will never quit.

He didn't quit on Peter. The devil's visits to this bold and confident disciple were quite regular. Jesus even warned him.

> "'Simon, Simon, Satan has asked to sift you as wheat. But I have prayed for you, Simon, that your faith may not fail. And when you have turned back, strengthen your brothers.' But he replied, 'Lord, I am ready to go with you to prison and to death.' Jesus answered, 'I tell you, Peter, before the rooster crows today, you will deny three times that you know me.'"
> - Luke 22:31-34

We looked at verses 31 and 32 in chapter 1. These verses not only help to identify our enemy and his scheming tricks, they also serve to identify what Satan is specifically targeting when temptations come upon us. We often forget this. However, Jesus, our Savior, does not forget. He knows Satan's target and in this instance He wanted Peter to know that Satan was crouching for an attack and ready to "sift him as wheat," to pulverize him! How would Satan do this? We find the answer in Jesus' loving prayer on behalf of this dedicated disciple. When Jesus said, "But I have prayed for you, Simon, that your faith may not fail," He was identifying clearly, for Peter and for us, His greatest concern. He saw Peter's faith in jeopardy. He saw Satan ready to challenge his faith. He saw Peter's faith as the great target upon which Satan was focused. He saw the greatest danger to Peter was the loss of faith! So Jesus prayed for him.

Notice that Jesus did not pray that the evil be removed. Nor did Jesus pray His heavenly Father to keep Satan from carrying out this assault on Peter. No, that day of evil would come. Jesus would be arrested. Peter would follow. Jesus would be found guilty of blasphemy and worthy of death. Peter would enter the courtyard surrounded by Satan's army of accusers. Jesus would die for our sins and Peter would deny his Lord. Knowing all this, Jesus still focused in prayer upon that which was of greatest concern to Him: Peter's faith. That is what Satan is always after. That is what Jesus wants us to protect most of all. This wasn't a test from God of Peter's faith. This was a challenge from Satan to Peter's faith and Satan's desire was to grind Peter's faith into dust. Jesus was warning him to help him focus in upon the danger lurking about him. Unfortunately, as it can also be said of us, Peter let Satan have his way with him.

On Maundy Thursday evening, the soldiers came to Gethsemane to arrest Jesus. Peter was there. After they took Jesus away, Peter followed. He went where he had been warned not to go.

> "Then seizing him, they led him away and took him into the house of the high priest. Peter followed at a distance. But when they had kindled a fire in the middle of the courtyard and had sat down together, Peter sat down with them. A servant girl saw him seated there in the firelight. She looked closely at him and said, 'This man was with him.' But he de-

nied it. 'Woman, I don't know him,' he said. A little later someone else saw him and said, 'You also are one of them.' 'Man, I am not!' Peter replied. About an hour later another asserted. 'Certainly this fellow was with him, for he is a Galilean.' Peter replied, 'Man I don't know what you're talking about!' Just as he was speaking, the rooster crowed. The Lord turned and looked straight at Peter. Then Peter remembered the word the Lord had spoken to him, 'Before the rooster crows today, you will disown me three times.' And he went outside and wept bitterly.'"

- Luke 22:54-62

Can you imagine yourself in Peter's shoes that dark and evil night? Can you imagine standing around that fire with people staring into your eyes, turning their heads constantly in your direction and then glaringly pointing you out as also being "one of them?" Can you imagine sneaking into that court-yard thinking you would be undetected? Can you imagine sneaking into that courtyard where you were told by your Lord not to go? Can you imagine yourself being that disobedient? Have you ever been that disobedient? Can you imagine? Can you imagine that you could sneak past Satan's detection? Can you imagine the devil just letting you sneak on by without trip-ping his trap? Can you imagine being caught and then trying to worm your way out? Can you imagine looking up after deny-ing your Lord and seeing Him seeing you? Can you imagine being there that night on the eve of evil's greatest roar? Can you imagine how your faith would have fared?

When Peter's eyes met the eyes of Jesus that night, it must have sent a chilling fear to the core of his heart and soul. It wasn't a fear based upon any kind of retaliation against him for what he had just done. He wasn't afraid in that sense. Jesus was the personification of love. Peter knew that. No, the fear that must have shot through him like a sudden spear piercing his heart was the knowledge of what giving into evil's temptation had won for him—nothing. His treasure chest, once so full of rich gifts from this man who had come to mean so much to him, whom he had once so boldly confessed, "You are the Christ, the Son of the Living God," that treasure chest was now emptied. Jesus had not taken those gifts away from him. As he peered into the eyes of his Savior, he could see all those gifts standing right there before him still. In Christ, they were all still there! Then he realized his personal treasure chest was emptied because he had turned it upside down. In denying his Lord, he had emptied the box, he had given up the faith, and he had cast all Christ's gifts to the ground. Peter saw everything he had forfeited by denying his Lord. Satan saw everything Peter had forfeited by denying his Lord. Jesus saw everything Peter had forfeited by denying his Lord. When their eyes met, it was too much for Peter to bear. He left the courtyard. He tried to get away from what he had just done, but he could not. Satan had him right where he wanted him and would not let go. "And he went outside and wept bitterly."

When the day of evil comes, do not go into battle without being fully armed. Did Peter go armed that night? Did he raise his shield? Did he wield his sword? No, instead, he laid his shield to the ground, he gave up his faith, and then everything else fell to Satan's attack.

That's just the way it is when Satan comes after us. He'll attack us where he can inflict the most damage. He attacks our faith because he knows that if we lose that, we will lose everything else God in Christ has won for us.

Yet, the relationship between evil, temptation, and faith is such that the three must coexist now for a while. Jesus gave us the reason why, in His Parable of the Weeds.

> "The kingdom of heaven is like a man who sowed good seed in his field. But while everyone was sleeping, his enemy came and sowed weeds among the wheat, and went away. When the wheat sprouted and formed heads, then the weeds also appeared. The owner's servants came to him and said, 'Sir, didn't you sow good seed in your field? Where then did the weeds come from?' 'An enemy did this,' he replied. The servants asked him, 'Do you want us to go and pull them up?' 'No,' he answered, 'because while you are pulling the weeds, you may root up the wheat with them. Let both grow together until the harvest. At that time I will tell the harvesters: First collect the weeds and tie them in bundles to be burned, then gather the wheat and bring it into my barn.'... His disciples came to him and said, 'Explain to us the parable of the weeds in the field.' He answered, 'The one who sowed the good seed is the Son of Man. The field is the world, and the good seed stands for the sons of the kingdom. The weeds are the sons of the evil one, and the enemy who sows them is the devil. The harvest is the end of the age, and the harvesters are the angels. As the weeds are pulled up and burned in the fire, so it will be at the end of the age.... He who has ears, let him hear.'"
>
> - Matthew 13:24ff

When I was a young boy, I worked for a truck and dairy farmer who was near where our family lived in Wisconsin. Every spring was, of course, the planting. Many fields I planted by hand: sweet corn, melons of various kinds, squash, potatoes, and tomatoes... the list could go on. It was hard work, back wrenching work at times and we didn't have a lot of modern machinery to get the job done. I can remember standing in many of those fields I had planted, looking down at the ground two to three weeks after planting, and wondering, "Where in the world did all these weeds come from?"

When you plow, the ground looks so bare. After you've disked and dragged the field, there's nothing there but just a smooth, even, level flow of beautiful brown earth. Then you go out and plant, and one by one, as the hoe opens the earth, the worker feeds the ground, and the earth takes in God's little miracles of life. While you're doing this you see practically no weeds at all, but if you should happen upon one while you plant, you immediately pluck it from the earth, roots and all. When you're done, you stand and gaze out over the huge field you've planted. There is a feeling of satisfaction in viewing it this way, and there is an eager anticipation of how the brown earth will soon be covered in green as the earth once again springs to life. You wait for rain. You wait for God's blessing. It comes, but with it also comes a curse—the curse of the weeds.

The weeds—how I hated the weeds. I would stand out in the field and curse those cursed weeds when they came. Why? Because they meant more work for me! They meant that the new plants could be choked out and an entire crop ruined. They meant some other forces were at work that I had to deal with, and often times, those other forces at work seemed to be gaining ground on me!

I always had trouble keeping up with the weeds and there were times when I just could not do anything about them. There were times when those weeds grew so close to the plants that I could do nothing but just let them grow and hope the plants would survive. There were times when the plants had grown to such a height that I was unable to get into the field to cultivate any longer, and the weeds had to be left to grow with the good plants.

As Jesus has taught us, this is the way it is with the world we live in. God has come to this earth in the gift of His Son, and has planted good seed in our hearts. We have from Him the life giving seed of His gospel of peace. It has taken root in the hearts of many and faith has sprung to life. But an enemy is also at work where we live. Weeds spring up in our lives. They come from evil seed of the devil and his host. Their seed is that of lies and deceit. They plant the seeds of doubt and unbelief and despair in people's hearts. Their works and their seeds are evil, designed to choke out God's good work of faith.

At times, we ask the same question God's angels may have asked when they saw evil enter the world and how it threatened everything good in God's creation. Like them, we sometimes ask, "God, why don't you get rid of this evil now? Why don't you rip away the weeds from this world so that only your goodness is left? Why don't you protect us from all this evil by just rooting out all of it so that it never threatens us again?"

God's answer to us today is the same answer He gave when evil first entered this world and corrupted His creation. God's answer is clear for us. He gives it to us in His Parable of the Weeds. "No," he tells us. "Leave the weeds alone for now. If you try to pull them up now you may root up and destroy good plants with them. There are plants I want to grow and nour-

ish. I will care for them and help them to survive even while
the weeds sprout up among them and threaten them. The time
for the final harvest has not yet come. When that day comes
and I have harvested all I can for eternal life, then you may
take the cursed weeds, pull them up roots and all, and cast
them into the fire to be destroyed once and for all."

A Blessed End

In short, God has a plan for you and for me. He has a plan for
this world. That plan is still in force. That plan has not yet
been completed. God still is planting His gospel seed in this
world. He is still nourishing that seed in the hearts of people
everywhere and watching faith sprout up. Until that last day
comes He will let evil live. For now, He will let it do its dirty
work because He knows that to rid the world of the problem of
evil permanently, would be devastating to those who remain
separated from God. It would be like rooting up and destroying
good plants with the weeds. It wouldn't accomplish what God
wants to accomplish.

God will save the lost from evil first—He has already done
that through the gift of His Son—then He will destroy evil itself once and for all, but not until as many hearts have been
changed as is possible. It will not happen until evil hearts have
been transformed by the life-giving power of God's Word. It
will not happen until faith has sprung to life worldwide and
His plan has reached completion.

We have a special term for this time God gives us to grow
and find nourishment in Him. We have a special term for this
time in which we as individuals can find deliverance from the
evil within us. We have a special term for this time God has
given to the world to find eternal blessings through the gift of

Jesus Christ. It is our *Time of Grace.* God wants us to use this time wisely, so that, in spite of the weeds, by His grace, our faith in Him grows great and strong.

Therefore, we must watch and pray. We must always be on the alert to the devil's schemes. We must be ready and armed like the soldiers God has made us to be so that when the day of evil comes and our faith comes under attack, our shields are raised and the whole of God's great gifts to us are protected and preserved.

> "Watch and pray so that you will not fall into temp-
> tation. The spirit is willing but the body is weak."
> - Matthew 26:41

Jesus spoke those words to his disciples after He found them sleeping in the garden that night He was betrayed. They needed to be watching. They needed to be praying for themselves and for one another. The day of evil suddenly came, and in fear, despair, and for some, unbelief, they scattered. Our loving God does not want that to happen to us.

> "So if you think you are standing firm, be careful that
> you don't fall! No temptation has seized you except
> what is common to man. And God is faithful; he will
> not let you be tempted beyond what you can bear.
> But when you are tempted, he will also provide a
> way out so that you can stand up under it."
> - I Corinthians 10:12, 13

As you read this, you may be wondering how you can bear up under the great evil challenge to your faith that September

11 brought. You may be inclined to think it is more than you can take. You may even be a friend or family member of one of those innocent victims who died that day. As you struggle to put your shredded life back together, you may be inclined to say, "It is more than I can bear."

Rest assured, God understands what you are going through. He's going through it too, and has been for centuries on end. Evil cost Him His one and only Son. Know that God understands your struggle. Recognize how that knowledge just makes Him uniquely and completely equipped to help you now. This too is part of His plan for you. Know also that He has already given you so much, so that you do not have to be the latest casualty in this great struggle with evil. He has given you everything you need so that you can be the latest victor. In Christ, the victory, through faith, is yours. This is the blessed end for all who believe.

- CHAPTER FOUR -

INSIGHT #4

The ultimate mission of evil is to change our mission, to alter our allegiance to God, to anyone or anything else, so that in reality, whether knowingly or unknowingly, our allegiance is to Satan and thus, our mission in life has changed.

PRAY in the Spirit for Everyone & Keep Praying

"Your mission, Mr. Phelps, if you choose to accept it. . ." Do you remember those words from the hit television series "Mission Impossible?" Once the mission was defined, the tape recording would self-destruct and the intrigue would begin. One of the things that made that series so interesting was that no one ever deviated from the mission. They would all work the scam to perfection, each team member doing his or her part. While they worked, always remaining one step ahead of everyone else, if a problem developed that threatened success, their quick wit and focus upon the mission would find some way to get out of the jam. Invariably, by the end of the show, "Mission Impossible" always ended up being "Mission Accomplished."

Then the first movie came along. What do you suppose happened? Good old Mr. Phelps changed the mission. While everyone else was trying to work together to accomplish the assigned task, Mr. Phelps started a scam of his own. He had his own agenda and was operating on a different page than everyone else. The scammers became the scammees, and the trusted Mr. Phelps was suddenly their betrayer. The result was total chaos.

That was, of course, make-believe, but in real life the principle holds true. If you change the mission, you change the entire nature of the battle, and chaos usually results. In the end, when the mission changes, the battle is usually lost. In fact, one theory, as to why General George Armstrong Custer met his demise at the Little Bighorn, is that on that fatal day he changed his mission. Originally, he was to simply locate and contain the enemy and then wait for reinforcements. At his command, the mission changed to discovering the enemy, surrounding the enemy, and totally conquering the enemy. As a result, his troops were divided in battle, General Custer rode into a trap, chaos ensued, and his army was annihilated.

Change the mission and you change the war, but not only the war—in all likelihood, you also change the outcome of the war. Do you suppose Satan is aware of this little fact? Oh, indeed, he is and he has exhibited a fair amount of success by employing this strategy against God's children down through the ages.

We noted briefly, in the last chapter that faith always takes an object. Christian faith saves, because it takes as its object Jesus Christ, the Savior of the world. Just as faith takes hold of all those other great gifts of God: truth, salvation, righteousness, the gospel of peace and the Word of God, so also faith takes hold of Jesus Christ as its object so that in Him all these great gifts from God to man are secured. In Christ, they all become personally ours.

So simple is this truth and so basic to the Christian religion, that it defines the very manner of our salvation. It is a concept that is easy to understand yet very profound in its implications. For instance, do you remember the account from the book of Acts where Paul and Silas were beaten and thrown into prison? With their feet in stocks, they were put in the inner cell where the jailer kept careful watch. At midnight, from their jail cell, Paul and Silas began to pray and sing hymns to God as other prisoners listened to them. Suddenly an earthquake struck that shook the very foundation of the prison. Just as suddenly, the prison doors flew open and everyone's chains came loose. When the jailer rushed in to see the prison doors open, he drew his sword to kill himself for he knew that empty cells meant his doom. But the prisoners hadn't escaped. They were all still there! He called for lights. Then he rushed into the cell where Paul and Silas stood with the door wide open and their feet no longer bound. He fell trembling before them and cried out, "Men, what must I do to be saved?" They replied with the simple saving message for the ages,

"Believe in the Lord Jesus, and you will be saved—
you and your household."
- Acts 16:31

It is the gospel in a nutshell and we know it best from the words of Christ Himself.

"For God so loved the world that he gave his one and
only Son, that whoever believes in him shall not perish but have eternal life."
- John 3:16

Christian faith saves because it takes hold of Jesus Christ, the object of saving faith and the author of our salvation. As was stated before, Satan takes hold of the same object but his purpose is to take Christ out of our lives and redirect our faith. We've already noted, based on II Corinthians 4:4, how Satan blinds the minds of unbelievers so that they "cannot see the light of the gospel of the glory of Christ." He does not want faith to see its saving object. He does not want mankind to see Jesus Christ as the Savior whom God our heavenly Father has sent into the world to deliver us from our imprisonment to sin and Satan. He does not want us to see how in Christ our chains have been loosed. He does not want us to see how on Easter morning the prison door to death's chamber had been rolled aside for everyone to see because the tomb was empty, and Jesus had risen from death to life! He does not want us to see that Christ's victory over death becomes our victory over death through faith. Instead, Satan continues to do what Jesus described in The Parable of the Sower.

> "Those along the path are the ones who hear, and then the devil comes and takes away the word from their hearts, so that they cannot believe and be saved."
> - Luke 8: 12

In a very narrow sense, Satan's goal is to rob us of our faith, but in a much broader sense, his goal is to change our mission by changing the object of our faith to something other than Jesus Christ. He knows that if he can change our mission, he can change the war, and prevent the gospel from advancing throughout the world. In this strategy, we discover our fourth insight.

INSIGHT #4

The ultimate mission of evil is to change our mission, to alter our allegiance to God, to anyone or anything else, so that in reality, whether knowingly or unknowingly, our allegiance is to Satan and thus, our mission in life has changed.

When the day of evil comes, we need to know the enemy and focus in upon him. We need to find strength in God's mighty power. We need to arm ourselves for the struggle, but lastly, we need also to do this:

> "And pray in the Spirit on all occasions with all kinds of prayers and requests. With this in mind, be alert and always keep on praying for all the saints. Pray also for me, that whenever I open my mouth, words may be given me so that I will fearlessly make known the mystery of the gospel, for which I am an ambassador in chains. Pray that I may declare it fearlessly, as I should."
> - Ephesians 6:18-20

Pray, Paul wrote, for everyone. Keep on praying! But pray for what? One might think that when Paul wrote these words during another period of imprisonment, that he would have asked people to pray that he be released from prison. You would think he would ask for prayers from the saints that might implore God to deliver him from the rod of suffering that he had to endure. You would think he would ask them to pray, focused in upon him, but no, he asked them to pray "for all the saints."

Paul was so focused upon his mission, that even while in prison, it was all he could think about. He wanted prayers that would enable him to continue spreading the gospel fearlessly! He wanted prayers that would enable him to continue to "make known the mystery of the gospel." He even referred to himself as God's "ambassador in chains." Even while in prison he could not help but speak about all he had seen and heard. His whole focus in life centered upon the task given to him by Christ. "This man is my chosen instrument to carry my name before the Gentiles and their kings and before the people of Israel. I will show him how much he must suffer for my name" (Acts 9:15, 16).

And suffer, Paul did. In his second letter to the church at Corinth, he wrote of his sufferings.

> "I have worked much harder, been in prison more frequently, been flogged more severely, and been exposed to death again and again. Five times I received from the Jews the forty lashes minus one. Three times I was beaten with rods, once I was stoned, three times I was shipwrecked, I spent a night and a day in the open sea, I have been constantly on the move. I have been in danger from rivers, in danger from bandits, in danger from my own countrymen, in danger from Gentiles; in danger in the city, in danger in the country, in danger at sea; and in danger from false brothers. I have labored and toiled and have often gone without sleep; I have known hunger and thirst and have often gone without food; I have been cold and naked. Besides, everything else, I face daily the pres-

sure of my concern for all the churches."
- II Corinthians 11:23-28

Suffering—Paul knew it well. Yet, of all the great men of faith he stands out so remarkably because he persevered in holding true to his charge. His mission, to bring the saving message of Jesus Christ to the Gentiles, was never relinquished, nor was it abandoned. It was never altered, nor was it compromised. How did he remain so strong in the midst of such great suffering? By God's grace, He remained focused on the object of his faith, Jesus Christ, and the great gifts that God in Christ had won for him. That is what enabled him to remain true to his mission.

The Object of Faith

Not every faith saves, but every faith takes some object as its greatest affection. Those objects can be many and quite varied, one from the other. Many gods are proclaimed through many religions in this world, but there is only one true God. Paul found this to be much the case when he visited Athens and was invited to speak at a meeting of the Areopagus. There he walked about and observed their many objects of worship and even found one altar with an inscription, "TO AN UNKNOWN GOD" (Acts 17:16f). They were very religious people, but they did not know the true God, so Paul told them, "Now what you worship as something unknown I am going to proclaim to you." He proceeded to share with them the saving message of Christ's death and resurrection.

Faith always takes an object, but faith can take a wrong object. Whatever that object is, that becomes your god. It has rightly been said that a person's god is whatever he regards as his highest good in life. The Apostle Peter put it this way,

> ". . . man is a slave to whatever has mastered him."
> - II Peter 2:19

What is the great object of your affection? What is your highest good in life? What has mastered you?

There can be many objects to faith: power, position, beauty, friends, family, religion, philosophy, self, materialism, money, wealth; these are just a few. Government and nation could be an object of faith. Even the law of God could be an object of faith.

The Scriptures are filled with warnings about making this world's trappings the object of our affection. John, in his first Epistle, wrote,

> "Do not love the world or anything in the world. If anyone loves the world, the love of the Father is not in him. For everything in the world—the cravings of sinful man, the lust of his eyes and the boasting of what he has and does—comes not from the Father but from the world. The world and its desires pass away, but the man who does the will of God lives forever."
> - I John 2:15-17

The person who has Jesus Christ as the object of his affection, will do "the will of God" and live forever. Jesus put it this way,

> "Do not store up for yourselves treasures on earth,

where moth and rust destroy, and where thieves break in and steal. But store up for yourselves treasures in heaven, where moth and rust do not destroy and where thieves do not break in and steal. For where your treasure is, there your heart will be also.... No one can serve two masters. Either he will hate the one and love the other, or he will be devoted to the one and despise the other. You cannot serve both God and Money."

- Matthew 6:19-21, 24

There is an important connection between the object of faith and one's mission in life. The object of faith determines the mission. If your highest good in life is to gain for yourself power and position, your life will be dedicated to finding any and all ways to rule over others. If the object of your faith is money and wealth, your mission in life will be to spend your waking hours accumulating as much as you can. If you must have everything that is the latest in fashion and your heart's desire is to maintain a youthful appearance, perhaps beauty has become your god. If family, friends, spouse, or children are more important to you than anything else in life is, then you will spend your time living for them, caring for them, making them happy, even to the exclusion of spiritual pursuits. Even if you are an atheist and proudly proclaim, "God does not exist," you have a god. Your highest good is yourself, specifically, your intellect that has led you to that conclusion, and it will govern the direction of your life. The object of faith is the determining factor in defining your mission in life. If Jesus Christ is the object of your faith, His mission for your life will take precedence over everything else.

On September 11, a great many people in our nation, and from other nations around the globe, lost friends and family who were very dear to them. Some are handling their loss better than others are. It will always be that way. No one is the same. Every individual's threshold for pain is different. When that New York firefighter so sadly uttered those spiritually bankrupt words, "If this was a test from God, I failed because whatever faith I had before is gone," I could hear his anguish over this great loss of life that had come upon him. But I also fear for him now and what this loss has come to mean in his relationship with God. Does it mean there is no saving relationship with Him any longer? Has the loss of family and friends who were so dear to him utterly shattered his love for his Creator who has done so much for him in life? Have their deaths robbed him of spiritual life? I hope and pray that this is not the case. I pray that after mourning this loss and after greater reflection upon God's goodness, even in the midst of this great evil, that faith will be restored to him, and hope for the future will overcome his current feelings of failure.

There is hope for the future when God and His will for us is first in life. The danger that hope will be lost, and replaced with feelings of failure and despair, is also very real if anyone or anything, except our Savior Jesus Christ, is regarded as our highest good in life. Sometimes family can become so important to us and we are so wrapped up in the joys, the obligations, and the responsibilities of caring for family and loved ones, that they become our highest good in life and the primary object of our affection. When this happens, these wonderful gifts from God end up replacing God in our lives.

There is great danger in that, for everything in this world, including life itself, is transitory. It can be lost in a moment.

Youth is lost to old age. Physical beauty can be permanently altered by an accident. Earthly treasure can be lost in an instant. Loved ones can be taken from us quite suddenly and unexpectedly. If then, in our lives, God has been displaced by some other priority, what will be our response? Will it be a response of strength and hope drawn from faith, with God in Christ as its object? Or, will our response be that of anger, bitterness, and resentment toward God that He would dare allow that which was most precious to us to be taken away?

God has warned us repeatedly in Holy Scripture, not to set our hearts on earthly things, even family. There is good reason for this. It is because everything that we have in life is not our own, but rather gifts, from the hand of God. They are never to be the prime objects of our affection.

> "The earth is the Lord's and everything in it, the world, and all who live in it."
> - Psalm 24:1

Why do we want to treat that which is God's, as if it were our own? Do we dare to think that we who are imperfect have the ability, the necessary wisdom, or foresight, to care for that which God has temporarily gifted to us, better than God can care for it Himself? In the framework of eternity, do we really believe that we have the ability to work through all the evil in this world, along with all of Satan's scheming, and all the sinful transgressions of mankind, in such a way, that it will end up working for the good of all God's children? Do we really think we can do what is possible for only God Himself to accomplish?

The answer to that question is this: YES! You may be

amazed but, yes, we do begin to think that way when God becomes displaced in our lives by other objects of faith, and Satan changes our mission in life from one of serving God and proclaiming His saving message of grace, to a new and entirely different mission. As bad as that is, it is not the worst of it, for with the new mission comes also a sense of pride that our new mission is better and more meaningful than God's charge for us. We can even become so bold as to think that our ways are infinitely wiser than God's ways for this world.

Is the object of your faith friends and family? Are they your highest good in life? Is caring for them, protecting them, nurturing them and providing for them your most important mission in life? If this is the case, then know that your whole reason for living can be swiftly snatched from you in an evil instant because your relationship with God and your mission in life is not what God has intended it to be. That is what Satan was trying to do with many people on September 11. The end result is anger toward God, faithlessness, hopelessness, and despair.

Jesus had some very interesting words to say on the subject of family and friends. They often seem very harsh and confusing to us. We'll discuss in a moment *why* that is the case. First, let's attend to *what* Jesus said.

> "As they were walking along the road... He said to another man, 'Follow me.' But the man replied, 'Lord, first let me go and bury my father.' Jesus said to him, 'Let the dead bury their own dead, but you go and proclaim the kingdom of God.' Still another said, 'I will follow you, Lord; but first let me go back and say good-by to my family.' Jesus replied, 'No one who puts

his hand to the plow and looks back is fit for service
in the kingdom of God.'"
- Luke 9:59-62

What's this? As Christians, can we not even take time to
bury our parents when they die? Are we not even allowed time
to say good-by to family? Must we spend every waking moment of every day focused in upon Christian service? That seems
a bit harsh, doesn't it? Isn't God being rather unreasonable
here? What are we supposed to be, religious fanatics?

The answer is yes and no. No, Jesus is not saying that you
can never take time to bury the dead and no, Jesus is not saying that there is anything wrong in saying good-by to family.
However, Satan would love to have you believe that God is that
unfair and that unreasonable. We know who our enemy is and
that he is the master of lies and exaggeration. Knowing that
this is but another of Satan's tricks to turn us away from God,
what then, is the true meaning of Christ's words?

The key to understanding these words from Luke's Gospel
is to note what is repeated by Christ concerning both individuals. For both of them, the word "first" is used to describe how
they will enter their relationship with Christ. Both of them
have something that they must "first" do before Christ can come
"first" in their lives. The second key point in understanding
this section of Scripture is to note that in both cases Jesus
underscores what their primary mission in life is to be. For the
first, that mission is defined as "proclaim the kingdom of God."
For the second, that mission is simply referred to as, "service
in the kingdom of God." However, both mean exactly the same
thing. God's mission for every person in life is that we are to be
of service to Him in His kingdom by proclaiming the saving

gospel message throughout the world.

Through hyperbole, an intentional exaggerated statement, Jesus shares an important lesson with us. If ever there is anyone or anything, other than Christ, who is "first" in our lives, we will not really be fit for "service in the kingdom of God" because another mission in life will take precedence over the mission Christ has given us, which is to "proclaim the kingdom of God." The object of faith determines the mission.

Therefore, if family, friends, or loved ones are the object of our faith, then our mission in life will be to care for them in every way possible as our greatest treasure. The treasure of Christ and His gospel will most certainly take secondary importance or, perhaps, Christ may find no importance in our lives at all! Then, the day comes when family, friends, and loved ones are suddenly taken from us. If they were our mission in life, suddenly life has no meaning any longer. Suddenly, we find ourselves left with a meaninglessness and hopelessness in living, that God never intended for any of us. On the other hand, if God in Christ comes first, then we always have meaning to life and we always have hope for the future, an eternal hope.

We need to ask ourselves an important question as we struggle in life keeping family and friends from occupying the most precious place in our heart, for it is a difficult struggle. We need to ask, "How can I best serve and care for my family, my spouse, my children, my co-workers and my neighbors? How can I best be my brother's keeper?" You do that best by keeping Christ first in your life so that through you the Christian mission is fulfilled. Through you, Christ is proclaimed to them in the hope that Jesus becomes first in their lives. When that happens, and the day of evil comes upon them, as it did on 9-

11, they will be prepared for it. They too will "fear no evil" for God will be with them, because you fulfilled your God-given mission and showed them Christ as "the way, the truth, and the life."

Jesus said,

> "Anyone who loves father or mother more than me is not worthy of me; anyone who loves son or daughter more than me is not worthy of me; and anyone who does not take his cross and follow me is not worthy of me. Whoever finds his life will lose it, and whoever loses his life for my sake will find it."
>
> - Matthew 11:37-39

These words also become easier for us to understand when we realize the important connection between Christ's place in our hearts and how that affects the fulfillment of His mission in our lives. If other people in our lives take first place over Christ, how can we be worthy servants to Him? If He is not first for us, how can we expect to carry faithfully His saving name to the lost of the earth?

As you read this, some of you may be struggling with mothers or fathers, sons or daughters, who do not share your Christian convictions. Perhaps you read this as one who does not yet believe, but you have a son or daughter, or maybe a mother or father, whom you just cannot understand, and their allegiance to Christ just baffles and frustrates you to no end.

Open your hearts to one another. If you know Christ, cling to Him but keep sharing His love with your unbelieving son or daughter, mother or father, but do so kindly and gently as Jesus Himself did when He walked this earth. Know that the

Holy Spirit works through you but let the Holy Spirit work in His own time and in His own way.

If you do not yet know Jesus Christ as your Lord and King, open your hearts to the words of Christ and the new life that your loved one wants to share with you. See how it guides their life and brings them peace with God and certainty of salvation. Know that through faith, all these gifts of God are there waiting for you too. Through faith in Christ, you can claim them as your very own. Your family simply wants you to have what they have.

In short, as Jesus said, if ever we find meaning to life in this world, so that we cling to anyone or anything in this world as our greatest gain, then we lose eternal life. However, if we ever come to see that in this world life has no lasting value through anyone or anything in it, but only in Jesus Christ, who came to us from heaven, we then find our greatest gain. Then we have found eternal life. With Christ as the object of faith, we will have a meaningful mission and purpose in living.

So many things, however, can displace Christ in our lives. So many things, and some, very unexpectedly, can alter our mission. For instance, as has been observed earlier in the book, some, in reaction to the events of 9-11, found reason to point the finger at others and say that they are at least partly responsible in setting the stage for this terrible evil that has befallen our nation. A way of thinking has been expressed that says God is being ignored, rejected in our nation's institutions, and that a secularization of America has become the norm. I suppose the idea that is being proposed is that we had this coming, given the fact that we have done so much as a nation over the last few decades to spurn God and cast Him out of the public eye.

As I contemplated this issue, I first asked myself, "Has this happened? Are we guilty of this as a nation?" I can think of times when Christ has been attacked in our land. It seems like it gets more and more frustrating every year when even simple Christmas decorations are no longer permitted in government buildings and in communities throughout our country. Certainly, I thought, I have not agreed with many of the decisions that have come out of our nation's courts. Roe vs. Wade has resulted in the loss of thousands upon thousands of innocent lives. Abortion is a very grievous sin in our nation. It is abhorrent to God and in every respect contrary to the sanctity of life as taught from Holy Scripture. I hope and pray that someday it will come to an end. So certainly, we have sinned as a nation, and we have sinned as individuals in this great land, Christian and non-Christian alike.

What do we say to this? How do we respond? What should we do? Well, as Christians, we have a mission, do we not? Jesus Christ is the object of our faith and the object determines the mission. The mission Jesus has given us is to go out into the world and proclaim the good news that in Him we have a Savior from sin and the gift of eternal life. The question then, becomes this: If Jesus is the object of faith and the believer's mission is simply to proclaim the gospel, can I do that without "spiritualizing" national institutions? The answer to this first question is very simply, yes. However, in leading more people to Christ is it also our responsibility to "nationalize" Christianity? Did Jesus ever command us to make Christianity into the official religion of the state? Here, the answer is unequivocally, no. We have no such command from our Lord.

Maybe the time has come for Christians across our nation to wake up and smell the coffee. Maybe it is time for us Christians to stop our whining when the principles of our faith are not practiced to our satisfaction across the breadth of our land. What should we expect to find? Jesus came to a world of sin and sinners. Why do we think we should find anything different in our nation and in our world today?

Maybe it is time for us as Christians to stop blaming the courts, to stop blaming the ACLU, to stop blaming the public schools, to stop blaming legislative bodies, to stop blaming those whom we perceive as wanting to "secularize" America and start pointing the finger where it really belongs: at ourselves and specifically, our lackluster, lackadaisical efforts to *spiritualize* America by touching the hearts of individual souls with the good news of Jesus Christ.

When Jesus came to this world, He wasn't interested in spiritualizing secular Roman institutions. He was interested in changing individual hearts through the proclamation of gospel truth. When the evangelists and the apostles began their worldwide campaign, it wasn't at Christ's command to transform the secular institutions of the day into a more spiritually acceptable form. They were to simply go out into the world and preach the gospel to every creature. So that's what they did! Change came as individual hearts were changed.

It is not the job of governments to proclaim the saving gospel of Jesus Christ. It is not the mission of public schools to proclaim the gospel of Jesus Christ. It is not the mission of legislative bodies to pass laws that make the gospel of Jesus Christ the law of the land. It is not the mission of the courts to proclaim Christ as Lord. It is not the mission of any public or private civic club or organization to proclaim the saving gospel. IT IS, HOWEVER, THE MISSION OF CHRISTIANS, IN-DIVIDUALLY AND COLLECTIVELY AS THE BODY OF

CHRIST, TO PROCLAIM THE GOSPEL OF JESUS CHRIST! Why would we want to change our mission? Is there another one of greater significance? Is there another mission of greater eternal importance? If God is the same, yesterday, today, and forever, then His plans for us are the same, yesterday, today, and forever. The irony in all of this, is that while Christians are being called upon to engage in such activities, via government bodies, the courts, etc., so that this nation becomes a more "Christian" nation, they are being called upon to do a work that is quite different than the mission Christ Himself has given them to do. In fact, by altering the mission, America appears to becoming less and less Christian!

Could it be that this is Satan's scheming? Could it be that Satan knows that if we make nation, government, or God's law, the object of faith, and our highest good, that Christ and His mission for us, that of proclaiming the saving gospel, will be put on the back burner? Could it be that by altering the mission—though trying to make the alteration appear so right and so holy—it is actually producing the opposite result? Perhaps that is evidence enough of why it is so wrong.

We need to remember what Jesus had to say on the issue of our relationship to nation and government, the relationship between the temporal and the eternal. Jesus said,

"Give to Caesar what is Caesar's, and to God what is God's."
- Matthew 22:21

Do you recall the circumstances under which Christ spoke those words? It was during Holy Week while Jesus was busy teaching in the temple grounds. The Pharisees laid a trap for

Him, to catch Him in His words so that they might turn the people against Him. They hoped to find Him either a political fanatic and an enemy of Rome, or a blasphemer living as an enemy of God and an ally of Rome. So they asked Him, "Is it right to pay taxes to Caesar or not?"

That same question is being asked of Christians today too, only with a slightly different twist. It really is nothing more than another of Satan's traps. "Should Christians be allowed to pray in public schools or not?" "Should the ten commandments be posted on the walls of public libraries, public schools and federal and state court buildings or not?" Do you notice the similarity between what was asked Jesus in His day and what is being asked us today? These are questions at the heart of our God-given mission.

For Jesus the mission was to save, to teach, to go the way of the cross. It was not to become an earthly king. It was not to get embroiled in all kinds of political arguments. It was not to make Christianity the state religion of the Roman Empire. He shunned all such notions. He said, "Give to Caesar what is Caesar's, and to God what is God's." In other words, government has a God-given task to fulfill and the children of God have another. Those tasks are quite different and it is not necessary to mix the two.

Many times, we are made to feel that if we, as Christians, do not support such initiatives, that we are not very good Christians at all. After all, why wouldn't a Christian support prayer in public schools and why wouldn't we want the Ten Commandments posted in buildings across our land? The answer is very simple. We can answer the same way Jesus did, "Give to Caesar what is Caesar's, and to God what is God's."

Neither necessarily has to be supported by Christians because they are not the tasks God has assigned to government nor are they the tasks assigned to us as Christians. These tasks do not represent our God-given mission! They are, in fact, diversions from the mission God has given us and Satan would love nothing better than to see us get off track from our mission of proclaiming the saving gospel of Jesus Christ.

You may struggle with this. You may ask, "But doesn't God want us to be a God-fearing nation? Doesn't God want us to be a Christian nation?" Yet, these questions too, almost beg a desire to alter the mission Christ Himself has given us. These questions assume that we will be a "Christian nation" if we display the great marks and symbols of Christianity across our land. We will be a "Christian nation" if we allow prayer in public schools. We will be a "Christian nation" if we post the Ten Commandments boldly in prominent institutions throughout our land. We will be a "Christian nation" to be favored and protected by God if we fulfill these and other "Christian-like" tasks from sea to shining sea.

This is a lie, and it is a trick of Satan to try to alter our God-given path. As Christians, we need to listen more closely to the object of our faith and recognize that our God-given task is to change hearts from within. It is to lead many more to Christ through the proclamation of the gospel. Our mission has never been to change the outward appearance of public buildings so that we end up with a nation whitewashed in the symbols of our faith. It was never supposed to be the manipulation and influence of government to lead individuals to Christ, but it has always been a mission to employ the power of the Holy Spirit, through God's life-giving Word, to lead many more to Christ. This is our task, the church's task, and not the government's task.

The Scriptures do say, "Blessed is the nation whose God is the Lord." This verse from the Psalms has been used almost as a mantra to rally Christians to a new Holy War, that of Christianizing our national institutions. This is, as we will see, not only unnecessary, as far as God is concerned, but it is misguided folly, as far as we should be concerned. It becomes a misuse of the blessed time of grace God has given us all. A careful examination of Psalm 33 helps to examine why this is so wrong and why this is such an important issue in the wake of September 11. So let's look at this Psalm now and see exactly what God is saying to us through it.

It is, first of all, a Psalm of praise to God from the lips of the righteous, and a song of celebration over God's gracious workings in the lives of His believing people everywhere.

1 Sing to the Lord, you righteous;
    it is fitting for the upright to praise him.
2 Praise the Lord with the harp;
    make music to him on the ten-stringed lyre.
3 Sing to him a new song;
    play skillfully, and shout for joy.
4 For the word of the Lord is right and true;
    he is faithful in all he does.
5 The Lord loves righteousness and justice;
    the earth is full of his unfailing love.
6 By the word of the Lord were the heavens made,
    their starry host by the breath of his mouth.
7 He gathers the waters of the sea into jars;
    he puts the deep into storehouses.
8 Let all the earth fear the Lord;
    let all the people of the world revere him.

9 For he spoke, and it came to be;
   he commanded, and it stood firm.
10 The Lord foils the plans of the nations;
   he thwarts the purposes of the peoples.
11 But the plans of the Lord stand firm forever,
   the purposes of his heart through all generations.
12 Blessed is the nation whose God is the Lord,
   the people he chose for his inheritance.
13 From heaven the Lord looks down
   and sees all mankind;
14 from his dwelling place he watches
   all who live on the earth—
15 he who forms the hearts of all,
   who considers all they do.
16 No king is saved by the size of his army;
   no warrior escapes by his great strength.
17 A horse is a vain hope for deliverance;
   despite all its great strength it cannot save.
18 But the eyes of the Lord are on those who fear him,
   on those whose hope is in his unfailing love,
19 to deliver them from death
   and keep them alive in famine.
20 We wait in hope for the Lord;
   he is our help and our shield.
21 In him our hearts rejoice,
   for we trust in his holy name.
22 May your unfailing love rest upon us, O Lord,
   even as we put our hope in you.

Yes, "Blessed is the nation whose God is the Lord," is the
pronouncement in verse 12, but who is this nation and how are

those of that nation so blessed?

Notice that no identifiable name for any particular nation is offered. Some have concluded that this means *any* nation. In other words: blessed is *any* nation whose God is the Lord. Yet, that is not what the Psalmist writes. He writes, "Blessed is the nation . . ." There seems to be a particular nation that the Psalmist has in mind. What nation is it? You do not have to look too far. The next phrase in verse 12 tells us. That nation is, "the people he chose for his inheritance."

In an immediate sense, we might think of the Old Testament nation of Israel. They were a *people,* a nation, chosen by God for a very special purpose. To them was given an inheritance, a land flowing with milk and honey. They were the nation of promise. The promised Messiah would come from their nation. He would come as a blessing for their nation and for all other nations. Through Jesus Christ, the Messiah who came, an even greater nation has grown. It is a nation of believers, a nation of God-fearing men and women who look to Jesus Christ as the giver of an even greater inheritance than what Old Testament Israel received in that physical land of promise. In Christ is given an inheritance of heavenly, eternal worth. The Apostle Peter wrote of this inheritance in his first epistle.

> "Praise be to the God and Father of our Lord Jesus Christ! In his great mercy he has given us new birth into a living hope through the resurrection of Jesus Christ from the dead, and into an inheritance that can never perish, spoil or fade—kept in heaven for you, who through faith are shielded by God's power..."
> - I Peter 1:3-5

Who then is this nation that is so blessed by God? Only the nation "whose God is the Lord." That nation is Christ's body of believers. That nation, so blessed, is the Holy Christian Church. That nation is made up of all people everywhere, of every race, of every nationality on earth, of every gender, of every age, and of every generation of peoples, past, present and future, who are "righteous" (vs.1) through faith in Jesus Christ, who are a direct result of the "plans of the Lord" and "purposes of his heart," (vs.11). He has eternal plans and purposes for us, namely, to believe in Jesus Christ and to be saved. If you are a follower of Jesus Christ, you are part of that great and blessed nation the Psalmist speaks of in Psalm 33. Peter also wrote of that nation.

> "But you are a chosen people, a royal priesthood, a holy nation, a people belonging to God, that you may declare the praises of him who called you out of darkness and into his wonderful light. Once you were not a people, but now you are the people of God; once you had not received mercy, but now you have received mercy."
> - I Peter 2:9-10

In Christ, everything is ours! In Christ we are that blessed nation of God! In Christ everything meaningful, everything living, everything eternal, is ours as a gift of God's mercy and grace through the blessing of His Son! There is no other "blessed nation." The only nation that will be so blessed by God, is the nation that is known only to God. It is made up of everyone everywhere whose hearts have been changed to see that in Christ we have a righteousness from God as our own, for our souls' salvation.

September 11 did not happen to the United States of America because we somehow lost our "blessed" status spoken of in Psalm 33. Furthermore, we will not gain back any kind of "blessed nation" status if we begin posting the Ten Commandments on public buildings and begin again offering up Christian prayers in public schools. Why not? Because, these are only the things man looks at, not God. "Man looks at the outward appearance, but the Lord looks at the heart" (I Samuel 16:7).

In Psalm 33, the Psalmist does not describe God as looking at individual nations; God is looking at individual hearts, their hope in Him, and the righteousness through faith that is there, (vs.1, 5, 8, 15, 18, 20, 21, 22). They look to God in Christ because through His resurrection they find someone who has the power "to deliver them from death" (vs.19) and one who can "keep them alive" through the great famine of spiritual deprivation and evil found throughout this sin infected world. Christ has provided the answer! Jesus provides the spiritual food we need the most! Thus we are fed, nourished, delivered and "God's plans" for the world, the spiritual "purposes of his heart" for generations, are fulfilled (vs.11).

This, God's mission through all generations, He now passes on to us. This is our mission and it will remain ours if we remain focused upon it. God is not a respecter of nations. God knows nothing of "most favored nation" status. His grace is to all and for all. Again, September 11 did not happen because we ceased to be that "blessed" nation of God. We were not that to begin with. We are letting Satan fool us if we become so proud as to think that God's favor is so cheaply earned. Good and evil will come to the faithful and the unfaithful alike as long as this world exists. That's what happened on September 11 and that day reminds us how important it is to remain true to Christ's mission so that when the day of evil comes, deliverance from death is realized for all who have come to believe.

So as Christians, we, especially now, need to keep our wits about us. We cannot change the mission and expect victory over death to be won. Posting the Ten Commandments will not speak to others the story of Jesus' victory over sin and death. Those commandments only show us our own sin and our many failures in the light of God's law. Fighting so long and hard for public prayer in public schools is not our Christian task. In fact, our children continue to pray in their schools daily, even though it may be done quietly, silently, and known only to God. Is this so terrible? Have we forgotten what Jesus said, "When you pray, go into your room, close your door and pray to your Father, who is unseen. Then, your Father, who sees what is done in secret, will reward you" (Matthew 6:6). We do not want to "strain out a gnat but swallow a camel" (Matthew 23:24). There are greater maladies to address, such as faithlessness, hopelessness, and despair that reign all too prominently in our nation and in our world.

September 11 is a reminder that Christ's mission to us is still of prime importance. The evil of that day reminds us that Satan is still very active. The loss of life that day reminds us that sharing the good news of deliverance from death, through Jesus Christ, needs to remain our primary focus and mission.

Yes, we can point to many ills and many sins throughout our country. Yes, we are laden with the guilt of abortion. It is a national tragedy. Yes, homosexuality, alcohol abuse, drug addiction, crime, and all other manner of sins grip us in a stranglehold, threatening to destroy us as a people and a free nation. However, these are not just problems our nation faces to-day. These are problems for the entire 21ˢᵗ century world. These are sins that are centuries old and they are sins that have al-ways been with us and will always be with us, as long as this world in its present state exists.

God wants us to be mindful of the truth that we will not change sinful habits without first working to change sinful hearts. We will not eliminate the sin of abortion without first changing the human heart to value the sanctity of human life from the moment of conception. We will not decrease sins of the flesh without first increasing the sum of the faithful. Sanc-tified living comes as a response of faith, which is a gift of the Spirit. All these workings happen as we go out into the world to fulfill our God-given mission. When we fail to do that, we fail ourselves, we fail others, we fail our nation, and we fail our God. We then, become as much to blame for this world's ills as anyone else.

It is too easy to become the moralists of this new century and make the law of God the object of our faith. It is an easy thing to point out sin all around us and spend all our time trying to create a more obedient society to God's laws. That is what is known as legalism and moralism. That is not Christi-anity. There were many people in Jesus' day who did that, and he found their deeds anything but God-pleasing. What follows is a very familiar example from Jesus' life and ministry. You may know this story quite well.

> "'Teacher, this woman was caught in the act of adul-tery. In the law Moses commanded us to stone such women. Now what do you say?' They were using this question as a trap, in order to have a basis for accus-

ing him. But Jesus bent down and started to write on the ground with his finger. When they kept questioning him, he straightened up and said to them, 'If any of you is without sin, let him be the first to throw a stone at her.' Again he stooped down and wrote on the ground. At this, those who heard began to go away one at a time, the older ones first, until only Jesus was left, with the woman standing there. Jesus straightened up and asked her, 'Woman, where are they? Has no one condemned you?' 'No one, sir,' she said. 'Then neither do I condemn you,' Jesus declared. 'Go now and leave your life of sin.'"
- John 8:4-11

Interesting, isn't it? Consider this: the first ones to walk away in shame were *the older ones!* The longer you live the more sin you see, not necessarily in others, but certainly in yourself. What it does is make you even more appreciative of God's great gift of forgiveness in Christ.

If our mission as Christians ever becomes that of rooting out sin wherever it is found, we will not only fail miserably, but we will have compounded sin's presence among us with our own sin of pride. If we are going to blame any particular sinners in our culture for the events of September 11, then I, for one, need some help in knowing where to begin for I have looked and I see sin everywhere, first in me and then everywhere else. Did my sins cause September 11? Did yours? Had someone at the Pentagon that day, or in the Twin Towers, committed some great sin that required such punishment that so many others were left in destruction's wake? What great sin was it that provoked such great punishment? Are we to believe that if we but root out sin from society as a whole, we will be healed of all our ills and God will smile down upon us again?

If this kind of arguing sounds ridiculous to you, it should. It is nonsense. The moralists and legalists of Jesus' day were constantly peppering Him with this kind of coldhearted, judgmental logic. Finally, Jesus had enough. This is what He said to the scribes and Pharisees, the legalists and moralists of His day. We would also do well to remember that Jesus most likely spoke these words on Tuesday of Holy Week.

> "'Woe to you, teachers of the law and Pharisees, you hypocrites! You travel over land and sea to win a single convert, and when he becomes one, you make him twice as much a son of hell as you are. Woe to you, blind guides!... You give a tenth of your spices—mint, dill and cummin. But you have neglected the more important matters of the law—justice, mercy and faithfulness. You should have practiced the latter, without neglecting the former. You blind guides! You strain out a gnat but swallow a camel.... Blind Pharisee!... You are like whitewashed tombs, which look beautiful on the outside but on the inside are full of dead men's bones and everything unclean. In the same way, on the outside you appear to people as righteous but on the inside are full of hypocrisy and wickedness.... You snakes! You brood of vipers!... I am sending you prophets and wise men and teachers. Some of them you will kill and crucify; others you will flog in your synagogues and pursue from town to town.... O Jerusalem, Jerusalem, you who kill the prophets and stone those sent to you, how

often I have longed to gather your children together,
as a hen gathers her chicks under her wings, but you
were not willing.'"
- Matthew 23: select verses

Three days later, these legalists/moralists completed their
mission and Jesus was put to death by crucifixion.

If the object of our faith ever becomes the law of God and
obedience to it as our highest good, then expect our mission to
change as well. The mission changed dramatically for the
scribes and Pharisees of Jesus' day when God's moral law took
center stage in their lives. Sinful pride took over where personal repentance and humility should have reigned. Legalism
and its ugly cousin, moralism, always find fault in others before it finds the sin within. The invariable result is a religious
spirit marked by bitterness, anger, and coldness toward others. That is not the way we are supposed to be. That is not the
way Jesus was.

Did you notice how He ended this justified scolding of these
self-righteous antagonists? He ended on a loving invitation of
mercy and forgiveness, ". . . how often I have longed to gather
your children together, as a hen gathers her chicks under her
wings, but you were not willing." Even at the height of their
hatred for Him, Jesus wanted to find them under His protective care to find life and salvation in Him. This was His mission. However, they would not turn to Him because their mission was quite different from that of their Messiah's. In a short
time, their mission would attain its climactic fury, and Jesus
would be dead. If only their mission had not changed. Maybe
then they would have seen in Christ the fulfillment of all that
the prophets of old had foretold. Sadly, that mission can and

does change because:

> The ultimate mission of evil is to change
> our mission, to alter our allegiance to
> God, to anyone or anything else, so that
> in reality, whether knowingly or unknow-
> ingly, our allegiance is to Satan and thus,
> our mission in life has changed.

When the object of faith changes, the mission changes, and when the mission changes, the whole direction of our lives changes—not for the better, but always for the worse.

The Object of Saving Faith: JESUS CHRIST

It's very simple but very powerful. It's life altering. The object of saving faith is JESUS CHRIST. To the jailer, the Apostle Paul simply replied,

> "Believe in the Lord Jesus, and you will be saved."
> - Acts 16:31

So now, we listen to Jesus. What is His mission for us? He not only gives us the mission, but He also sets its marvelous tone.

> "Go into all the world and preach the good news to all creation."
> - Mark 16:15

> "Therefore go and make disciples of all nations, bap-
> tizing them in the name of the Father and of the Son

and of the Holy Spirit."
- Matthew 28:19

". . . you will be my witnesses... to the ends of the
earth."
- Acts 1:8

That is the mission! It is a message of peace with God and
a message of life, hope, forgiveness, and salvation. It has been
the mission of God for us down through the ages. Some have
tried to change it. Don't you be one of them! Don't let Satan
replace it! Don't let anyone or anything take its place. Nothing
else is worth it because everything else pales in comparison.
Instead, live it, and share it, because this is a message of victory over evil. It leads us from terror to triumph through Jesus
Christ, the Lord of life.

CHAPTER FIVE

INSIGHT #5

The ultimate triumph over evil begins when we first of all recognize the God of our salvation as our greatest ally and friend.

Know Your Allies and Friends

Linus sat out in the great pumpkin patch waiting for the Great Pumpkin to arrive. His eyes were wide open in anxious anticipation. Sally sat with him. She had forfeited the evening's trick or treating to be with her sweetheart, this innocent, kindhearted, and exceptionally insightful childhood friend.

Meanwhile, the rest of the gang was hastily making their rounds. Door to door they went in their traditional Halloween getups. At the opening of every door came that common innocent and prankish reply, "Trick or treat!" Thump, thump, thump—you could hear the candy being dropped into their sacks. As they gathered along the sidewalk to see what each had received, one said, "I got a gumball!" Another added, "I got a tootsie roll!" Still another, "I got a candy bar!" Then, invariably, Charlie Brown would look up, after searching deep inside his bag of treats, and say, with that forlorn yet disgusted tone to his voice, "I got a rock."

Perhaps some of you are familiar with that scene from the Charles Schulz Halloween special, "It's The Great Pumpkin, Charlie Brown!" Poor Charlie Brown—it always seems to happen to him, doesn't it? While everyone else gets the candy, he gets the rock. Isn't there ever a faithful friend for Charlie Brown? By contrast, there is Linus, out in the great pumpkin patch, waiting for the arrival of The Great Pumpkin, with Sally, his dear friend, who is always at his side to support him in his every endeavor, no matter how impossible and unrealistic it might sound. I guess having friends is a good thing and it pays to know who those faithful friends are.

We have seen how the Apostle Paul, at the end of that great section from Ephesians, chapter 6, encourages us to pray without ceasing. However, to whom should we pray and for what should we pray? The first might seem obvious to everyone. We pray to God. Yes, but do we always understand clearly why?

As to the second, we are often very mistaken in determining what we should pray for. Lest we end up like Charlie Brown, with a bag full of rocks, we need to know for what we are to pray. Jesus has given us some wonderful guidance.

> "Ask and it will be given to you; seek and you will find; knock and the door will be opened to you. For everyone who asks receives; he who seeks finds; and to him who knocks, the door will be opened. Which of you, if his son asks for bread, will give him a stone? Or if he asks for a fish, will give him a snake? If you, then, though you are evil, know how to give good gifts to your children, how much more will your Father in heaven give good gifts to those who ask him!"
> - Matthew 7:7-11

Call it silly, but whenever I read this beautiful discourse on prayer, which came from the sweet lips of our Savior, I cannot help but think of poor little old Charlie Brown. All he was asking for was a simple piece of candy, yet all he got in its place was a rock. Jesus asks rhetorically, "Who would do such a thing? Who would be so unkind as to laughingly substitute a stone for a piece of bread or a snake for a fish? What parent or friend would do that?" Charlie Brown knows. Poor Charlie Brown— he knows all too well. Do you suppose Mr. Schulz had this section of Scripture in mind when he wrote that story about Charlie Brown? It almost seems like he did. It fits so very well.

Lest anyone think that all prayers offered are prayers received, there is a need to listen more closely to what Jesus is saying. Lest anyone think that all things requested in prayer are good things, there is also a need to listen more closely to what Jesus is saying. For success in prayer, we need to know to whom prayer should be offered and for what we should be praying.

We live in an age where there is increasing pressure upon people of all faiths to compromise their convictions by acknowledging all gods as equal gods and the same gods. "All roads lead to Rome," it was once said. Today, a similar kind of religious cry has gone up for everyone to hear, "All faiths lead to the same god." September 11 not only reminds us of how untrue that statement is but how important it is for us to be praying to the God who does truly exist.

Is it factual that with all the different religions of the world, that still, everyone is essentially praying to the same god? I hope not. In fact, I know that is not true. You know it too, in spite of all the pressure around you these days to think to the contrary. You too know that is not that way.

You know it from history long past. You know that the Roman gods were a figment of man's convoluted imagination. If those Roman gods were still being worshiped today, would you feel compelled, by today's social, religious, and political standards, to acknowledge them as gods whom we must accept to be just as real as any other, and to whom we can rightly pray?

In most recent history, if the god the September 11 terrorists worshiped and adored—the god for whom they committed this evil deed—is as real and true as any other is, by today's religious rationalizations, then perhaps nothing should dissuade us from joining with them and members of al-Qaida in prayer to their god. After all, what does it matter, if all gods and all religions lead to the same place?

If doing that seems abhorrent to you as a Christian, it should, because you have the God of life and truth at your side and none other will ever take His place. If doing that also seems abhorrent to you and you are not even a Christian, it is understandable, because even without faith in Christ as Lord, you know by nature that not all gods are true.

Why, then, this great effort that stretches from one corner of the globe to the other, to meld all religions and all faiths together as if all were as equally valid as the next? If by nature we know this is not true, then why this great effort to lead people to think to the contrary?

There are many reasons why, some social and some political. However, one of the primary reasons why we see this happening, especially in nations of the free world, is that we have come to a point in time where we are confusing our religious freedoms with our political freedoms. This is unfortunate. We are confusing the "right" of people to believe what they believe with the "rightness" of what is believed. We have somehow come to a point in time where many feel that it is expedient, and for some even necessary, to meld the two together. Religious distinctiveness and unyielding firmness in conviction is viewed not so much any longer as a right to be enjoyed in our nation, but as a threat to our unity as a nation. This too is very unfortunate and sadly unnecessary. It is not only religious folly but, as we will see, it is also religious suicide.

As a Christian, therefore, I will firmly, but also politely, disagree with anyone who would try to convince me that all faiths are "right" in their own distinctive ways. Yet, at the same time, I would fight to the death, as patriots from our past have, for the free right of anyone in our nation to practice their religion as they see fit. As Americans, we are obligated to defend our right to practice freely our religion, no matter what our religious persuasion might be. Freedom of religion is a great blessing. However, as Christians, we are also obligated to defend the rightness of our faith. There is nothing wrong in that. As Christians in 21st century America, we dare not yield in this struggle to compromise the convictions of our faith when others would make us feel that it is expedient to do so. It is not.

We noted earlier in the book, that after the attacks of September 11, President Bush made it his primary focus as our Commander in Chief to identify the enemy. This was a necessary first step. His second step was like it. He began forming what has become known as the coalition of nations against terrorism. In doing so, he was taking the next logical step, identifying our allies and friends who would join us in this war on terrorism.

When the day of evil comes, from a spiritual perspective, we also need to know who our friends and allies are. We need to know who is true and who is not. We need to know who hears our cries and who is able to help. We need to know so that when we pray, we receive that which we need the most in our struggle against the forces of evil around us. We need to know so that we receive bread and not stones, fish and not snakes. We need to know not only the enemy, we need to know who is our greatest friend and greatest ally in this great spiritual struggle that bears such eternal significance. We need to know who will remain by our side throughout the struggle and who will never tire when our arms begin to grow weak. We need to know who has the power and strength to lead us to victory.

Jesus has told us who is true and to whom we must turn. Through prayer, He invites us to turn to our Father in heaven who will give us good gifts. He invites us to ask of Him in prayer, to seek Him out, to knock at His door, which He will open wide to us for aid and strength. This is our next insight. It is so important because it is where the road to triumph over evil begins.

INSIGHT #5

The ultimate triumph over evil begins when we first of all recognize the God of our salvation as our greatest ally and friend.

THE WAY TO TRIUMPH: *Knowing God as Friend*

It might seem simplistic but it is not. Knowing God as our friend is NOT NATURAL for us. By nature, we see God through sin colored spectacles that have darkened His appearance to us. With our sin blinding us to His nature, we see Him only in part and the part that we see, by ourselves, does not look very appealing. We see His strength and we see His power—we see our sin and we see our failures. We see His anger over sin and we see Him moving closer to us—we see Him coming closer, not always to help us, but to punish us. This is what we see if we are left to view Him by ourselves, and that is why all other religions of the world offer, in some way or another, a method that man can employ to appease His wrath. It has been that way from the beginning, not the beginning of time but from the beginning of sin.

> "Then the man and his wife heard the sound of the Lord God as he was walking in the garden in the cool of the day, and they hid from the Lord God among the trees of the garden. But the Lord God called to the man, 'Where are you?' He answered, 'I heard you in the garden, and I was afraid because I was naked; so I hid.'"
> - Genesis 3:8-10

When I was only two or three years old, I remember visiting my grandparents farm a few miles north of Yankton, South Dakota. Many other relatives were there on that particular occasion: cousins, aunts, and uncles. The farmhouse and grounds were just what you might picture in your mind's eye of an established farm in the 1950s. The house was white, two stories high, with a cellar to boot (that's where all the poisonous snakes and creepy crawly spiders would hang out).

My Uncle Tommy was visiting as well, and to me he was almost as scary as the cellar underneath the house. He was a World War II veteran and one tough guy, at least that's what I saw at the age of three. He had a deep, almost thunderous voice when he spoke; when he did, you listened. Uncle Tommy was a powerful presence in any room. He was one of those uncles that you didn't want to look at directly, because as long as your eyes didn't meet, you were hidden from his view. So I never wanted to draw attention to myself when Tommy was in the room. That way, I thought, I would remain invisible to him.

One day I was playing outside, around the west side of the house. I was by myself, trying to find something to do. At my grandparent's farm there were, of course, cats everywhere. A friendly little feline happened my way and I started thinking, "Is it really true that cats always land on their feet when they fall to the earth?" Having established the hypothesis, I decided to begin the next phase: experimentation. I picked up that cute little fur-ball and with all my might threw it up into the air as high as I could. Down it came and sure enough, it landed on all fours! Oh sure, it seemed somewhat dazed but it landed all right.

Like any good scientist, I realized that all reliable hypotheses are established under repeated experimentation. So, I scooped up that cat and let her go again. Down it came, and again on all fours! Suddenly, "Rap—rap—rap!" The sudden rapping on the window startled me. I looked up and there through the window I could see my Uncle Tommy staring down at me and shaking his finger. I can still hear his booming voice through the pane of glass, with its thunderous warning, "If you throw that cat up into the air one more time, I'll come out there and throw you up into the air!" Gulp. I was found out.

I quickly started petting that cat as if it was the best friend I ever had. I could see Uncle Tommy step away from the window and I could see only darkness now inside the house. "That was close," I thought to myself, "But I'm safe now." Now remember, if our eyes didn't meet, I was invisible to Uncle Tommy.

He was gone. I was safe. So I picked up the cat and let it go one more time!

Suddenly, in an instant, in the twinkling of an eye, something grabbed me and I was lifted up! No sooner had that cat come back to earth that I found myself raised above ground! Then I heard it: the voice, that deep, solemn, demanding voice that I had come to fear so desperately and it said this: "Didn't I tell you to stop throwing that cat up into the air? Here's what it feels like." And suddenly I was airborne.

My heart sank. My stomach tightened. Up, up into the air I went, so high it seemed to me that I was flying higher than the roof itself! Then gravity began to take over. My momentum slowed and soon I felt myself falling—falling down to earth again. Terrified, I thought I'd hit the ground hard and break every bone in my body. But just then, as the earth seemed to have me completely in its grasp, something amazing happened. In mid-air, everything ended. It was over. What happened? What was going on? I tried to catch my breath. Then it dawned on me. He caught me, Tommy did! He didn't let me fall to the ground! He was nicer to me than I was to the cat and boy was I glad! I was afraid, but I was sure glad! "Are you going to throw that cat up into the air anymore?" I can still hear that voice. "No," I answered quite sheepishly. "OK," he said, "Because that's what it feels like." He was right and I knew it.

Since that day, I have never again thrown a cat up into the air and I don't think I ever will again. You see, I learned that day what it feels like to be thrown up into the air with the prospect of coming down to nothing but hard earth. It is not a good thing; believe me. Besides, I also know that Uncle Tommy might be there right around the corner. I know that I can't hide from him anymore.

Adam and Eve got the picture too, like me, the hard way. After sin had entered the world, they didn't gain the knowledge that Satan, that crafty serpent, had promised them. They lost knowledge. They thought they could hide from God! Can you imagine it? Have you ever tried to do it?

Jonah once tried to run away from God. It didn't work. Pharaoh foolishly tried a more direct approach. He tried to fight God. That didn't work either.

When Adam and Eve finally came out from behind the trees and answered God's call to them, which was, by the way, God's first call to repentance, Adam could only say, "I was afraid because I was naked; so I hid." Afraid, because he was naked—really? How honest was Adam being? His nakedness never prompted any feelings of fear before. Why was he experiencing such fear now?

No, what Adam feared was God Himself and he feared what God was now going to do with him. He feared God's power and wrath over his sin. He no longer saw a merciful, kind, and loving Creator. He saw a powerful, angry judge. He now saw God only through the eyes of sin and to him it was not a pleasing sight.

Moses too, had seen God from a similar vantage point. Psalm 90 is the only Psalm within the Psalter attributed to Moses. In it, Moses prayed,

> "We are consumed by your anger and terrified by your
> indignation. You have set our iniquities before you,
> our secret sins in the light of your presence."
> - Psalm 90:7, 8

Can you imagine what must have been going through Mo-

ses' mind when he witnessed the power of God at work in part-
ing the waters of the Red Sea and then watching those same
waters come rushing in as a flood upon Pharaoh's great army?
In the desert, Israel had repeatedly rebelled against God. Moses had witnessed God exercising His awesome power against
an unbelieving people who did nothing but rebel against the
very God who had delivered them from their bondage in Egypt.
Moses witnessed how they were literally "consumed" by God's
anger. Moses and all the nation of Israel had been "terrified"
by God's righteous indignation against their sin. No wonder
Moses wrote the words he did. Those 40 years of wandering in
the wilderness had provided many opportunities to witness this
awesome and terrifying side of God's nature.

Paul too, understood something of this picture of God that
is imprinted in the minds of all of us. In the second chapter of
Ephesians he wrote,

> "As for you, you were dead in your transgressions
> and sins, in which you used to live when you followed
> the ways of this world and of the ruler of the king-
> dom of the air, the spirit who is now at work in those
> who are disobedient. All of us also lived among them
> at one time, gratifying the cravings of our sinful na-
> ture and following its desires and thoughts. Like the
> rest, we were by nature objects of wrath."
> - Ephesians 2:1-3

That really is not a very pleasant thought. To be spiritually
dead because of our sins and by that, unable to make ourselves
alive to God, is bad enough. Then, to imagine that because of
sin we are now by nature "objects of wrath"—God's wrath—

that can be almost too much to bear.

We don't want to think that things are that bad in our relationship with God. We would like to think that He just ignores sin and will eventually just make it all better for us. Calvary's cross reminds us that He did not just ignore our sin. There we see His righteous indignation against it. There we see the Father abandoning His Son when He became sin for us. In that sacrifice we see the full consequence of spiritual death: separation from God. It caused Jesus to cry out, *"Eloi, Eloi, lama sabachthani?'* which means, 'My God, my God, why have you forsaken me?'"* (Matthew 27:46). Jesus, that day, as our perfect Redeemer, knew what it meant to be an object of God's wrath. Every Good Friday we are reminded of God's fury over sin and every day of our lives we see our own sins staring back at us, reminding us of this fact. It is simply not natural for us, in view of our sin, to think of God as friend. At best, by nature, we might think of Him as a watchful superior who is not very pleased with our performance from one day to the next and we are ever wondering, "When is the ax going to drop?"

Where might we be today if Christ had never come to this world to deliver us from our bondage to sin and from the fear that sin's residue leaves in our hearts? Would the world be very changed, from what it is now, if it had never heard the good news of Christ's loving sacrificial death and victorious resurrection? Without Christ's historical presence, what kind of love would we find in the world today? Without Christ, would it be even more ruthless than it is today?

The last example we have of a world without Christ was the Roman world. Is that world, the pre-Christ world, better than what we have today in the post-Christ era? Would we continue to be worshiping gods drawn from nature and idols made from stone? How would those notions affect our relationships with one another? How would we be dealing with death? Would it be in fear, in hopelessness and ignorant superstition? Would our nation, or for that matter other nations like ours, be entirely different without the Christian principles upon which so much in our nation has been built? Would we even recognize our nation as the land of freedom and opportunity that so characterizes it today? Do we realize how much the world changed when Christ became known to the world as the Lord of life and love, as the Savior of the nations, and the King above all kings? Do we realize why He made such an impact? Do we see that in the revelation of Jesus Christ, a new age dawned, and a completely new way of viewing our Creator emerged that had never been known to the world before? Do we appreciate the positive impact the gospel has made upon the lives of people everywhere, and not just spiritually, but also from social and political perspectives? Do we see that left on our own, our lives had been and still would be to this day, marked by fear, superstition, and spiritual ignorance?

Jesus' entrance to this world completely changed everything! Yes, September 11 reminds us how quickly one event can change the world and 9-11 will change things for us in many ways, but Jesus' arrival changed the world even more. He wanted it to change. It needed to change for we were in Satan's grasp.

> "Since the children have flesh and blood, he too shared
> in their humanity so that by his death he might de-
> stroy him who holds the power of death—that is, the
> devil—and free those who all their lives were held in

slavery by their fear of death."
- Hebrews 2:14, 15

God cursed the world with death for a very good reason, so that death could become, through the gift of His Son Jesus Christ, the gateway to new, perfect life again! God doesn't want us to be afraid of death. Satan, however, wants us to fear it. As long as we remain slaves of Satan and bound by sin, there will be great fear of dying. That is because, as we have already seen,

"The god of this age has blinded the minds of unbelievers so that they cannot see the light of the gospel
of the glory of Christ, who is the image of God."
– II Corinthians 4:4

Satan wants us to remain blind and ignorant of the gospel. He does this, as we noted in chapter 3, by attacking faith and keeping people in a natural state of unbelief. He wants us to stay the way we are by nature for if, in unbelief, we remain blind, we will not see Christ. If we do not see Christ, we will not see the light of spiritual truth and if we do not see the light of truth, we will remain in the darkness. If we remain in the darkness we will continue to live in fear, in fear of God, in fear of our sin, in fear of the guilt that it works in our hearts, and we will continue to live in fear of death. So, these three agents: Satan, sin, and guilt, are continually working together to keep us from knowing God as our friend. In our natural state, we cannot, and we will not, be able to see God in any other light.

Something, however, has happened to the world and us. God has come to us and has revealed Himself to us as friend. This is the good news.

THE WAY TO TRIUMPH: *The Truth Revealed*

"You see, at just the right time, when we were still
powerless, Christ died for the ungodly. Very rarely
will anyone die for a righteous man, though for a good
man someone might possibly dare to die. But God
demonstrates his own love for us in this: While we
were still sinners, Christ died for us. Since we have
now been justified by his blood, how much more shall
we be saved from God's wrath through him! For if,
when we were God's enemies, we were reconciled to
him through the death of his Son, how much more,
having been reconciled, shall we be saved through
his life!"
- Romans 5:6-10

Living in constant fear does interesting things to people.
Living in fear tends to warp all kinds of perceptions. Living in
fear of God warped our perception of God. Fear made our view
of God far too narrow. He was in fact much greater and much
more complex than our fear was ever able to perceive. Fear
does that to people. Fear of God changed our spiritual understanding of God.

Now might be a good time to finish telling you the story
about my Uncle Tommy. The childish fears of my uncle had
narrowed my view of him. Eventually, as I grew older, I came
to know my Uncle Tommy better. He was a strong and a dy-
namic man but he had a good heart, a very loving heart too. He
died relatively young, in his 50s, from a heart attack. I will
always remember him fondly and what I learned from him that

day when I tossed the cat and he tossed me. But I have come to realize that he typified for me what we see about God on our own and what we can see about God as we get to know Him more fully, as He reveals Himself to us through His life giving Word.

Sometimes we view people incorrectly because our understanding is limited. By nature, through spectacles tainted by sin, we see God incorrectly too. Sin permits us to see only one side of God. In Christ, through the gift of His Son, we see Him in His full glory, as the God of our salvation and a loving, merciful redeeming God. We see Him as our greatest ally and friend.

That is what Paul was writing about in these verses from his epistle to the Romans. He tells us about the circumstances under which God turned to us and delivered us. He did it when we were afraid of Him. He did it when we were denying Him. He did it when we were rejecting Him. He did it when we were fighting against Him. He did it when we were His enemies. When we were His enemies, He came down to us to show us that He was our greatest friend.

When flight 93 crashed into the farmlands of Pennsylvania, something happened, something very special. We need to mark it. We need to mark it well, for it can help us understand what Christ has done for us in an even greater historical context.

What happened that day in the skies of Pennsylvania was very important and very significant. It happened even before anyone realized it had happened. I'm not talking about the crash itself. What happened on September 11 was not just about death. If that is all we see, the crash and the lives that were lost, then we are truly missing the mark. What happened that day was life. What happened was sacrifice. What happened was salvation. In an instant, in that moment in time, the events of one day, one hour, one minute, one second, became a living, breathing, real, historical manifestation of salvation won through the willing sacrifice of others. Those events will forever remain that, and nothing can ever alter that marvelous sacrificial truth.

You see, after the plane hit the first tower in New York, then after the second tower was hit, and then after the Pentagon was attacked, it became obvious to those aboard flight 93 that they were going to be played as pawns to yet another villainous act. The terrorists on board their flight were targeting other innocent lives. Those passengers chose to say, "Enough is enough. This will end. We may be dead by the end of the day but on this day no more lives will be lost if we have anything to do about it." As we know now, they did much about it. They sacrificed their lives for the sake of others.

The events on board flight 93 are still, and forever will be, shrouded in mystery. What we do know is that these terrorists suddenly found themselves under attack. In the narrow confines of the cabin and in the crowded cockpit of that airplane a struggle began that resulted in the saving of many more lives by a tremendous sacrifice. Somewhere in that struggle, the goal to wrestle the controls of the airplane away from these madmen was lost, but the most important goal of saving lives was won.

We do not know what the intended target of flight 93 was. Many suspect it was the White House. We may never know for sure. Whatever it was, the truth is this: somewhere today, there are people out there who are kissing their loved ones good bye in the morning and heading off to work; there are people who are living life to the full, celebrating birthdays, anniversaries,

Christmas, and the New Year; there are people who are nurturing their children and caring for their aging parents; there are people worshiping and still telling the saving news of Jesus to others; there are people living life to the full, because on September 11, 2001 certain people, aboard a certain flight, under a certain set of circumstances, made a certain decision that they were going to sacrifice their lives, if need be, to save the lives of others. Others are living today because those aboard flight 93 chose to sacrifice their lives on September 11.

Who were the people who sacrificed themselves? We now know their names. Who was saved that day? It is amazing— we don't know the name of a single one of them! You may be one of them. As you read this book now, you may be one for whom the sacrifice was made and you don't even realize it. When you tuck your baby daughter in and kiss her good night, you may not realize that even that small, blessed privilege is yours today because a sacrifice was made for you. The life you live now is being lived because a life had been sacrificed on your behalf. It is immaterial whether you realize it or not. It is immaterial whether you believe it or not. It is a historical fact that stands on its own merit in time.

In human history, another reality stands just as true and it has even greater life-giving implications. "You see, at just the right time, when we were still powerless, Christ died for the ungodly." We were targeted. Our enemy, Satan, had his sights set on us. We were walking dead people. Not only that, but we were sinners and enemies of God.

Then something happened; something unexpected happened to mankind. A sacrifice was made. Another died so that many more might live. "While we were still sinners, Christ died for us." This is how God demonstrated His love for you. It is immaterial whether you realize it or not. It is immaterial whether you believe it or not. It too is a historical fact that stands on its own merit in time. Jesus died for you so that you would be saved through His life! It is a historical reality just as valid as the sacrifices made aboard flight 93, only Jesus' sacrifice carries with it a far greater eternal significance. That historical reality exists in and of itself: through the sacrifice of one, life and salvation is won for all.

Through Jesus Christ, that is how you best know God is your friend! He is the best friend you could ever have. Most of us might consider giving up our lives for a spouse, a son, a daughter, someone we know, or maybe even someone we do not know, like a soldier going off to war, willing to give his life for his neighbor and his country. However, not many of us would be willing to give up our lives for that criminal on death row or that mass murderer whom we feel deserves to die. We wouldn't offer up our lives for an enemy like Osama bin Laden who has already killed so many and wants only to kill so many more. No, we would not die for anyone like that, "but God demonstrates his own love for us in this: While we were still sinners, Christ died for us... when we were God's enemies, we were reconciled to him through the death of his Son."

Jesus sacrificed His life, not for friends, but for those who were sinners and enemies of God. He died for you before you came to faith, in the hope, that through His gift of sacrificial love, love for God might begin to shine in your heart. He died for you so that through faith in Him, life from death would be yours. "We love because he first loved us" (I John 4:19). It may even be, and there is substantial evidence for this, that the sacrifice made aboard flight 93, on September 11, was made by people who were strengthened in the knowledge of Christ's sacrifice for them. Knowing Jesus Christ as their friend gave them the strength to be like Christ and live their lives not only for themselves, but also for others! That is amazing grace!

The God of Our Salvation: Our Greatest Ally and Friend

Let's start here then, in thinking about what constitutes a good friend. What are the characteristics we look for in a friend and ally? There can be many and probably more than we can list. For everyone, the emphasis may vary. What is important in friendship to one person, might not be that important to another. There are, however, qualities that mark those whom we would regard in life as good friends.

First, they are people who are active in our lives and there for us. They care about us. They are reliable, compassionate, empathetic, and attentive to our needs. Therefore, they are also helpful people in our lives and if they are also fearless in their approach to life, they often fill us with confidence. We like to think of friends as forgiving, encouraging, merciful in nature, understanding, trustworthy, and faithful to us. We like friends who can sympathize with us, remain loyal under difficult times, and we like friends who will defend us from those who would harm us or speak ill of us. We like friends who can console us when we're down in spirit. They are caring, patient, humble, and unselfish. Above all, we need them to be truthful and honest with us, for if they are not, we will feel betrayed. Yet, as they deal honestly with us, we want friends who are considerate, unashamed to call us their friend, and protective of their relationship with us. They are not rude or insulting toward us but for the most part, complimentary of us, even if at times our faults glare out for everyone to see. They will stand by us to the end.

It can become quite a list. The job description for a good friend can be very long and the expectations far greater than what is found in real life. Nonetheless, we expect certain things from our friends and they expect certain things from us too. In fact, when you start thinking about your friends, you might come to see many, if not all these qualities in them. You might also begin to feel a bit guilty, knowing that you have not always lived up to these expectations yourself.

When Joseph Scriven wrote the text to that now famous hymn "What a Friend We Have In Jesus," he must have had in mind these many characteristics of friendship. He beautifully penned how we find them all perfectly fulfilled in the God of our salvation. He wrote, "Can we find a friend so faithful, who will all our sorrow share? Jesus knows our every weakness—take it to the Lord in prayer."

From the beginning, God has proven Himself our greatest ally and friend, though we, by nature, do not always view Him that way. Nonetheless, He was and always will be a perfect friend and the kind of friend we need the most. We need to see this about our God, our Creator God, and our Saving God, because events like 9-11 can easily shake our confidence in God as our great friend. Satan, our greatest enemy, does not want us to view Him that way, so we need reminders. We need to see everything that God has done for us in the past and all the ways He has remained a faithful friend, so that we will continue to approach Him confidently in the future. When the day of evil comes, we need desperately to know the God of our salvation as our greatest ally and friend. It can make all the difference in the world. It made all the difference for Adam and Eve. In the words God spoke to the great Tempter, we see how intent God was in maintaining His friendship with mankind in spite of sin.

> "I will put enmity between you and the woman, and between your offspring and hers; he will crush your head, and you will strike his heel . . ."
> - Genesis 3:15

Even before a single word of discipline was spoken against the woman or the man for their disobedience, God's promise of grace and forgiveness was offered to them. These words represent the first gospel promise. From the offspring of the woman would come one who would do marvelous things. He would crush the head of the serpent. He would destroy Satan who worked this great temptation against mankind, and this great evil against man and against God. However, in destroying Satan's power, the great Serpent would strike at the heel of this great Deliverer and inflict his venomous poison. That offspring of the woman was Jesus Christ.

On Good Friday, Satan struck at Him hard so that by Friday evening He lay dead in that cold, dark tomb. However, on Easter morning the final blow was leveled on Satan, sin, and death. Christ rose from death to life. He rose to crush Satan's power and to overcome sin as death's sting. Now, in Christ, we are delivered from death's curse. In Christ, we are no longer held in slavery to Satan. Sin no longer separates us from God. Today, life, liberty, and forgiveness reign through Jesus Christ. He is the God of our salvation. This is now the way it is for us because God kept His first promise from millennia past, and remained our greatest friend down through the ages.

If Adam and Eve were not able to detect God's love for them

in that first gospel promise spoken by God, they could certainly see His love for them in the many ways He continued to care for them. Remember, their reaction had been to cower and hide from God. After sin had entered the world, and them, they were literally afraid to death of what would happen next. They had forgotten what a friend they had in their Creator God.

> "The Lord God made garments of skin for Adam and his wife and clothed them. And the Lord God said, 'The man has now become like one of us, knowing good and evil. He must not be allowed to reach out his hand and take also from the tree of life and eat, and live forever.' So the Lord God banished him from the Garden of Eden . . .'"
>
> – Genesis 3:21-23

After September 11, we may be tempted to think of God in ways other than what is still true. Like Adam and Eve, we may blame Him, and we may even be afraid of Him. We may tend to think He is our enemy or a powerful Judge who has now exercised His hand of correction against us. But that way of thinking is a mistake, for our God is not a god of evil. Adam and Eve saw Him incorrectly when their day of evil came upon them. We do not want to make the same mistake.

Then, God showed mercy and love. He clothed them and cared for them. Yes, He banished them from the Garden too, but not as punishment. He did it to protect them. It is a mystery that is known fully only to God, but it seems that somehow it would have been possible for man to live forever in this state of sinfulness and depravity that he had created for himself. God had a greater plan in store for mankind, a saving plan, and so God forced man out of the Garden. In God's plan, death would come, necessarily, so that God's power would lead to new life and realized through the resurrection from death. This new life would be won, through the offspring of the woman, Jesus Christ, who would be the first to rise from the curse of death. We will be the next to rise. This will happen when our friend and risen Savior Jesus Christ calls us home to be with Him forevermore.

Repeatedly, throughout the pages of Old Testament history, we see God reminding His chosen people Israel of His great love for them. We see Him living and working in their lives as their greatest ally and friend. From ancient times, when they were living in slavery in Egypt, God was mindful of their condition. Evil existed, yes, but God's loving presence also existed in their lives. God spoke these words to Moses who had been sent by God to lead them out of bondage:

> "The Lord said, 'I have indeed seen the misery of my people in Egypt. I have heard them crying out because of their slave drivers, and I am concerned about their suffering. So I have come down to rescue them from the hand of the Egyptians and to bring them up out of that land into a good and spacious land, a land flowing with milk and honey.... And now the cry of the Israelites has reached me, and I have seen the way the Egyptians are oppressing them. So now, go. I am sending you to Pharaoh to bring my people the Israelites out of Egypt.'"
> - Exodus 3:7-10

God was mindful of their condition. He had "seen the misery" of His people. He had "heard them crying." He was "concerned about their suffering." He was coming to "rescue them" and to "bring them up" to a better land. They were assured that their cry had "reached" Him. He was mindful of it and so now He would be "sending (Moses) to Pharaoh" to bring His people to freedom.

If ever we are tempted to think that God does not hear our prayers, that He is insensitive to our circumstances, or that He has withdrawn His grace from us, we can look to His attentiveness from the past to see how much He cared then and know how much He cares now. Then, He saw His children's conditions and acted. He sees our situation now and will act.

Don't be fooled by evil's heyday on September 11. Don't ever think that evil will win the war. When all is said and done, God's good will for His children will prevail. Evil will be vanquished and God's loving intentions for His children will be realized. It will happen in God's good hour. It will happen either now or in eternity, but it will happen.

Our Friend in heaven is not so feeble and weak in His concern for us, that if we should fail Him, He will quickly abandon us. We may not always be such good friends to God, but He is always the best of friends to us. Nor should we think of Him as so gentlemanly in His dealings with us, that if we should but err in walking away from Him for a time, that He will ever so politely step away from us. That is nonsense. God is not that way and He does not act that way. He is a much greater friend to us than that. He is so much more.

He is constantly working in our lives, constantly watching, constantly trying to draw us closer to Him. Why is He so persistent? Because He loves us that much and His concern for our spiritual well-being is that strong. He is the kind of friend that you just cannot shake. He keeps holding on and simply will not let go.

Think of how His chosen people Israel rebelled against Him time and time again. The misery and evil they so often suffered as a nation was not of God's origin but of their own making. Yet, in spite of their rebellious ways, God clung to them as a dear friend. He does the same with us and in the day of evil is not quick to abandon us.

We can see the walk of God in the lives of people from ancient times. He walks as Friend, still, with us today. He walked proudly with David, even though David himself was far from perfect. Yet, from the beginning of David's life as a shepherd in the hills of Bethlehem, to the end of his reign as Israel's greatest and most faithful king, God remained his ever-present ally and friend. For David, that friendship and that walk with God began in a very dramatic way. You may know the story very well.

"A champion named Goliath, who was from Gath, came out of the Philistine camp. He was over nine feet tall. He had a bronze helmet on his head and wore a coat of scale armor of bronze weighing five thousand shekels; on his legs he wore bronze greaves, and a bronze javelin was slung on his back. His spear shaft was like a weaver's rod, and its iron point weighed six hundred shekels. His shield bearer went ahead of him. Goliath stood and shouted to the ranks of Israel, 'Why do you come out and line up for battle?... This day I defy the ranks of Israel! Give me a man and let us fight each other.'... Then he (David) took his staff in his hand, chose five smooth stones

from the stream, put them in the pouch of his shepherd's bag and, with his sling in his hand, approached
the Philistine.... He said to David, 'Am I a dog, that
you come at me with sticks?' And the Philistine cursed
David by his gods. 'Come here,' he said, 'and I'll give
your flesh to the birds of the air and the beasts of the
field!' David said to the Philistine, 'You come against
me with sword and spear and javelin, but I come
against you in the name of the Lord Almighty, the
God of the armies of Israel, whom you have defied.
This day the Lord will hand you over to me, and I'll
strike you down and cut off your head.... All those
gathered here will know that it is not by sword or
spear that the Lord saves; for the battle is the Lord's,
and he will give all of you into our hands.'"
- I Samuel 17: select vs.

You know what comes next, don't you? If it has been a long
time since you have read the account of David and Goliath in
full, I might suggest that you put the book down now, take out
your Bible, and read the 17th chapter of I Samuel before going
any further. It is a remarkable story of victory through the
presence of God in our lives. It is worth reading again.

This Philistine must have appeared to the Israelites as a
huge, evil monster, wearing his 125 pounds of armor and wield-
ing that 15-pound spear. Yes, the stone struck the forehead of
the great warrior Goliath and he fell facedown to the ground.
The Philistine died that day by David's hand, but not by David's
might. David knew it was the Lord Almighty who had given
the enemy into his hands.

"The battle is the Lord's." It was true for David that day,

long ago, in the hills of Judah and it is true for us today. "The battle is the Lord's," and always will be His for He stands with us as our ally, victor, and friend. Evil may growl at us, with its ugly face, and want us to scamper away like frightened sheep about to be slaughtered, but "the battle is the Lord's." We don't have to be afraid of evil—the Lord Almighty is at our side! We don't have to wonder the outcome—the Risen Christ is at our side even in the face of death! We don't have to turn tail and run—we can stand our ground with God the Holy Sprit present to bless us with gifts that only He can bring! The victory over evil is assured!

The prophets of old understood what it meant to fall under the protective cover of the Almighty. They learned, in their lifetimes, how the battle against evil was fought and won. Those prophets fought as faithful servants of God and found great refuge in His presence. He was indeed their greatest ally and friend. Daniel is just one example of many.

> "So the king gave the order, and they brought Daniel and threw him into the lions' den. The king said to Daniel, 'May your God, whom you serve continually, rescue you!' A stone was brought and placed over the mouth of the den, and the king sealed it with his own signet ring.... At the first light of dawn, the king got up and hurried to the lions' den. When he came near the den, he called to Daniel... Daniel answered, 'O king, live Forever! My God sent his angel, and he shut the mouths of the lions. They have not hurt me, because I was found innocent in his sight.'"
> - Daniel 6: select vs.

A certain death awaited Daniel when he was thrown into that den of lions, at least it seemed that way. Though King Darius was reluctant to render such harsh judgment against Daniel, a decree had been issued and the king was obligated to live up to the standard of the law by his own example. So when Daniel was found guilty of praying to God and asking God for help, after the king's decree had specifically forbidden such prayers, the king was forced to give the order to cast Daniel into the lions' den. Yet, even the king knew that the only way Daniel would be delivered would be by the God whom Daniel served continually. It happened just that way. "God sent his angel," and the mouths of the lions were shut.

Yes, we've learned to know our enemy. He too "prowls around like a roaring lion looking for someone to devour" (I Peter 5:8). We too, like Daniel, are to resist him by standing firm in our faith. We do so with faith that looks to God as our ally and friend, for "the God of all grace, who called you to his eternal glory in Christ, after you have suffered a little while, will himself restore you and make you strong, firm and steadfast" (I Peter 5:10). Our strength comes from Christ who is present daily in our lives, then and now.

There is something else, though, about Daniel that we dare not miss. Did you catch it, that glimmer of prophecy announcing greater victories to come? Here are the clues as drawn from Daniel 6: 1) other administrators of the king hated Daniel because the king wanted to "set him over the whole kingdom." 2) "Men went as a group to the king" and reminded the king that Daniel's violation of the law required a sentence of death. 3) It was "sundown." 4) Daniel was thrown into the lion's den and 5) "a stone was brought and placed over the mouth of the den." The king then 6) "sealed it" with his ring. Then, 7) "at the first light of dawn," the king rushed to the den.

Does this sound at all familiar to another time, another day of evil, and another day of even greater triumph? It should, because that greater day of victory came. It came on Easter morning.

Jesus, Our Living Savior & Friend

> "Joseph took the body, wrapped it in a clean linen cloth, and placed it in his own new tomb that he had cut out of the rock. He rolled a big stone in front of the entrance to the tomb and went away.... 'Take a guard,' Pilate answered. 'Go, make the tomb as secure as you know how.' So they went and made the tomb secure by putting a seal on the stone and posting the guard.... After the Sabbath, at dawn on the first day of the week, Mary Magdalene and the other Mary went to look at the tomb.... The angel said to the women, 'Do not be afraid.... he has risen, just as he said.'"
>
> - Matthew 27 & 28: select vs.

The resurrection of Jesus Christ on Easter morning lifted those first disciples from the depths of despair to new and marvelous heights, heights they had never known before. Their Savior, their friend, was alive! He was their hope and He was their future. This was true for them, suddenly and surprisingly, that first Easter morning, not because they just wished Jesus was alive. It was because He actually was alive. The grave could not hold the Son of God. On Easter morning, the great friend of sinners everywhere, rose from death to life.

That event permanently changed the lives of those first disciples. That event has changed the lives of thousands upon thousands and ten thousands upon ten thousands since that time, because Jesus lives to be our greatest ally and friend.

Samuel Medley, who wrote the text to the famous Easter hymn, "I Know That My Redeemer Lives," understood this great truth. He understood it so well that he had to write about it. What can we expect from Jesus as our living resurrected Savior and friend? Medley wrote this:

I know that my Redeemer lives!
What comfort this sweet sentence gives!
He lives, he lives, who once was dead;
He lives, my ever-living head!

He lives triumphant from the grave;
He lives eternally to save;
He lives exalted, throned above;
He lives to rule his Church in love.

He lives to grant me rich supply;
He lives to guide me with his eye;
He lives to comfort me when faint;
He lives to hear my soul's complaint.

He lives to silence all my fears;
He lives to wipe away my tears;
He lives to calm my troubled heart;
He lives all blessings to impart.

He lives to bless me with his love;

He lives to plead for me above;
He lives my hungry soul to feed;
He lives to help in time of need.

He lives, my kind, wise, heav'nly friend;
He lives and loves me to the end;
He lives, and while he lives, I'll sing;
He lives, my Prophet, Priest, and King!

He lives and grants me daily breath;
He lives, and I shall conquer death;
He lives my mansion to prepare;
He lives to bring me safely there.

He lives, all glory to his name!
He lives, my Savior, still the same;
What joy this blest assurance gives:
I know that my Redeemer lives!

What does Easter morning have to do with September 11, 2001? EVERYTHING! From the comfort Jesus brings to us as our loving friend, to the salvation His sacrifice won—from His rule as our Resurrected Lord and King, to His attentiveness to our prayers—from His guidance through His gift of the Holy Spirit, to the courage He instills in us when we grow faint— from His merciful intercessions for us before His Father's heavenly throne, to the nourishment He provides us through His life-giving Word—from His unending love for us, to the life He breathes into us and our children as our Creator—from the heavenly home He prepares for us, to His walk with us as we journey through life to that eternal home—in all these ways and many more like them, Jesus proves to us that He is our greatest ally and friend. We need Him more than anyone or anything else.

September 11 is a reminder to us of why we need Him so much. Evil is too great an enemy for us to battle on our own. We need Jesus, our living Savior and friend, at our side so that whenever the day of evil comes, the battle will be the Lord's and, in Him, the victory ours.

It wasn't long after the attack on September 11, that the mayor of New York, Rudy Giuliani, was pronouncing victory. When he saw the resolve of his fellow New Yorkers, the unity of the American people as a whole, and the support from our allies and friends from nations across the globe, he expressed hope that everyone could see that the war had already been won.

However, his words rang true in an even greater spiritual sense. September 11 was a day of great evil and a time of great mourning for our nation but in Jesus Christ, the victory has already been won! In Him, those who die, live! In Him, evil has no eternal hold on us any longer! In Him, our battle with evil is sealed with the victorious triumphant cry of Easter morning, "He is risen!"

To this day Jesus lives to be at our side with His strength, His gifts, and His blessings. They aid us in this great struggle. He is just the kind of friend we need. He gave His all for us and that kind of friend is very special indeed. He spoke of His close friendship with us on the night He was betrayed into the hands of His enemies. There, in the upper room, He met with His disciples and told them,

"Greater love has no one than this, that one lay down his life for his friends. You are my friends if you do what I command. I no longer call you servants, because a servant does not know his master's business. Instead, I have called you friends, for everything that I learned from my Father I have made known to you. You did not choose me, but I chose you to go and bear fruit—fruit that will last."

- John 15:13-16

We were once slaves to sin, but now, we are friends of God! Jesus was about to sacrifice His life for His friends. He loved them that much. It needed to be done for them. We too are His friends and prove ourselves friends of God if we but do what He commands us, and His command to us is not burdensome. It is light and a great joy to do. For the work He has given us is simply to spread this precious news of life and joy to others so that many more might know Jesus as Savior and Friend. Our Redeemer would have us bear this fruit because it is the fruit that lasts. It multiplies and produces a greater yield of fruit from the life of one believer to the next, and in the end, yields an eternal bounty. All this comes from the hand of our sacrificial friend, Jesus Christ.

That night, Jesus also told His friends of even greater gifts that He would impart to them. He would leave them, for a time, but He would send another to guide them, instruct them, and strengthen them for their task. Through the special gift of the Holy Spirit, they would find peace and rest, even in the midst of all kinds of evil. In Christ, they would find life. He assured them,

"I will ask the Father, and he will give you another Counselor to be with you forever—the Spirit of truth... I will not leave you as orphans; I will come to you.... Because I live, you also will live.... But the Counselor, the Holy Spirit, whom the Father will send in my name, will teach you all things and will remind you of everything I have said to you. Peace I leave with you; my peace I give you. I do not give to you as the world gives. Do not let your hearts be troubled and do not be afraid."

- John 14: select vs.

During the course of our lives, if we do not receive from God exactly as we expect, we should not be surprised. Within 24 hours, those first disciples would receive from Jesus a gift that was quite unexpected, even though Jesus had tried to prepare them for it. The lifeless body of their dear friend would be taken down from the cross of Calvary and laid in the chilly darkness of death's cold tomb. Indeed, Jesus does not give as the world gives. However, Jesus always brings a blessed result through all His works. Within 72 hours, the stone would be rolled away from the entrance, the tomb would be empty, and Jesus would be standing, alive again, with these same disciples on the evening of that first day of the week.

It is true; Jesus does not give as the world gives. Thank God for that! He gives to us a gift that the world cannot possibly give: the gift of life from this world's sentence of death. In Christ, we can say much more than just, "We live and we die." In Christ, we can say, "We live, we die, and we live again, eternally, with Christ."

To this day Jesus continues to counsel us through the gift

of the Holy Spirit. September 11 has come, but the Holy Spirit came long before that evil day. The Holy Spirit has come to remind us that all God's gifts to man remain firmly in place whenever any day of evil comes. Therefore, we live without fear. We need not be troubled because we are not alone. God, in Christ, and through the living presence of the Holy Spirit within us, is at our side. We are not living as orphans in this world. God has not abandoned us. We find strength in communion with Him through prayer. We find peace and rest in His Word of truth that remains with us to this day. The Bible is the Holy Spirit's gift to the world so that we are armed with the sword of truth as we struggle against that which is evil and false. Furthermore, we are confident even in the face of death, because we know that if death comes to us, we will live again. Jesus said, "Because I live, you also will live." This is our friend speaking to us. He does not lie. This is our friend and He is not dead but alive to render assistance and aid whenever it is needed.

If we know Christ as our personal Savior, we will be thankful for all He has done for us, for we know that we have not received from Him as our sins deserved. Nevertheless, it is for this purpose that Jesus came to this world, to save, not to condemn. Remember, He does not give as the world gives.

> "God did not send his Son into the world to condemn
> the world, but to save the world through him."
> - John 3:17

In spite of all the times we have failed God, failed family, failed friends, failed strangers in need, failed one another, our friend, Jesus Christ, did not condemn us. He came and saved us. He came to this world and forgave us. Our sins nailed him to the cross, yet from its pain and misery, He prayed as our loving friend, "Father forgive them, for they do not know what they are doing" (Luke 23:34).

What does all this mean for us in relation to September 11? It means that September 11 had nothing to do with punishment from God for sins committed. There was only one time in history when God rendered just satisfaction for sin. It was not September 11. It was long before then. It happened on Good Friday when Jesus became sin for us.

September 11 happened because Satan and other agents of evil still want to be heard. They still want to undo all the good that God in Christ has done. They will try to do this by leading us to think that God is not our dearest friend. They wreak physical havoc in the world, to wreak spiritual havoc in our souls. We can be glad that we have this word of truth from the lips of Christ, "God did not send his Son into the world to condemn the world, but to save the world through him."

You have a choice since 9-11. Either you may believe the Son of God and Savior of the world or you may believe him who is known to the world as "the father of lies."

It is also important for us to realize that on September 11, Jesus, as our compassionate friend, was very much at work. He always has been.

> "When Jesus landed and saw a large crowd, he had
> compassion on them and healed their sick."
> - Matthew 14:14

As time passes, I am confident we will begin to hear more stories of the miraculous workings of God in the lives of people since September 11. It is already beginning to happen. However, more and more stories will become known as God continues His activity in the lives of people everywhere. This is bound to happen because we have in Jesus a compassionate friend who takes an active interest in our lives. He will ever remain the Great Physician to the world's sick and suffering. He worked as the compassionate friend to the sick and dying during His ministry on this earth. From His rule in heaven, He will continue in this work as our best and greatest friend.

His ways can at times be very mysterious. Just as Jesus often tried to hide His miracles from view during His three years of ministry on this earth, so it seems that even today, His miracles, and works of compassion often remain hidden from our view. However, if we open our eyes to view the events in our lives from a deeper spiritual perspective, we can see God at work among us on a daily basis.

How many lives were spared from the brave acts of firefighters and police officers who faithfully carried out their God-given responsibilities to serve and protect? Will we ever really know? How many lives were spared when flight 93 went down before it even had a chance to close in on its intended target? Will we ever really know? How many lives were spared when the plane struck the Pentagon in an area of the structure that was not fully occupied because it was under renovation? If this flight was intended by the terrorists to target the White House, why was the pilot, seemingly, unable to locate it from the air? Will we ever really know? What of endless aid and rescue workers, volunteers, counselors, and just everyday bystanders who reacted with love and compassion to help, to comfort, and to save? Why do things happen the way they do? Why are people in given places at given moments in time? Do such things happen by accident? Are all things only by chance?

The Scriptures tell us that our times are in God's hands. David confessed this truth in Psalm 31:15. That means God will work through people to accomplish His ends. Sometimes they are His people through faith, and sometimes they are not, but God can and does work in and through them all.

Before Jesus ascended into heaven He spoke to His disciples the very comforting words, "And surely I will be with you always, to the very end of the age" (Matthew 28:20). The truth is this: Jesus is always present in our lives, and present in ways that we are often not even cognizant. Yet, He is there as our constant companion and compassionate friend, sometimes intervening directly, and other times intervening through the lives of others.

We have in Jesus a loving and empathetic friend. He feels personally our losses and knows our every hurt. We see Jesus' heart in the beautiful account of the death of Lazarus.

> "When Mary reached the place where Jesus was and saw him, she fell at his feet and said, 'Lord, if you had been here my brother would not have died.' When Jesus saw her weeping, and the Jews who had come along with her also weeping, he was deeply moved in spirit and troubled. 'Where have you laid him?' he asked. 'Come and see, Lord,' they replied. Jesus wept. Then the Jews said, 'See how he loved him!'"
> - John 11:32-36

Yes, these words, "Jesus wept," might make up the smallest verse in all of Scripture, but it is also one of the greatest verses because it underscores Jesus' love for us. It underscores

His deep empathy for our lost condition and how troubled He was in spirit that death had such a stranglehold on mankind. We see in these two words the motivating force behind why Jesus was willing to go the way of the cross for us. We see in them His love and His great desire to deliver man from the curse of death.

The death of His dear friend Lazarus brought Him to tears and He wept, unable to control His emotions. See how He was so "deeply moved in spirit" and "troubled" in heart. When the people saw His reaction, they responded to what was so very clear to them, "See how he loved him."

How do you suppose Jesus reacted from heaven on 9-11 to the evil, the suffering, the death, and the destruction that marked that day? He lives, still, to this day, human in every way, just as we are. He knows that feeling of loss. He suffered death and rejection Himself. He knows the terror of sin and the power of hate. Is he still deeply moved in spirit? Is he deeply troubled in heart still? Does He still weep for us today?

Yes, He does, but now He can do something more for us. He paid the ultimate sacrifice for our sin. Through His death and resurrection, He has won victory over death. Now, He also extends to us His hand as our resurrected Lord and lovingly invites us, "Come to me and I will give you rest." Now the angels of heaven cry out, "See how He loves them still—those for whom He died!"

In Jesus, we find a sympathetic, understanding, and merciful friend. In the period of the Old Testament, the High Priest was primarily responsible for interceding before God on behalf of the people, watching over them, and administering to their spiritual needs. But those priests of old were sinful like us, and imperfect in fulfilling all their responsibilities. In Jesus Christ, we have a High Priest who perfectly meets our every need.

> "For we do not have a high priest who is unable to
> sympathize with our weaknesses, but we have one
> who has been tempted in every way, just as we are—
> yet was without sin. Let us then approach the throne
> of grace with confidence, so that we may receive mercy
> and find grace to help us in our time of need."
> - Hebrews 4:15-16

Since 9-11, have you felt angry with God? Have you blamed Him for what happened? Have you argued with Him? Have you turned your back to Him because you feel He has turned His back on you? Did you lose faith after 9-11?

Our response may not always be the godliest response when the day of evil comes. We are often failures in maintaining our relationship with God. We often wrongly accuse Him when the bad seems to overtake the good around us. We may even shake our fist at Him as if to say that our way would have been the better choice. If you would do that to a spouse, you might end up with a broken marriage. If you did that to your boss at work, you'd be fired. If you did it to a police officer, you may find yourself with a hefty fine to pay or even end up in jail.

With Jesus it's different. He took a lot of abuse from man during His years on this earth. Then, He reacted with a calm and sympathetic mercy that even rattled the worst of His enemies. He has been taking a lot of abuse from mankind since He left the confines of this world and ascended to rule as King. Yet, He still reacts with a calm and sympathetic mercy to our ranting and raving against Him, even when our own evil ways threaten us with ruin and destruction.

He can "sympathize with our weaknesses" because He is one of us. He knows where we are coming from. He was tempted as we are tempted. He knows how hard it can be. Therefore, though we are wrong, and though He is without sin, He understands and lovingly works to mend our hurting hearts. He is patient with us and tries to keep leading us down the right path, though we may be kicking and fighting Him all the way.

When we see this love our Savior has for us, this patience and forbearance should humble us. It should lead us to express our sorrow to Him for our own shortsightedness and plead His forgiveness. He will give it because He loves us. It will be real and effective for us because He died for us so that now, in Him, we can "receive mercy and find grace to help us in our time of need."

This is the one to whom we can turn in every time of need and every period of sorrow. This one humbled Himself to become our most helpful friend.

> "But we see Jesus, who was made a little lower than the angels, now crowned with glory and honor because he suffered death, so that by the grace of God, he might taste death for everyone.... Both the one who makes men holy and those who are made holy are of the same family. So Jesus is not ashamed to call them brothers.... Since the children have flesh and blood, he too shared in their humanity so that by his death he might destroy him who holds the power of death—that is the devil—and free those who all their lives were held in slavery by their fear of death.... Because he himself suffered when he was

tempted, he is able to help those who are being tempted."

- Hebrews 2: select vs.

Did you ever notice how ants begin to scurry when you stomp your foot on the ground around them? I sometimes wonder what the ant sees, or feels, or senses when we are standing there, looming so large and powerful above them. Are they afraid? Do you suppose our presence strikes terror into every fiber of their puny, frail frames? I've never known anyone who wanted to trade places with the ant. It just doesn't seem a fair trade. There doesn't seem any sense to it. Wait—I take that back. I do know someone who traded places with the ant. His name was Jesus.

When God looks down upon us from His grand throne in heaven, we must appear to Him like a bunch of busy ants always racing around, scurrying here and there, and frantically trying to complete all our pressing tasks in life. Yet, Jesus became one of us. Jesus became an ant like us so that He could live like us and be one of us, so that "he might taste death for everyone." God became man. The eternal made Himself subject to death and He did it willingly, gladly, and so much so that He is not ashamed to call us brothers.

Jesus, the Son of God, did this for us because He saw us as more precious than ants. He saw us as children of God, people created in the image of God, who were in need of help and deliverance. So He became one of us to deliver us from evil, by suffering in our stead and freeing us from our fear of death. When God became the ant, we received the friend and ally we really needed the most. When that happened, the great Goliath of sin and Satan, who stood before us threatening to stomp us out, met his match, and victory became ours.

Now we see the field of battle that is before us. We have identified our enemy. We also know who is our greatest ally and friend. Let us now do the right thing in the wake of September 11. Let us do the most important and necessary thing of all.

> "Let us fix our eyes on Jesus, the author and perfecter of our faith, who for the joy set before him endured the cross, scorning its shame, and sat down at the right hand of the throne of God. Consider him who endured such opposition from sinful men, so that you will not grow weary and lose heart."
> - Hebrews 12:2, 3

The message from Calvary is this: Do not grow weary. Do not lose heart. "Consider him who endured such opposition from sinful men" and was victorious. The message from the cross is this: Be victorious with Him. When the day of evil comes, we have the victory already in hand if we do not lose faith, if we remain focused upon Him who is the author of our salvation and the perfecter of our faith. He is Jesus Christ our Resurrected and ever-living Lord. He will always be there for us when the day of evil comes for He has promised,

> "Surely I will be with you always, to the very end of the age."
> - Matthew 28:20

Jesus will be there for us. The question is, will we be where we need to be, at His side, with the sword of the Spirit drawn, which is His Word of truth to us. We will be there at His side and He will be there with us, if we know this truth:

> The ultimate triumph over evil begins when we first of all recognize the God of our salvation as our greatest ally and friend.

- CHAPTER SIX -

INSIGHT #6

The ultimate triumph over evil is realized in every act of God where He exercises His almighty power and infinite wisdom to use, frustrate, or overturn the forces of evil at work in this world, so that finally, His saving purposes for mankind are accomplished.

Two Important Characteristics of God

My father passed away a few years ago and those of you who have lost a parent through death know the empty hole that it leaves inside you. However, as time passes, you reflect more and more upon days past and many wonderful memories start springing to life. They help like a balm over an open wound. This is a wonderful gift from God—this gift of memory—for it can help us to weather through the bad times with remembrances of better times from the past. So I prefer to remember the life my father lived and all the ways in which he was a blessing to his family and the people in his community while he was alive.

There is much to remember about him, but one thing in particular comes to mind in the context that I am writing now.

He said something to me one day that caught me by surprise and even confused me for a while. It was a little saying he had come across, somewhere, in the latter years of his life, and he had grown quite fond of it. He would love to speak it from time to time in situations where he would find it to be appropriate.

On that particular day, he was recounting for me something he had read from the newspaper that struck his fancy. Someone had gotten himself into a strange pickle by doing something quite ridiculous. Whatever it was, I cannot recall now, but it doesn't matter because what is important was my dad's response. He found it all quite humorous and then turned to me and asked, "Dwight, you know what that man's problem is, don't you?" I had no clue and responded, "No, what?" He began to chuckle and then could hardly get the words out as he started laughing so hard, "That person is educated beyond his intelligence!" I cracked up. I had never heard that before. It sounded like such an amusing contradiction in terms. Then I started to think about it and I began to wonder more seriously, "What does that actually mean?"

The phrase has stuck with me now for years and I've come to realize the many situations in which it aptly fits. Have you ever come across anyone who is *educated beyond his or her intelligence*? Sometimes such a person can be identified whenever their knowledge is applied incorrectly, or not at all, in a given situation. I've come to realize that sometimes the person who manifests himself as *educated beyond his intelligence* is someone who has the smarts but lacks good common sense. As a result, the knowledge gained is often applied inappropriately. It is akin to the difference between knowledge and wisdom. A person can be very smart and possess great knowledge but never be wise. Wisdom has been defined in a variety of ways.

However, it might best be defined as the "proper application of knowledge." In that sense, there are people in this world who are *educated beyond their intelligence*—smart but never wise. When we question God's ways for our lives, we are questioning not only His intelligence but also His wisdom. We need to understand clearly, it is not a complimentary thing to do. It is almost as though we are accusing Him of being *educated beyond His intelligence!* (Uh, oh—did you see the lightning strike and hear the thunder crack?) It is, in fact, a blasphemous thing. Indeed, when we question God's ways for us and challenge Him, that is exactly what we are doing, blaspheming God! It is an impious and irreverent utterance against God.

Has there been any questioning of God's ways for us since the events of September 11? You bet there has been and it's not just that people are asking, "Why?" they're asking, "Why bother with God? Does He even care? Does He really know what He is doing?" The observation was made in Chapter 2 that Satan, our great enemy, loves to tempt us to question God's providence. He would have us believe that God is weak—weak in being honest with us, weak in His power to help us, and weak in His love for us.

In the last chapter, we noted that in Jesus Christ, the God of our salvation, we have the ally and friend that we need the most. He does love us dearly and cares about us most deeply. Now we are ready to examine two all-important attributes of our great ally and friend that make all the difference between total defeat and total victory when the day of evil comes. They are critically important for us to know and to believe, with all our heart and with all our mind. These two characteristics of God, together with His great love for us, enable us to be transported from the terror of evil to the triumphant victory of life, peace, and rest when the final battle has at last been fought. These two important characteristics of our great ally and friend are His almighty power and His infinite wisdom. Let's first briefly examine His almighty power.

> "'How will this be,' Mary asked the angel, 'since I am a virgin?'... The angel answered, '...nothing is impossible with God.'"
> - Luke 1:34, 35

We stand amazed every Christmas over the story of the virgin birth of Christ. Mary was amazed too when the announcement came to her from the angel Gabriel. "How will this be?" she asked. The announcement defied knowledge and common sense.

Down through the ages, people have stood amazed at this account of Jesus' birth. Remember, also, who recorded this event for us. It was Luke, the physician! Luke's Gospel contains so many miracles from Christ because as a physician himself, he could only stand in utter awe and amazement of the many ways in which God, through His almighty power, was able to perform the impossible. But that is what makes God, God. God is omnipotent. Therefore, as the angel Gabriel assured Mary, "Nothing is impossible with God." Expressed positively: everything is possible with God! After September 11, we need, desperately, to know this.

Secondly, the Apostle Paul, among many others, stood amazed and confounded over the infinite wisdom of God.

> "Oh, the depth of the riches of the wisdom and knowledge of God! How unsearchable his judgments, and

his paths beyond tracing out!"
- Romans 11:33

"Don't ask me to explain it, just do it!" Did you ever say that to someone, perhaps one of your children? Sometimes explaining is just too hard. It takes too long. It feels too unnecessary. Wisdom knows that just "doing it" will suffice.

It has been said that science is the art of thinking God's thoughts after Him. That is an interesting way of looking at it and, in many ways, very accurate. No wonder scientific inquiry and study are such time consuming, detailed, mind-bending pursuits. To follow behind God and try to figure out why He did what He did; to try to understand His judgments and follow behind on His paths is "beyond tracing out!" His wisdom is often just too deep for us to grasp. It is beyond our understanding and ability to rationalize.

We live in a universe, the dimensions of which we cannot even define. Yet, as it is His creation, He has measured it all. We live in a world that we can easily destroy but, so often, have no idea how to fix after we have so carelessly abused it. Yet, He who brought everything into existence, knows its workings in intricate detail. Even today, we can flick the switch that turns on the light but we can only harness the power of electricity. We cannot create it at will or even completely explain what it is. Only God can do that. "Oh, the depth of the riches of the wisdom and knowledge of God!"

Combine God's almighty power with His infinite wisdom and then add to the mix the sweetness of His unending love and you have the formula that we need when evil enters our lives. It is the formula for triumph and these parts combine to form our sixth insight.

INSIGHT #6

The ultimate triumph over evil is realized in every act of God where He exercises His almighty power and infinite wisdom to use, frustrate, or overturn the forces of evil at work in this world, so that finally, His saving purposes for mankind are accomplished.

God USES the Forces of Evil

There are so many places one could start in examining the ways in which our God, the God of all wisdom, power, and grace, is able to work His good purposes in the face of evil's dark designs. However, through Joseph we find a most profound setting in which God is not only repeatedly challenged by the forces of evil, but lays a path to triumph through evil's road blocks that is amazing to behold. The story of Joseph is as profound in its spiritual implications for us, as it was for Joseph himself when he lived through these events so many years ago.

If, as you study this account now with me, you feel compelled to weep as Joseph wept, do so. If you feel compelled to shake your head in amazement at the suffering he had to endure, then do so. If you feel compelled to wonder why all this happened to him, as he must have wondered himself at times, then wonder and read and learn the truth. As you study this section of Holy Scripture now, whatever you feel with Joseph through this warp in time that Holy Scripture provides us, then feel it now. However, in the end, above all else, believe what Joseph came to believe about God's grace, God's power, and God's wisdom in the face of evil's terror. If you go away with faith like that of Joseph, you will go away a powerful, healthy, wise, and mature child of God. Like Joseph, you will be able to withstand whatever evil Satan and his forces of darkness might cast your way. This is his life under God's direction and the road he walked, from terror to triumph.

THE STORY OF JOSEPH
Genesis 37-50

From the outset of the 37th chapter of Genesis, you know trouble is brewing. We first read something about Joseph that isn't very flattering.

> "Joseph, a young man of seventeen, was tending the flocks with his brothers... and he brought their father a bad report about them." - 37:2

It appears Joseph was a bit of a tattletale and no one likes a tattletale. Then we're told something about Israel (Jacob), Joseph's father.

> "Now Israel loved Joseph more than any of his other sons . . ." - 37:3

Can you begin to see where God is leading us? Next, we're told something about Joseph's brothers as well.

> "When his brothers saw that their father loved him more than any of them, they hated him and could not speak a kind word to him." - 37:4

A tattletale, a favored son, and eleven jealous brothers; in this setting the web of Joseph's tumultuous life is spun. Note carefully, this is what God uses as His mold, to create something from nothing. This is what God has to start with. But is there anything here worth having? Does jealousy, anger, bitterness, hatred, favoritism, backstabbing, or gossip have any redeeming qualities? They have none whatsoever. They are all sins before God. They are all just the opposite of how He would have us live. Yet, God is good. God is holy and God is love. Carefully and lovingly, this is what the God of unlimited power and infinite wisdom will use to mold Joseph into the kind of man He intends him to be. This is also, what the God of unlimited power and infinite wisdom will use as the beginnings of His grand plan of salvation for the world. It all begins here, in the hills of Canaan. It all begins with this evil in the lives of Jacob, Joseph, and his brothers. It will all end in triumph as God uses this evil to win a greater good.

Joseph thickened the mix when he added the sin of indiscretion to the soup. Joseph had a dream, on top of everything else, and he was both pompous and foolish enough to share it with his brothers. In the dream, he and his brothers were "binding sheaves of grain out in the field." Suddenly the sheaf of Joseph "rose and stood upright." Then the sheaves of the other brothers gathered around Joseph's and "bowed down to it." The implication was clear for all his brothers to see. Angrily, they queried him, "Do you intend to reign over us? Will you actually rule us?" You can taste the venomous words of hatred spewing from their mouths against him. Now they despised him even more.

Joseph didn't stop there. A second dream followed. He shared this one with his brothers too. "I had another dream, and this time the sun and moon and eleven stars were bowing down to me." This one, he told his father as well. Though disturbed over the implications of it, that even Joseph's mother and father would bow to him, Jacob mildly rebuked his favorite son and sent him off. However, just as Mary "pondered in her heart" the news to her from the angel Gabriel, Jacob also "kept the thing in mind."

It is interesting that in both Mary's case and in Jacob's—two critical junctures in human history when God is about to act in miraculous ways to advance His saving plan for the world—the way in which God will work sounds so impossible. Yet, two dedicated children of God, first Jacob and then Mary, do not dismiss the account. It is as though they are faithfully fixing their eyes on the heavens, waiting, watching, and wondering, "What is this great thing God is going to do now?" There is a kind of perplexing freshness to their wonderment, for in both cases we see faith perceives something great is coming even though it cannot identify exactly what it is.

In days of evil it is good for us to do the same thing and ask not "God, where are you now?" but "God, what great thing are you going to perform now through all this evil?" We can ask that after September 11. We need to ask it. It is spiritually healthy if we do. It will be good for us all to wait upon God and see what wonders He will perform in the days and months and years after September 11. I believe He is going to surprise a great many people who ever doubted Him.

So the stage had been set for disaster, and that day came with great vengeance and fury. These brothers were out grazing their father's flocks. Jacob sent Joseph out on another spying mission to see how his brothers were doing. Joseph was to return promptly and report to his father. Upon receiving news that they had left the fields of Shechem and were grazing the flocks near Dothan, Joseph went after his brothers. Then we read this,

"But they saw him in the distance, and before he
reached them, they plotted to kill him. 'Here comes
that dreamer!' they said to each other. 'Come now,
let's kill him and throw him into one of these cis-
terns and say that a ferocious animal devoured him.
Then we'll see what comes of his dreams.'... So when
Joseph came to his brothers, they stripped him of his
robe—the richly ornamented robe he was wearing—
and they took him and threw him into the cistern."
- 37:18-20, 23, 24

"We'll see what comes of his dreams," they said. Jesus' words
come to mind, "Father forgive them for they do not know what
they are doing." Evil can never foil the works of God. God will
stomp evil into the ground, use it for His sacred purposes, or
overturn it, but it can never stop the good and noble purposes
of God.

It is certain that these brothers had no idea what they were
saying and how factual their brother's dreams actually were.
They were a hot pot, boiling over with steaming malice and
hatred. Nothing would stop them. However, for a moment,
Reuben tried. It was to no avail. The deed was done. Into the
deep, dry, hard cistern, they threw their brother. Callously, "they
sat down to eat their meal."

Hated and abused by his brothers, at the tender age of 17,
Joseph now began a most uncertain future. It is hard to imagine such evil being carried out, but that's what happened then,
and here we are today. Man has not changed very much in the
centuries that have passed. We're quite a mess—so much for
the evolutionary advances of our species.

For Joseph, help would come. In fact, it had already come,

only no one recognized it. Just as when Jesus came, no one recognized Him as our great help sent by God. On that day, in Joseph's life, help from God came in the form of Midianite merchants who were on their way to Egypt. If they had not come by, in all likelihood, these misguided wretches would have finished their meal and murdered their brother. It was Judah, however, who spoke up. What he said wasn't very noble, but nonetheless, it did save Joseph's life. Interestingly, it was from Judah's line of descent that Jesus, our Savior, was born, in Bethlehem, in the land of Judah.

> "Judah said to his brothers, 'What will we gain if we kill our brother and cover up his blood? Come, let's sell him to the Ishmaelites and not lay our hands on him; after all, he is our brother, our own flesh and blood.' His brothers agreed. So when the Midianite merchants came by, his brothers pulled Joseph up out of the cistern and sold him for twenty shekels of silver to the Ishmaelites, who took him to Egypt."
> - 37:26-28

So, for 20 pieces of silver, Joseph was betrayed by his brothers. Still, evil did not win. For 30 pieces of silver, Jesus was also betrayed by one of His own, but evil did not win.

Joseph was handed over to Gentiles who became his means of salvation, though that fact was shrouded in mystery at the time. Jesus too was handed over to Gentiles and He has become our means of salvation, though that fact was shrouded in mystery on Good Friday.

God sent Joseph to Egypt, to find safety there, having been harassed by evil. The child Jesus was also sent from Bethlehem to Egypt to find safety, being harassed by the evil King Herod.

The selfish, evil rationalizing of Judah led him to assert, "What will we gain if we kill our brother and cover up his blood?" He didn't know how prophetically true his words were. Preserving Joseph's life would one day mean life for them and deliverance from a famine that would sweep across the land. Likewise, in Jesus' day, the selfish, evil rationalizing of Caiaphas the high priest led him to assert, "You know nothing at all! You do not realize that it is better for you that one man die for the people than that the whole nation perish" (John 11:49, 50). He didn't know how prophetically true his words were either. Jesus' death would mean life and deliverance for all from the dry famine of sin that leads to spiritual death.

See what God wants you to see here. See in Joseph the victory over evil that is ours in Jesus! In both of these dramatic, life-altering events from our history, God has shown that evil will never win the day. At best, it can only appear to win for a while. Then, with the breath of God's power, wisdom, and goodness, evil is swept away like a dark cloud that swiftly moves across the sky so that the sun is able to shine again and bring to us its comfort and warmth. Yes, even Joseph was as good as dead, but he lived. Jesus was actually dead, but He lived. He rose to life on Easter morning. Joseph's sacrifice, brought life for his brothers. Jesus' sacrifice, wins life for all. Because He lives, we too will live.

Oh, one more important thing: the lie. These brothers, after ruthlessly selling their brother into slavery, spread the lie that a ferocious animal had devoured him. They presented, to their father, Joseph's blood stained robe that they had dipped in goat's blood as proof that he was dead. Before their own father, they cold-heartedly concocted and spread this lie. Joseph, in fact, was alive and they knew it well.

Three days after Jesus' crucifixion, death, and burial, the chief priests and elders, upon hearing on Easter morning that the tomb was empty, spread the lie that Jesus' disciples had come in the night and stolen His body from the tomb. They wanted everyone to believe that Jesus was still dead. Before their own Father in heaven, they cold-heartedly concocted and spread this lie. Jesus, in fact, was alive and they too knew it well. The soldiers who had been guarding the tomb, whom they bribed with a large sum of money, knew it. From the very testimony of these Roman guards, they knew it too, but they didn't want anyone else to know. Their story was also a lie and meant to cover up the truth that in Christ a new day had dawned, for through the gift of His Son, God was victorious over evil, sin, and death.

Hated and abused, then enslaved and separated from his family, Joseph must have wondered desperately why, "Why is this happening to me?" Nonetheless, the journey continued and he was taken down to Egypt where he was sold again into the service of an Egyptian master by the name of Potiphar.

> "Potiphar, an Egyptian who was one of Pharaoh's officials... bought him from the Ishmaelites who had taken him there. The Lord was with Joseph and he prospered, and he lived in the house of his Egyptian master."
> - 39:1, 2

In spite of his enslavement and in spite of still being separated from his family against his will, we read that the Lord was with Joseph. We read no word that Joseph in any way blamed God for his misfortunes. We read nothing of Joseph complaining to God about his sufferings or despairing of God. His Creator was allowing all these terrible events to transpire in his life, yet no anger or bitterness swelled up in his heart against God. Through it all, God was honing Joseph to be someone God needed him to be. Though misfortune continued, God's love for Joseph was still evident to see.

From a favored son to nearly being a dead son, from being thrown into a cistern and then sold into slavery, by God's handiwork Joseph experienced a rather remarkable emergence from this dark night. The Lord was with him and blessed everything he did so that Potiphar "entrusted to his care everything he owned" (39:4). It seemed things were beginning to come back together for Joseph and he must have hoped that one day he might even be able to return to his father. However, evil came after him again, this time through the back door.

You have probably heard the story of Potiphar's wife. Joseph caught her eye. "Come to bed with me," she begged him, day after day, without end. Repeatedly, Joseph rejected her advances, "How could I do such a wicked thing and sin against God?" (39:9). Joseph tried to keep his distance but she was relentless in her pursuit of him. Finally, one day, when Joseph "went into the house to attend to his duties" she found herself alone with him. She grabbed him by his cloak and as she tried to reel him in, Joseph shook loose from her hooks, shed his robe, and ran out of the house as fast as he could. Infuriated and frustrated, this was the last straw for her. If this devil-woman could not have her way with Joseph, and have him in her pillow bed, she would do away with him, and cast him into a prison bed.

So she screamed, she clung to his robe, and she waved it for all to see. She cried aloud for all the other household servants to hear. "Rape! Help me! He's attacking me! Look at his garment that he left behind!" They came running to her aid. With evil lies spewing from her mouth like the repeated thrusts and jabs of a vengeful dagger, she spread her poison. They were all lies, of course. Did everyone believe her? Did they empathize with her? Did they all comfort her in her deceitful distress? Had she fooled them all? There is one whom we know was fooled—Potiphar, her husband. It wasn't long before shock and sympathy turned to burning anger and hatred.

> "When the master heard the story his wife told him, saying, 'This is how your slave treated me,' he burned with anger. Joseph's master took him and put him in prison, the place where the king's prisoners were confined. But while Joseph was there in the prison, the Lord was with him; he showed him kindness and granted him favor in the eyes of the prison warden. So the warden put Joseph in charge of all those held in the prison."
> - 39:19-22

Now, falsely accused and imprisoned, Joseph found himself in what would be considered the most deplorable of conditions. To be a prisoner was even worse than being a slave. However, one condition remained, for even in the midst of all this evil swirling about him like a whirlwind, "the Lord was with him." In the midst of all this evil, God was there, at his side, and working a mysteriously great work.

Interestingly, he was placed "where the king's prisoners

were confined." Under most circumstances, this would be the worst place to be held. These prisoners were watched most closely and incarcerated most securely. The hope for escape was practically zero. For Joseph, this became a great blessing. Joseph came under the watchful eye of the prison warden who came to look upon Joseph with favor and understanding. So much so, that as time passed, he placed Joseph in charge of everyone held in the prison. Amazingly, Joseph was in charge again!

Here we see a progression that is hard to miss. First, Joseph was used as overseer of his father's flocks. Then, he was placed in charge of everything in Potiphar's household. Next, he was made responsible for everything done in the prison where he himself was confined. In the most horrific of circumstances, God had provided an important training ground for Joseph. By using the evil that seemed to envelop him completely, God was providing the means for ultimate freedom and ultimate rule.

Years passed by and there was no change in Joseph's situation. Did he think the Lord had left him? Was this to be his lot in life? Would deliverance be a gift never to be realized? We read nothing of Joseph approaching the evil in his life that way. In fact, from what we read, he appears to have grown stronger in his faith day by day with an uplifted spirit that was the envy of his fellow inmates. For one day, when Joseph came upon the king's cupbearer and the king's baker, two fellow prisoners with him, with faces saddened and dejected, Joseph asked them, "Why are your faces so sad?" Each of them had dreamed. They were disturbed by their dreams and were distraught because no one could interpret them. Joseph said to them, with a trust in God that only faith can express, "Do not interpretations belong to God? Tell me your dreams" (40:8).

Both dreams were similar in nature but each quite different in conclusion. The meaning was this: in three days the chief cupbearer would be restored to his position before Pharaoh, but after those same three days, the chief baker would be put to death. It happened for each of them just as Joseph said it would. God had been with him and guiding him again. Sadly, chapter 40 ends on this sour note, "The chief cupbearer, however, did not remember Joseph; he forgot him." Sometimes, forgetting the blessings that come to us through the people we associate with in life, is as great an evil as anything else is. It can be as hurtful and as damaging as the most violent of deeds. Thankfully, God did not forget Joseph. The day of victory was gradually drawing near, but two more years would pass.

After that time, Pharaoh himself had a dream. No one could interpret it—not the wise men of Egypt, not the magicians, or the sorcerers. No one could help. Then the chief cupbearer remembered, "Oh yes, Joseph!" He spoke to Pharaoh favorably of this young Hebrew who had been in prison with him and with the chief baker. This man had interpreted their dreams correctly when no one else could. Pharaoh sent for Joseph and he was brought forth from the dungeon. Shaved, and given a change of clothes, they led him before Pharaoh.

There now was Joseph, standing before the most powerful ruler on the earth. How could this have come to be, given all the evil that had befallen him in his life? Pharaoh spoke. "I had a dream, and no one can interpret it. But I have heard it said of you that when you hear a dream you can interpret it" (41:15). What would you have said in response? Understand, your freedom is on the line. Perhaps you would have said, "Yes, yes I can! I can interpret your dream, my king! I would be glad to help my Pharaoh in any way I can!" Would you be thinking of the freedom that would soon be yours? Wouldn't most of us

be inclined to be thinking about that—thinking about ourselves?

Here is what Joseph answered: "I cannot do it." Do you believe it? Was he nuts? "I cannot do it," he said. What in the
world is going on here? Well, what's going on here is the power
of faith. What's going on here is trust. What's going on here is
spiritual maturity. What's going on here is righteousness. What's
going on here is the joy of salvation. What's going on here is a
blessed end to a long road of sorrow. What's going on here is
the amazing work of God. What's going on here is the triumphant victory of God over evil. What's going on here are Satan's devices being firmly leveled and the plans of God being
victoriously exalted.

Joseph, son of Jacob, of Hebrew descent, despised brother,
servant, slave, prisoner—hated, abused, threatened with death,
separated from family for years, falsely accused, imprisoned,
forgotten—this man—no, this man of God—now stood before
Pharaoh himself, and all his highest ranking attendants. There
were priests, administrators, magicians, and religious men of
all kinds present. He stood before them all, after all he had
been through, and humbly, yet powerfully, confessed the truth
before them all,

> "I cannot do it, but God will give Pharaoh the an-
> swer he desires."
> - 41:16

If, after September 11, you can do what Joseph did that
day, those hundreds of years ago, and in the face of all the evil,
remain firm in faith and in the end give glory to God, then you
will have accomplished, by God's power and might, what the

Apostle Paul wrote about centuries later: "Therefore put on the full armor of God, so that when the day of evil comes, you may be able to stand your ground, and after you have done everything, to stand" (Ephesians 6:13).

It is so important that all of us grasp what a meaningful, powerful, and victorious confession Joseph uttered that day. Evil could have ruined him. It could have destroyed his faith. All that he suffered in life could have made him a bitter and angry empty shell of a man. The point is not that **he** did not let this happen to him. Even more accurately, the point is that **God** did not let this happen to him.

Through it all, God remained with him. Through it all, God created blessings for him. Through it all, Joseph found ample reason and opportunities to thank and praise God. He didn't let evil eat away at his spiritual armor like a decaying rust on his soul, but he remained strong in faith by God's continued grace and presence in his life. He did not blame God for the evil nor did he see God as the source of the evil. He saw God working His good purposes through it all! Therefore, at the end, when evil finally met its match in God, evil also met its match in Joseph when he confessed, "I cannot, but GOD CAN!"

After 9-11, we need to pray for the strength of Joseph, which is the strength of God at work in the heart of man. Then we too will stand our spiritual ground in the face of this great evil that has come upon our nation today.

God's interpretation of Pharaoh's dream through Joseph predicted seven years of abundance throughout the land and then seven years of famine. It would all begin soon. God not only accurately interpreted the dream through Joseph, but as God had honed him to be an effective administrator and manager, through the years of evil that had befallen him, He now used Joseph to instruct Pharaoh on how all of Egypt should prepare for the difficult years of famine to come. So Pharaoh reasoned,

> "'Since God has made all this known to you, there is no one so discerning and wise as you. You shall be in charge of my palace, and all my people are to submit to your orders. Only with respect to the throne will I be greater than you.' So Pharaoh said to Joseph, 'I hereby put you in charge of the whole land of Egypt.'... Joseph was 30 years old when he entered the service of Pharaoh king of Egypt."
> - 41:39-41, 46

Thirteen years had past. Thirteen years of evil had ended and Joseph was released from his prison chains. What a glorious end to a dark and evil road.

It must have been easier for Joseph now. I'm sure it was. Yet, it wasn't a perfect time. He was still separated from his family and he had not seen his father in 13 years. However, Joseph had a job to do now and he knew that this was the work to which God had called and prepared him all those years past. So he stayed in Egypt and fulfilled his God-given responsibilities.

Joseph married and was blessed with children. The seven years of abundance came and went. Joseph managed a remarkable system of agricultural abundance and preservation that enabled Egypt to become the breadbasket for the entire civilized world over the next seven years of famine. Yes, the years of famine also came, just as God had revealed through Pharaoh's dream. Something else came with the famine. His brothers came, and with them came a day of reckoning.

> "When Jacob learned that there was grain in Egypt,
> he said to his sons, 'Why do you just keep looking at
> each other?' He continued, 'I have heard that there is
> grain in Egypt. Go down there and buy some for us,
> so that we may live and not die.'"
> - 42:1, 2

Some interesting parallels here are worth noting. Like Joseph, "Jesus himself was about **thirty years old**, when he began his ministry" (Luke 3:23). Also, the knowledge that there was abundant grain in storage in Egypt prompted their father to send his sons there. Little did they realize the complete salvation that they would find there, not only in the form of grain for bread that won deliverance from famine, but there they would also find a message of great forgiveness from their long lost brother, against whom they had sinned greatly. It was there waiting for them. God's work was now complete. They needed just to go and find the truth. Their father's words to them indicate some perplexity as to why they still were just standing around with this great salvation accomplished for them. "Why do you just keep looking at each other?... Go," he said to them.

After Jesus ascended into heaven, having completed his great work of salvation for us, we read in Acts 1 about the two men dressed in white (angels) who suddenly appeared and stood next to the disciples. They had been "looking intently up into the sky" witnessing Jesus' departure from the confines of time and space. When the angels saw Jesus' disciples doing this, they asked them a question strikingly similar to what Jacob asked his sons. They inquired, "Why do you stand here looking into the sky?"

It's a remarkable parallel that further underscores Joseph as an Old Testament type of Christ and a shadow of the greater gifts that were to come through God's Son, Jesus Christ. Salvation from famine, through Joseph, awaited them in Egypt. They needed to stop staring at each other, wasting precious time, and go! Salvation from sin, through Jesus Christ, is accomplished for us. We too need to go to Christ in whom life is found. We too need to stop standing around gawking at one another and idly standing around waiting for Christ to return. He will come again, but until then, our work is to waste no more precious time but to go and spread the good news everywhere!

So they went, as their father had commanded them. They went unknowingly, into an amazing work of God that had already been accomplished for them. They were moving into such a realm of power, wisdom, and grace that it would leave them speechless and terrified. In the end, however, they would find peace and deliverance for they would discover that a far greater saving purpose had been accomplished for them through their original evil intent against their long lost brother. However, only ten of them went. The youngest, Benjamin, Joseph's only other full-brother, was left to stay in Canaan to be with his father. You may want to read the full details of this account in Genesis 42 through 45. It is rich in drama and full of meaning for our lives. For our purposes here, we summarize this day of reckoning.

When they met, Joseph stood before them as governor of the land and he recognized his brothers but they did not recognize him. As Joseph's dream in his youth had accurately foretold, "they bowed down to him, with their faces to the ground"

(42:6). At first, Joseph almost seemed to taunt them just as they had so often taunted him in his youth. He accused them of being spies. They assured him they were not and had only come to buy food. They spoke of their family: twelve brothers of one father, one brother was left behind, and another who was no more. It was not good enough. Just as they had cast Joseph into the dry cistern, he now cast them into prison for three days. We might wonder why Joseph would play this game with them. It almost seems vengeful on his part. Why not just reveal himself immediately and then let them go? This appears to have been the only way to get them to deal truthfully with him. This may also have been the only way he hoped to ever again be united with his father. Remember, they had told Jacob that Joseph was dead. Even if Joseph had revealed himself to them and let them return to Canaan, what guarantee was there that they would own up to their sin and tell their father the truth regarding his lost son? Their treacherous ways were entrenched in their souls. Joseph knew it all too well. He would deal with them in a way that would ensure a blessed reunion with his father.

After three days the brothers were brought up from their prison cells. Joseph told them that Simeon would remain in Egypt. The rest were to return to Canaan and bring back with them the youngest, Benjamin, as proof that their story was true and that they were not spies. Only then, would Simeon be released.

This turn of events prompts an interesting response from the brothers. Speaking in their native language, in the hope they might not be understood, they said to one another, "Surely we are being punished because of our brother. We saw how distressed he was when he pleaded with us for his life, but we would not listen; that's why this distress has come upon us" (42:21). Joseph, of course, understood every word they said. They believed all this was happening as punishment for their sin! In fact, it was all happening to work a great blessing for them!

Simeon was bound and led away. Joseph turned away from them and was moved to tears; touched deeply by this amazing turn of events. His heart had been softened over the years to understand the pain in suffering, and so he could sympathize with what his brothers were now going through, just as Jesus our good friend is able to sympathize with us when the terror of our sin glares back at us. Jesus doesn't want us to feel that way. He wants to bring us relief through forgiveness. Joseph had similar plans for his brothers, to replace their terror with his grace that would lead to triumph for them. He began this benevolence toward them by giving orders to "fill their bags with grain and then to put each man's silver back in his sack, and to give them provisions for their journey" (42:25).

As it was commanded, so it was done. They left for Canaan. That night, they discovered that their silver had been returned to them. Even that filled them with fear and they blamed God, thinking that He was again exercising some divine punishment against them for their sin. Surely, they thought, they would be accused of trickery and theft when they returned to Egypt.

Isn't it amazing how far afield we can go in viewing God's activity in our lives? In our ignorance, we not only think God to be the source of evil, but also are often unable to recognize His blessings when they are extended to us. This is an amazing example of how sin and guilt are used by Satan to blind us to the goodness of God at work all around us. Whenever any day of evil comes upon us this can happen. We dare not let the events of 9-11 so cloud our vision of God.

Upon their arrival, the brothers relayed to their father, everything that had happened in Egypt. Simeon was now being held in prison and was as good as dead. They had returned but with orders to go back to Egypt and present Benjamin. Only then would Simeon be released.

At this news, Jacob's heart sank. Not only had he lost Joseph, his favorite son, but now it appeared he had lost Simeon as well, and he refused to let the same happen to Benjamin. At first, he refused to let him go. Eventually, however, the grain ran out and Jacob was forced to relent. With Benjamin, these brothers now made their way back to Egypt a second time.

They left Canaan with gifts in the hope of appeasing the governor's (Joseph's) wrath. They came to him to honor him with gifts, gifts of "balm and a little honey, some spices and myrrh" (43:11). They brought back double the amount of silver that had been returned in their sacks. Does this sound at all familiar? It should. "Then they opened their treasures and presented him (the infant Jesus) with gifts of gold and of incense and of myrrh" (Matthew 2:11). Joseph is a true type of Christ, a shadow of Christ. In Jesus, the greater salvation is won.

When they arrived in Egypt Joseph saw that Benjamin was indeed with them. He ordered a dinner prepared and all the brothers to attend a noon feast with him. Then Joseph's steward led them to Joseph's house. They were all filled with fear as to what might happen to them there, and could not understand why so much attention was being extended their way.

Upon entering the palace, they were given water to wash their feet, their donkeys were attended to, and when Joseph came home, they presented him with all their gifts. He spoke kindly to them. He asked them of their father, which must have puzzled them greatly. Then he saw his dear brother Benjamin. This was the first time in thirteen years he had laid eyes upon him and he extended to him a greeting, "God be gracious to you, my son" (43:29). Joseph could not control his emotions any longer and he hurried out of their presence, went quickly to his private room, and there he wept.

After he had pulled himself together, he returned, and gave orders for the meal to be served. He ate alone, other Egyptians in the room ate by themselves, and his brothers ate with one another. They were astonished when they noticed that all of them had been seated before Joseph in order of their ages. How could this man know such a thing? In addition, Benjamin received a portion five times greater than anyone else did. Why was that? This was all very perplexing to them.

The next morning the brothers made ready to be on their way. They had not gone far from the city when Joseph sent his steward after them to stop them and search their sacks for Joseph's silver cup. The sacks were lowered to the ground, each one opened, and there the cup was found, in Benjamin's sack. However, it wasn't Benjamin's doing. Joseph had ordered that the cup be secretly placed in his younger brother's sack. Now they were all forced to return to the city, back to Joseph's residence, to face charges of theft.

"What is this you have done?" Joseph asked. They had no defense. They could not prove their innocence. They offered themselves as slaves to Joseph but he replied, "Far be it from me to do such a thing! Only the man who was found to have the cup will become my slave" (44:17). Benjamin!

In an instant, Judah, who had reasoned with his brothers to sell Joseph to the Midianite traders so many years before, stepped forward, and pleaded on Benjamin's behalf. He told him how such a thing would break his father's heart. He begged Joseph to be merciful for if they did not return to Canaan with the boy, his father would most certainly die. Judah confessed that he had guaranteed the boy's safety. He could not let this happen. Therefore, Judah offered himself as slave in place of his brother Benjamin in order to deliver him from this great evil.

It was a noble gesture, but, as he would soon see, quite unnecessary. Yet, centuries later, another would offer Himself, in the place of his brothers and sisters, for the sins of the world. A very necessary sacrifice would be made. He too would be from the tribe and lineage of Judah. His name was Jesus Christ and He delivered us from our slavery to sin when He became sin for us.

So Judah pleaded, "No! Do not let me see the misery that would come upon my father" (44:34). Next, we read this:

> "Then Joseph could no longer control himself before all his attendants, and he cried out, 'Have everyone leave my presence!' So there was no one with Joseph when he made himself known to his brothers. And he wept so loudly that the Egyptians heard him, and Pharaoh's household heard about it. Joseph said to his brothers, 'I am Joseph! Is my father still living?' But his brothers were not able to answer him, because they were terrified at his presence. Then Joseph said to his brothers, 'Come close to me.' When they had done so, he said, "I am your brother Joseph, the one you sold into Egypt! And now, do not be distressed and do not be angry with yourselves for selling me here, because it was to save lives that God sent me

ahead of you. For two years now there has been famine in the land, and for the next five years there will
not be plowing and reaping. But God sent me ahead
of you to preserve for you a remnant on earth and to
save your lives by a great deliverance.'"
- 45:1-7

That must have been quite a moment. Suddenly these
eleven brothers viewed Joseph in an entirely different light. At
first, it was in fear because of their sin. They were "terrified at
his presence" and had every reason to be struck with fear. But
Joseph wanted them to see what he had come to see during the
course of his life! He wanted them to see with eyes of faith, like
him! He wanted them to feel the deliverance that he had felt.
He wanted them to know the grace of God in the face of evil, as
he had come to know it. He wanted them to view their brother
Joseph, not as an angry judge ruling against them for all their
evil, but as a blessed deliverer for them, and sent by God!

Therefore, he shared with them what God had done through
him. He told them how God had used the evil against him,
repeatedly, to work a greater good. Everything had been planned
out this way by God. No longer did they need to be distressed.
No longer did they even need to be angry with themselves over
the evil they had committed against their brother. *GOD HAD
DONE MUCH MORE!*

That is what we find so amazing in Joseph's explanation of
his past. He told them, "God sent me ahead of you... God sent
me... to save your lives by a great deliverance." God was not
the evil, but God was using the evil for a greater good! God was
using His infinite power and infinite wisdom to work a great
deliverance and to save lives! He told them that they were not

the ones who had sent him to Egypt. God did! "He made me father to Pharaoh... God has made me Lord of all Egypt" (45:8, 9).

Perhaps you've seen, through this study of Joseph's life, some truths that you have never seen before. I hope so, but more than anything, I hope you are able to see the great power and wisdom of God at work in our lives.

As intricate and complex as they can sometimes be, and even though the forces of evil might be working overtime to undo what God has done in our lives and in our hearts, nothing is able to prevent God from carrying out His noble purposes. His power and His wisdom will prevail. And if He must, He will use the evil acts of Satan and of men, to work His blessed purposes. He did it for Joseph and for Joseph's brothers. He has been doing it since the beginning of time. He will do it again through the events of 9-11. It is simply a matter of waiting upon Him, as Joseph did so patiently, and trusting that a greater good will be accomplished after all is said and done.

As we wait for God's good purposes in our lives to be fully revealed in space and time, we will have setbacks. We will have doubts. We will relapse. This may happen whenever evil returns to harass us. Satan is not idle. Though he knows God is strong, he also knows we are not.

Expect attacks upon your faith to continue until your last day. They continued for Joseph's brothers for years. In fact, when the day came that their father Jacob died, their fears resurfaced. They thought, "What if Joseph holds a grudge against us and pays us back for all the wrongs we did to him?" (50:15). So they sent word to Joseph that before he died, Jacob, his father, had left specific instructions on how he was to deal with his brothers, "I ask you to forgive your brothers the sins and the wrongs they committed in treating you so badly" (50:17). The brothers begged Joseph's forgiveness all over again and we're told that when the message reached him, he wept. Their sins continued to haunt them. They still feared retribution. They doubted the forgiveness Joseph was extending to them. So they came and threw themselves down before him saying, "We are your slaves" (50:18).

Why would Joseph weep? Why shouldn't he? How do we feel when our love for someone is questioned? How do we feel when people suffer with guilt over sins against us, in spite of assurances to them that sins of the past are history and that all has been forgiven, never to be spoken of again. We ache inside for them. We want so much for them to live in peace knowing how much they are loved and how total and complete our forgiveness is for them. It tears us up inside when we see that they are not at rest. If they would just trust us and forgive themselves as we have forgiven them, then peace and rest would come.

This is why Joseph wept. They doubted his love for them and the forgiveness he was extending to them. It was an evil plague upon their souls that he wanted removed permanently. So he reminded them of his love and he assured them of his benevolence.

> "But Joseph said to them, 'Don't be afraid. Am I in place of God? You intended to harm me, but God intended it for good to accomplish what is now being done, the saving of many lives.'"
> - 50:20

September 11 may have caused some people to question

God's love for them. It may have caused you or someone you know to doubt how full and complete God's forgiveness for us really is. The God of our salvation sent His Son to this world to face the forces of evil head on and accomplish for us a great work that would result in the saving of many lives from an eternity of separation from God. Jesus did this for us. He did it by rendering satisfaction for our sins upon Calvary's cross. His forgiveness is total and complete, never to be repeated, never to be taken back. It is ours.

If we find in September 11 some notion that God is punishing us for sins we have committed as a nation, as a people, as individuals, or for whatever reason we might imagine, then we have gravely missed the mark and we are guilty of the mistake Joseph's brothers made. Then we question God's love for us, though He has assured us of it. Then we question the completeness of Christ's sacrifice for us, though He assures us that all is forgiven. Then we grieve the Holy Spirit who is alive and at work within us. Then we are letting evil continue its foul and rancid work of eating away at our faith. This makes God weep for us.

Rather, let us make Him glad as He sees us trusting in Him now and finding our strength in Him. This is what God wants. He wants us to live without fear of any further retribution for our sins. He wants us to find peace and rest in Him when the day of evil comes. He wants us to know that evil arrives in our lives not as punishment for sin but as a byproduct of sin itself. It is not of God. It is of Satan and his host, and of man's continuous rebellious ways. We need to see that God is greater than sin and evil in every way, but especially in power and in wisdom. He will use evil to destroy evil. He will use it to work a greater good. As He did it for Joseph, and as He did it in

Christ, He will do it again now, for us, after September 11.

We have spent a fair amount of time examining the life of Joseph because it offers so much insight in leading us to a more complete and rounded understanding of how God wages this great war with evil on our behalf. Yet, God does not always work so mysteriously and on such a grand scale as He did with Joseph. Evil may come in many sizes, shapes, and forms. God is able to work through every situation to bring about a blessing. We find a wonderful example of that in our next study from John's Gospel, the story of the man born blind.

John dedicates an entire chapter of his Gospel to this one remarkable individual and all that was accomplished through him. In it, we see the love of our Savior at work through the suffering of His children, and the immediate blessings that God can reap in the lives of people everywhere when God's power and wisdom are so magnificently bestowed.

THE STORY OF THE MAN BORN BLIND
JOHN 9

"As he went along, he saw a man blind from birth.
His disciples asked him, "Rabbi, who sinned, this man
or his parents, that he was born blind?"
- vs.1, 2

We might find it somewhat humorous that His disciples would ask such a question of Jesus but we shouldn't laugh too long. The world has not changed very much since then, and the thinking of natural man remains much the same. People repeat that question often today when evil, suffering, sorrow, and misfortune come. "I must have done something terribly wrong that God is punishing me so." "What did I do to deserve this?" This is how people respond even today when the day of evil, suffering, and misfortune comes upon them. Jesus came to set the record straight.

> "'Neither this man nor his parents sinned,' Jesus said,
> 'but this happened so that the work of God might be
> displayed in his life.'"
> – vs. 3

How many of us think this way when we visit people suffering in the hospital? How many of us think this way when we are the ones suffering? How many of us, when we see the disabled, think like this? Many times, we busy ourselves wondering why some people suffer so, and why some live such abnormal lives with physical handicaps. But how often do we stop to ask ourselves, "What great work might God want to display through those lives?" Yet, that is exactly what Jesus wants us to ask and then open our eyes to see. He wants us to see how the working of God's power and wisdom is so amazingly displayed in people's lives through suffering.

So now, as we work through this story of the man born blind, let's count. Let's count how many lives are touched by this man's affliction and let's keep track of the many ways in which the work of God was displayed in his life the day Jesus entered his world. Maybe it will give us some idea of the many ways in which the work of God can be displayed in our lives when Jesus enters our world today. Start counting.

#1 – JESUS HIMSELF and #2 – THE MAN HIMSELF

"Having said this, he spit on the ground, made some mud with the saliva and put it on the man's eyes. 'Go,' he told him, 'wash in the pool of Siloam' (this word means Sent). So the man went and washed, and came home seeing."
– vs.6, 7

What a strange thing this is that Jesus does. This is what I call the "EUW" miracle because whenever people read about what Jesus did here—especially children—they go, "Eeeuuuwww!" Why did He do it this way? Why mud mixed with saliva? Believe me, if you try it, it will not do anything for you. Interestingly enough, that is the very reason Jesus did it that way. Remember, God will often use the simple things of the world, the plain things, because then we know all things depend on His great power alone.

This is what we have happening here. Dirt, mixed with saliva, to make mud is no healing potion, especially for the condition described here: blindness from birth. Why then, did Jesus use mud? To accentuate the very point He made at the beginning of His discourse: "This happened so that the WORK OF GOD might be displayed in his life." Jesus is the first one whose life is affected by this man's condition because it affords Jesus an opportunity to reveal His power as God, through this man's life. The mud didn't heal this man. Everyone knew mud had no such healing powers. Jesus healed this man. Everyone soon came to know that. This man suffered this blindness from birth for a reason and that reason was now standing before him. That reason was Jesus Christ.

The man himself is the second individual who is affected

by this affliction. He was the one who suffered this condition from birth and now he was the one miraculously healed. He suffered this affliction so that at the proper moment in time he might become the means for Jesus to reveal Himself to the world in a very powerful way. Soon he would see something even greater. He would realize the total healing that Jesus works in the lives of those born blind.

He didn't have to go far. As Jesus commanded him, he went to the pool and back, and suddenly he was changed. Everyone he knew had to take notice.

#3 – NEIGHBORS and #4 – OTHERS WHO KNEW HIM
  "His neighbors and those who had formerly seen him
  begging asked, 'Isn't this the same man who used to
  sit and beg?'"
  – vs.8

It didn't take long. Soon they were all staring at him, neighbors, many of whom probably knew him from birth, and others who knew him, all wondering if this could possibly be the same man. Look at all the lives this man touches almost immediately! Already we are unable to count them all. The word spread like wildfire among neighbors and acquaintances. Many of them began to wonder how this could possibly be the same man, but he insisted, "I am the man" vs.9. They demanded to know more, "How were your eyes opened?" vs.10. He told them exactly what had happened. The man named Jesus made mud, put it on his eyes, and told him to go wash. He simply did as he was told and suddenly he could see!

By this time, news of this glorious work of God had spread even further, to a place where it would not meet a very positive response.

#5 – THE PHARISEES

"They brought to the Pharisees the man who had been born blind. Now the day on which Jesus had made the mud and opened the man's eyes was a Sabbath. Therefore the Pharisees also asked him how he had received his sight. 'He put mud on my eyes,' the man replied, 'and I washed, and now I see.'... 'He is a prophet'"
— vs.13-15, 17

The Pharisees were the fifth group whose lives were now touched through this man's affliction and subsequent healing. As they discussed among themselves what had happened concerning this man, they were divided in their opinions as to how this man had actually been healed.

Look closely at verse 14. Isn't there something in that verse that is so simplistic in nature, yet so strange in content, that makes you wonder why it is mentioned at all? Look at it again: "Now the day on which Jesus had made the mud... was a Sabbath." Who cares on what day Jesus had made mud! Amazingly, the Pharisees cared a great deal! This is how out of focus they had become when the object of their affection had become God's law. Therefore, they reasoned that Jesus could not be from God because He was working on the Sabbath. He had healed—AND—he had made mud! If he was breaking the Sabbath, then He was also a sinner, and no sinner could perform such miraculous signs.

Do you remember what we learned in Chapter 1 about spiritual focus and in Chapter 3 about the object of faith? The object of these men's faith was the law of God. Their focus was on Christ, not as friend, but as the enemy. Also, so enamored were they of their obedience to the law, that they had convinced themselves that they were without sin. They had become the worst of the moralists and legalists of their day. Take note of how it affected their whole spiritual viewpoint. See how it sadly rendered them unable to see the glory that was being revealed in Jesus Christ.

This is what can happen to anyone, even to us, when Christ is no longer the object of faith. Therefore, they would not believe and sought to prove the man a liar, a charlatan, and a sinner. Next up: the man's parents.

#6 – HIS PARENTS

". . . they sent for the man's parents. 'Is this your son?' they asked. 'Is this the one you say was born blind? How is it that now he can see?'"

– vs.18, 19

Now we find this man's parents touched by these events in his life. They answered affirmatively, yes, this was their son, but they denied having any knowledge of how it happened. In actuality, they knew the truth but they were afraid to acknowledge that Jesus had healed their son because already it had been decided that anyone who acknowledged that Jesus was the Christ would be put out of the synagogue.

Look at all the people who ended up being touched by this man's life. All these people were touched by Christ's presence in their lives, through this one man, in the span of only a few hours! We find Jesus, for whom this man had been set aside for a very special purpose, the man himself, neighbors, acquaintances, his parents, very likely other relatives, and even Jesus' enemies. Within a very short period, the reason for this man's life of suffering was made known to all these people, now to you and me as well, and to countless others down through the ages. It was for the exact purpose Jesus had announced, "so that the work of God might be displayed in his life." A terrible affliction was used by God for a very glorious purpose, to reveal Jesus as the Christ, the chosen Son of God, and promised Messiah.

John graphically portrays the final exchange between this man and the Pharisees in his Gospel. It is sadly comical in terms of the Pharisees response but profoundly uplifting in the fearlessness that is exhibited by this bold new servant of Jesus Christ.

> "A second time they summoned the man who had been blind. 'Give glory to God,' they said, 'We know this man was a sinner.' He replied, 'Whether he is a sinner or not, I don't know. One thing I do know. I was blind but now I see!' Then they asked him, 'What did he do to you? How did he open your eyes?' He answered, 'I have told you already and you did not listen. Why do you want to hear it again? Do you want to become his disciples, too?' Then they hurled insults at him and said, "You are this fellow's disciple! We are disciples of Moses! We know that God spoke to Moses, but as for this fellow, we don't even know where he comes from.' The man answered, 'Now that is remarkable! You don't know where he comes from, yet he opened my eyes. We know that God does not listen to sinners. He listens to the godly man who does his will. Nobody has ever heard of opening the eyes of a man born blind. If this man were not from

God, he could do nothing.' To this they replied, 'You
were steeped in sin at birth; how dare you lecture
us!' And they threw him out."
– Vs.24-34

What an exchange! Though his parents had shown hesitation and fear, this man was not about to give up on the one who
had done so much for him. You can almost hear the fearlessness in his voice, "Challenge this man and you challenge me!"
At every point where they try to cross him up and lead him
away from a clear and dedicated focus on Jesus, he responds
with simple, yet remarkable strength in conviction. He will not
be turned.

They say, "This man is a sinner!" He responds, "I was blind
but now I see!"

They say with unbelieving sarcasm, "What did he do to you?
How did he open your eyes?" It appears almost as if they sus-
pected he and Jesus were working some kind of scam. He fights
back their sarcasm with bold, biting humor of his own, "I have
already told you... Why do you want to hear it again? Do you
want to become one of his disciples, too?" What a perfectly cut-
ting response!

They spit back at him, "You are this fellow's disciple! We're
disciples of Moses!... but as for this fellow, we don't even know
where he comes from." He proudly stands his ground and doesn't
hesitate for a moment to defend his Great Physician. Firmly
he sets them in their place, "Now that is remarkable! You don't
know where he comes from, yet he opened my eyes.... If this
man were not from God, he could do nothing."

Infuriated, they replied, "How dare you lecture us!" and they
threw him out. Yes, truth can make a bold and noticeable exit

after it has manifested itself like this.

It was an interesting day for this man, wouldn't you say? Imagine if this had been you. You get up in the morning. You groom yourself, get dressed, and go out. You meet a man named Jesus. You are healed of your blindness from birth. You now can see. You notice that suddenly others can no longer see you for who you are, in fact, they think you are someone else. Friends, neighbors, and acquaintances of all kinds examine you. You tell everyone what has been done. You stand before the religious leaders of your day. You are told this cannot be true though you have clearly been healed. You see your parents brought in and questioned because of you. You are called in a second time to stand before religious leaders. You are accused. You are jeered. You are mocked and insulted. You are strong. You put them in their proper place. You become the object of great scorn and hate. Last, you are thrown out. Yes, this is what it means to stand your ground when the day of evil comes. It will be a relentless attack on your faith and on you personally for what you believe about Jesus Christ and all the good He has accomplished in your life.

That is what is so meaningful about this story. In the beginning, we see nothing but the love and grace of God in Christ through this miraculous healing. This man has suffered this evil for so many years, then suddenly comes healing and relief. But you see, when God's grace and love for man is revealed, it is just as quickly challenged. This day of miraculous glory becomes another day of evil, in an instant, when the dark forces at work in this world challenge this man's newfound hope. It can happen that quickly and that unexpectedly.

It came quickly on 9-11. It can happen at any day and at any time. We need to be ready for the challenge for we never know when it will come.

This man was ready and he learned a great lesson about his life; it was not just his own. His life was being lived to benefit others. Even the blindness that he suffered from birth was meant for a good end. God used it for that purpose. How many there were who came to know Jesus as their Savior through this man, we do not know, but he certainly was a testimony to many of Christ's power, wisdom, and love.

Our lives are never meant to be our own. In many ways, God uses them to benefit others. Yielding to God, means letting Him use our lives in whatever way He chooses, to His glory and for the good of others. Sometimes God will choose to use the evil times, the times of sorrow, the times of want, the times of suffering, the times of hardship, and the times of loss to work a greater good in our lives and the lives of others around us. Sometimes that is what it takes to save a lost soul. It may be ours. It may be someone else's. Isn't it worth it? God thinks it is. We need to think as God thinks and keep spiritual and eternal priorities in mind. We need to have the mind of Christ.

Oh, one other blessing came to this man on that special, miraculous day. A second miracle was realized in his life. It was the miracle of faith, with Christ as its object.

> "Jesus heard that they had thrown him out, and when he found him, he said, 'Do you believe in the Son of Man?' 'Who is he, sir?' the man asked. 'Tell me so that I may believe in him.' Jesus said, 'You have now seen him; in fact, he is the one speaking with you.' Then the man said, 'Lord, I believe,' and he worshiped him."
> - Vs.35-39

Both were important. Both were valuable. However, which was most precious: the physical sight this man received on that day or the spiritual sight he gained in knowing Jesus Christ as his Lord and Savior? He had been born not only physically blind but also spiritually blind. He needed a two-fold healing.

The greatest miracle came not when Jesus walked into his life but when Jesus entered his heart. Had he never been born physically blind he may never have received his spiritual sight. We see that God used evil in his life to work a great good. That is what God does and that is what God will do again for us after 9-11.

PETER

Holy Scripture offers us so many examples of how God will often use the forces of evil for His saving purposes. We can think, for instance, of Peter the most bold and courageous of Jesus' disciples. Yet, Peter had failed his Lord when the day of evil came upon him. He denied his Lord. After the resurrection, Jesus sought to test Peter's zealous confidence in himself. "Do you love me more than these?" Jesus asked him. It must have been obvious to Peter what Jesus was doing, for Peter had at one time boasted a greater faith and love for Jesus than any of the others. Yet Peter had denied his Lord. Again, Jesus asked, "Do you love me?" Peter answered affirmatively. Then, Jesus asked the same question of Peter a third time, "Do you love me?" We then read this:

> "Peter was hurt because Jesus asked him the third
> time, 'Do you love me?' He said, 'Lord, you know all
> things; you know that I love you.' Jesus said, 'Feed

my sheep. I tell you the truth, when you were younger
you dressed yourself and went where you wanted;
but when you are old you will stretch out your hands,
and someone else will dress you and lead you where
you do not want to go.' Jesus said this to indicate the
kind of death by which Peter would glorify God. Then
he said to him, 'Follow me!'"

- John 21:17-19

Tradition has it, that Peter died at the hands of the Romans and was crucified upside-down. This tradition may be
entirely accurate. If his time in this world ended by such a
means, it would correlate quite well with what Jesus told him
on that day when they met together on the shore of the lake
after Jesus' resurrection. On that occasion, Jesus told him, ". . .
when you are old you will stretch out your hands, and someone
else will dress you and lead you where you do not want to go."

Even in death Peter glorified God and through a death that
was like his Lord's, by crucifixion. Even though Jesus warned
him that such a death would come, even though a great evil
would befall him, still Jesus spoke the invitation to him, "Follow me!" Jesus would allow this evil death to come upon this
beloved disciple, because it would redound in a meaningful way
to God's glory. It would become a source of inspiration and hope
to many other novice Christians in the first century and beyond. In Peter, they would see what it means to be committed
to Christ. In Peter, they would not see another denial, but the
proof of a heart that was firmly committed to spreading the
glorious gospel no matter what the circumstance or personal
sacrifice.

Today we still marvel over the sacrifices those early disciples made. We marvel over how they became changed men so suddenly. Some of them fled as cowards on Good Friday and others, like the Apostle Paul, were enemies of God. Yet, in the end, something dramatically changed them, and that change came about after Jesus' resurrection.

In life and in death they glorified God. They knew that becoming Christians would not mean a life of ease by any means. They knew that becoming part of *The Way* would not protect them from experiencing the reality of evil in the world. In fact, as Christians, the onslaught of evil against them would increase. God knew it and they knew it, but they didn't back away from the challenge, because after the struggle was ended the glorious victory over death would be fully realized and they would be forever with their Lord. They didn't back away from the challenge, and by standing up to evil, they have set a glorious example of faith for others to follow. Through their example, the faith of many has been encouraged and God is glorified.

PAUL

For the Apostle Paul, faithfulness to the gospel of Jesus Christ would mean a host of troubles including beatings, imprisonment, and death. Evil repeatedly tried to break him. Yet, from prison, this is what he wrote as evil surrounded and threatened him:

> "Now I want you to know, brothers, that what has
> happened to me has really served to advance the gos-
> pel. As a result, it has become clear throughout the

whole palace guard and to everyone else that I am in chains for Christ. Because of my chains, most of the brothers in the Lord have been encouraged to speak the word of God more courageously and fearlessly. It is true that some preach Christ out of envy and rivalry, but others out of good will. The latter do so in love, knowing that I am put here for the defense of the gospel. The former preach Christ out of selfish ambition, not sincerely, supposing that they can stir up trouble for me while I am in chains. But what does it matter? The important thing is that in every way, whether from false motives or true, Christ is preached."

- Philippians 1:12-18

In chains, suffering, persecuted, and falling directly under Satan's evil hand—yet notice what Paul says about everything that happened to him; everything had served to "advance the gospel." He was glad to suffer for Christ and glad that even the "palace guard" and "everyone else" who was there knew why he was in chains. It was "for Christ." Through his chains, they were being introduced to their Savior! If Paul had never been imprisoned, many of them may have died without ever hearing the good news of their Savior. Paul recognized that he was in prison for a noble purpose, a saving purpose. Furthermore, he recognized that his chains were serving the purpose to encourage others in the Christian community throughout the Roman world to "speak the word of God more courageously and fearlessly."

Stamina against evil can be a very powerful tool used by God to strengthen faith. Paul's imprisonment served this noble purpose. He was there for "the defense of the gospel." Paul was even able to recognize that if people preach Christ out of evil motives or selfish ambition, God can still create blessings. No matter what the circumstance, what is always foremost is that "Christ is preached." Whenever Christ is preached, even under the most unfortunate and evil of circumstances, a good and blessed working of God will result. The Savior's name is being proclaimed to create the blessing of saving faith.

What will be accomplished in this regard from the events of 9-11? Already we have heard some of the stories of Christian faith being challenged that day, individuals losing beloved mothers, fathers, spouses, children, and loved ones. Those accounts bring to our ears the message of the gospel in which children of God placed their hope. We hear of the Lord's Prayer spoken aboard flight 93 before it went down and we hear of survivors witnessing their Christian faith to hundreds upon hundreds of men and women in a variety of settings throughout the world. Even 9-11 is serving to "advance the gospel" and this is a good thing, a blessed thing, and a glorious thing. I believe we are only in the early stages of seeing some of the great blessings that will come out of this terrible tragedy. Rest assured, God will see to it that, in one way or another, "Christ is preached" and that many more have the opportunity to come to faith in Him.

However, we dare never forget that we find the ultimate example of God using the forces of evil for His saving purposes in Christ Himself. We return to John's Gospel to look at how the words spoken by Jesus' enemies prophetically uttered the great good that would be accomplished through His sacrificial death.

JESUS CHRIST, THE SON OF GOD

"Then one of them, named Caiaphas, who was high
priest that year, spoke up, 'You know nothing at all!
You do not realize that it is better for you that one
man die for the people than that the whole nation
perish.' He did not say this on his own, but as high
priest that year he prophesied that Jesus would die
for the Jewish nation, and not only for that nation
but also for the scattered children of God, to bring
them together and make them one. So from that day
on they plotted to take his life."

- John 11:49-53

The evil of betrayal, of vindictiveness, of jealousy, of treach-
ery, of lies, of hatred, of torture, of murder, and of death would
culminate on one day outside the walls of the holy city of Jerusalem. On that day Jesus died. On that day, a world filled with
sin and sinners received deliverance.

Caiaphas, the enemy of Christ, who plotted to take Jesus'
life, was very right about one thing. It was better "that one
man die for the people" than that a whole nation, indeed a
whole world, perish. God viewed our situation that way and
we can be glad. It was good for us but a terrible sacrifice for our
heavenly Father when He sacrificed His Son on our behalf.

It will forever be impossible to view evil correctly without
Good Friday and Easter Sunday. Human philosophy tries and
has never come up with any kind of satisfactory answer. Religions of the world take up the issue and always arrive at some
exercised measure of human goodness and kindness that is
supposed to overcome evil's power in this world. It has never

been enough because they fail repeatedly to recognize that man, by nature, is part of the problem, not part of the solution. Man's attempts to flush evil away by works of love and kindness are nice, and they impart some degree of temporary relief to the world's suffering, but those works only take care of part of the problem and not nearly enough. It's like putting a band-aid on a wound that is 100 times the size of the patch. It simply will not do.

Evil days, like September 11, still happen, and over the last century seem to be occurring with increasing and alarming frequency. We need to ask why. Could it be true—what the Scriptures have always testified—that we are not the solution but part of the problem? Could it be that we cannot work a resolution to the problem of evil in this world by ourselves?

Evil is a problem in this world because of the evil one who reigns here. Evil is also a problem in this world because man is still too inclined to take what is to his advantage and remove anything from his path that prevents him from getting what he wants. This is sin at work. Acts of sin happen because of enslavement to sin. That's what Jesus meant when He said, "Everyone who sins is a slave to sin" (John 8:34). In other words, mankind, by nature, is evil too. We are part of the problem and unable to find the solution to our dilemma.

The good news is that we no longer need to try to attain what has always been impossible for us to accomplish. That is because Jesus has come, Jesus died his sacrificial death, Jesus rose, and Jesus is alive to assure us that the victory is established. Jesus will return to make all things new again.

God has shown us, through the gift of His Son, the resolution to our struggle with evil. With almighty power and infinite wisdom, God used evil to crush the evil one and to destroy sin's enslaving power upon us and within us. Without Good Friday and the victory of Easter morning, evil is endless, and there is no positive resolution to any of it. But Jesus' sacrifice teaches us, better than anything else does, that God can use the evil intents of mankind and the evil of Satan and his host, to create the ultimate good of life from death, and salvation from the curse of sin.

Jesus' sacrifice on Good Friday gives us the assurance that there is a positive and blessed resolution to the struggle between good and evil in this world. That resolution has a name, Jesus Christ, the King of kings and Lord of lords, the Prince of peace.

God FRUSTRATES the Forces of Evil

God will continue to aid us in our struggle while we stand up to the forces of evil at work within us and outside of us. He will continue to use evil to accomplish a greater good when it will serve to advance His grand saving plan for the world. However, sometimes God finds it desirable and necessary to simply frustrate the forces of evil at work in this world and stop them dead in their tracks. How often does God do this? Probably much more often than we realize because most of the time we see only what happens in this world. We cannot see what is never allowed to happen. God, however, sees it all. Some evil He allows, for reasons known only to Him. Many more times He will prevent it, and this too can be attributed to His almighty power and infinite wisdom.

Scripture provides numerous examples of God's direct intervention in the affairs of mankind to prevent evil from advancing. God sets bounds, and when His saving purposes are threatened, He acts.

We find such direct intervention in the exodus of God's chosen people from their bondage in Egypt. We know the story well. Through Moses, God led them out of Egypt and they miraculously crossed the Red Sea. However, Pharaoh's heart was hard and as vain as it might sound, he actually thought he could wage war with God and win. However, Israel was to play a critically important role in God's plan of salvation for the world. Their nation would be established because from this nation and people, the Savior of the world would come. Therefore, when Pharaoh tried to prevent this intent purpose of God from being realized, God reacted with clear and decisive swiftness.

> "When the king of Egypt was told that the people had fled, Pharaoh and his officials changed their minds about them and said, 'What have we done? We have let the Israelites go and have lost their services!' So he had his chariot made ready and took his army with him.... The Egyptians pursued them, and all Pharaoh's horses and chariots and horsemen followed them into the sea.... The Lord said to Moses, 'Stretch out your hand over the sea so that the waters may flow back over the Egyptians and their chariots and horsemen.'... and the Lord swept them into the sea... not one of them survived."
> - Exodus 14: select vs.

It was a day of divine judgment for Pharaoh and his army. God's chosen people would be freed. This evil against them came to a clear and decisive end when God intervened that day. There would be many more challenges to God's people Israel. Their struggle with the forces of evil surrounding them and their struggles with the evil of sin within them is well documented in Holy Scripture. It would be a long and hard road for them. But on that day of deliverance, God acted directly and decisively to frustrate this evil challenge to His providence. It threatened His saving plan for the world. He still works today in similar ways but often His activity is either invisible to us or simply unrecognized by us.

At another key juncture of history, when God's plan of salvation was to take a major leap forward through another of God's chosen servants, a similar direct act of God thwarted the advancement of evil against Christians in the early church. It too happened in an extraordinarily miraculous way. A man was stopped dead in his tracks, and from that moment on, the course of his entire life was changed, for him, and for us. His name was Saul and he was a persecutor of Christians. We know him best as the Apostle Paul, the greatest missionary the Christian church has ever known.

"Meanwhile, Saul was still breathing out murderous threats against the Lord's disciples.... As he neared Damascus on his journey, suddenly a light from heaven flashed around him. He fell to the ground and heard a voice say to him, 'Saul, Saul, why do you persecute me?' 'Who are you Lord?' Saul asked. 'I am Jesus, whom you are persecuting,' he replied. 'Now get up and go into the city, and you will be told what you must do.'... Saul spent several days with the disciples in Damascus. At once he began to preach in the synagogues that Jesus is the Son of God."
- Acts 9: select vs.

The mission, of course, for Paul that day, was to go to Damascus, find any Christians he could, and prevent their movement from spreading any further. Imprisonment, confiscation of property, even death might be used to prevent them from spreading the news of Jesus Christ as the Son of God and Savior of the world. Saul had been very aggressive as a Pharisee in his campaign to wipe out Christians wherever they were found. He was even present at the death of the first Christian martyr, Stephen. When Stephen was put to death by stoning, we're told that Saul (Paul) was there giving approval.

However, Saul's mission changed quickly and dramatically. God could have struck Paul dead right then and there on that dry and dirty road but he did not. God knew it was unnecessary to do so and it was not expedient. He had a special path chosen for this man. Instead, God chose to change the course of his life by changing his heart.

God intervened directly. Jesus appeared to him on that road in His glorified state, and it changed the direction of Saul's life profoundly. From that day forward, he was so astonished at God's undeserved grace and mercy toward him, that he could not speak of himself in any way but in the most humble and self deprecating of terms. He wrote, "I am the least of the apostles and do not even deserve to be called an apostle because I persecuted the church of God. But by the grace of God I am what I am" (I Corinthians 15:9, 10). We are thankful, that by God's grace, he became the great ambassador of the gospel that God made him to be.

As God continues to frustrate the forces of evil around us, He does not always act alone. Sometimes He works through others. It may be through His angels whom He discharges at His will. However, He also works through people, many of whom have been established directly by God for this special purpose, to serve Him in a unique way. Through governments and agents of government, we are protected from the evil around us that would threaten our welfare and livelihood. They are God's servants, whether they believe in Him or not. He establishes them and God calls upon us to accord them the honor and respect they deserve.

> "Everyone must submit himself to the governing authorities, for there is no authority except that which God has established. The authorities that exist have been established by God. Consequently, he who rebels against the authority is rebelling against what God has instituted, and those who do so will bring judgment on themselves. For rulers hold no terror for those who do right, but for those who do wrong. Do you want to be free from the fear of the one in authority? Then do what is right and he will commend you. For he is God's servant to do you good. But if you do wrong, be afraid, for he does not bear the sword for nothing. He is God's servant, an agent of wrath to bring punishment on the wrongdoer."
> - Romans 13:1-4

The renewed patriotism and pride in America that is a positive byproduct of 9-11, has brought about another great blessing in our nation. It is a deeper appreciation for and a renewed respect for our leaders and everyone in positions of national and community service throughout our land. This is as it should be for these are not ordinary servants among us, they are "God's servants" at work.

They are represented by our President and Vice-President, members of Congress, governors, and state legislators. They are the men and women in our armed forces, National Guard, and Coast Guard. They are the police officers and firefighters in communities throughout our nation and in communities throughout the world. Some are elected by the people and others enlist themselves in the service of preserving and protecting our nation and its people, but all of them are selected by God and established by Him. It is not only a basic role and responsibility of government to protect its citizens; it is also a divine right. That is what God is teaching us, through the pen of the Apostle Paul, in these verses from his letter to the Christians in Rome.

September 11 came on the heels of one of the most trying elections in our nation's history. It is good to see how America has come together in support of our President, after an election that still has many raising their eyebrows and wondering if the right man is sitting in the oval office. Put all the chads aside, hanging, dimpled, pregnant, or otherwise, because it's a mute point. Whatever they indicated is immaterial now. This is not even a political issue anymore. It matters nothing if you are Democrat, Republican, or Independent. The point is, God made His choice as to who was to be our next President and he sits in that seat of honor and responsibility now because, as God makes clear to us through Holy Scripture, "the authorities that exist have been established by God." He is our public servant and Commander in Chief now, because he is first of all, God's servant. The fact that George W. Bush is there and others are not says nothing negative about the other choices. It simply is proper, from the Christian perspective, to acknowledge that our last election ended the way God intended it to end.

We can also be thankful to have a man sitting in the White House who will approach his responsibilities to God and our nation from a Christian perspective. He will know where to draw strength. He will know where to find wisdom. In this great struggle to defend our nation from this onslaught of evil that threatens our freedoms and the very existence of our nation, He will know where to turn for help because through faith in Jesus Christ, our President is a child of God. For him and for all others who serve like him, let us be very thankful. They are God's representatives among us.

As our constant protector, God is always there, always able to use evil, when it comes, to achieve a blessed end, or to frustrate evil and prevent its advance whenever His saving purposes for us require Him to do so. He is our source of refuge when the day of evil comes and our constant strength. We can look to him as the psalmist did.

> "God is our refuge and strength, an ever present help in trouble. Therefore we will not fear, though the earth give way and the mountains fall into the heart of the sea... The Lord Almighty is with us; the God of Jacob is our fortress."
> - Psalm 46:1, 2, 7

On September 11, it seemed as though that day, spoken of by the psalmist, had come. The earth was giving way and the mountains were falling into the heart of the sea. It was a terrible day. But we do not have to be afraid of what man can do to us, or even Satan and his host. God is greater. In life, He provides us everything we need in our struggle against the evil that is all around us. In death, He will deliver us to Himself and on the day of Christ's return, raise us up to live with Him forever in a new heaven and a new earth where evil will never have another day. In the God of our salvation, through Jesus Christ our Good Shepherd, we really lack nothing. David wrote so beautifully of this truth in the 23rd Psalm.

> "The Lord is my shepherd, I shall not be in want.... Even though I walk through the valley of the shadow of death, I will fear no evil, for you are with me; your rod and your staff, they comfort me."
> - Psalm 23:1, 4

We walked through that dark and gruesome valley on September 11. Death was everywhere. Death's dark shadow fell over our nation and our hearts. We mourn those lives lost. We pray for those who found their lives and families changed in an instant. For a while, we were afraid of all that might come.

When on such a day as September 11, and you enter "the valley of the shadow of death," you enter a place where you do not want to be, but a place, nonetheless, through which you must walk. We entered its deep valley floor that day and now the shadows of its steep, disturbing, and ominous walls loom over us. It is an uncomfortable place to be, a frightening place, because you never know what will leap out from the shadows. When will evil strike again? What direction will it come from?

Our President has told us to be vigilant and well we should. Our leaders encourage us to walk through this dark valley together, united as a nation, with a common goal, and this we also must do. However, only the God of our salvation can take away our fears as we walk. Only He can do that because only in Him is the fear of death removed. Only in Him is the promise of life made sure. Only in Him is there the wisdom to walk through the valley of the shadow of death in such a way that we come through to the other side, still spiritually whole. Only in Him is there the strength we need to overcome the powers of darkness that constantly move threateningly all around us. Only in Him will we be successful while we live and when we die, because only He is our Good Shepherd—the Shepherd who gave His life for the sheep. Love such as this is found in no one else but Jesus Christ. He takes our hand and will lead us to quiet waters for drink and to green, tranquil pastures for rest.

God OVERTURNS the Forces of Evil

So now we walk. We walk without fear. We walk lacking nothing for this journey. We walk, in fact, with confidence and with victory assured. We do this because "the Lord Almighty is with us" and He is our refuge and strength. He is present with us to help us now, in this our time of need. We have His assurance that whatever happens, as we walk with Him at our side, all things will work for our good, in life and in death. The Apostle Paul had this confidence during his walk and he was proud to shout out the good news.

> "And we know that in all things God works for the good of those who love him, who have been called according to his purpose.... What, then, shall we say in response to this? If God is for us, who can be against us? He who did not spare his own Son, but gave him up for us all—how will he not also, along with him, graciously give us all things? Who will bring any charge against those whom God has chosen? It is God who justifies. Who is he that condemns? Christ Je-

sus, who died—more than that, who was raised to life—is at the right hand of God and is also interceding for us. Who shall separate us from the love of Christ? Shall trouble or hardship or persecution or famine or nakedness or danger or sword? As it is written: 'For your sake we face death all day long; we are considered sheep to be slaughtered.' No, in all these things we are more than conquerors through him who loved us. For I am convinced that neither death nor life, neither angels nor demons, neither the present nor the future, nor any powers, neither height nor depth, nor anything else in all creation, will be able to separate us from the love of God that is in Christ Jesus our Lord."

- Romans 8:28ff

What powerful, uplifting, and soul inspiring words to take with us on our walk through life—especially now! They are appropriate any time our walk brings us into "the valley of the shadow of death."

Christ Jesus is with us and is our Good Shepherd. He will not leave us. He will not let any eternal harm come to us. None can, if we are at His side and He is at ours. If we live, we continue our walk with Him at our side to protect us and keep us renewed day after day as we live in service to Him. If we die, we live—we live eternally with Him—because He lives and is risen from death! So, of what do we have to be afraid? Whom should we fear? What can anyone or anything do to any of us if we are the Lord's?

Do we see fallen angels bent on evil and demons in service to Satan? Yes, now we see them. We know they are there. The

King of kings is more powerful and wise than all of them combined! We also see the past, so filled with our sins. We see the present, visible, yet often so hard to understand. We look to the future, invisible, uncertain, and unknown. In Christ, our past is made clean as our sins are removed. In Him, the present finds meaning for in Him, we find blessings and purpose for our lives. Through our Savior, even the future is certain and sure. Jesus has made it so.

How do we react to these powers that stand before us to crush us and strike terror within us like an electric current rushing to every nerve of our body? Do we fear them? Let these fallacious, counterfeit Goliaths come! We have nothing to fear! The Lord Jesus Christ is our right arm of strength and is always at our side! From the highest mountain peaks to lowest parts of the earth and the deepest depths of the sea, there is nothing to be found anywhere in all the earth, indeed in all of creation, that is able to match the power and wisdom of our God who does all things well. Nothing can be found, because nothing in all of creation exists, that is able to "separate us from the love of God that is in Christ Jesus our Lord." Therefore, everything is ours in Christ and the victory over evil is ours too!

We are safe in God's hands because nothing can separate us from His love. This Savior God, in His almighty power and His infinite wisdom is able to turn the tables on sin and overturn every misfortune, every wound, every hurt, and every act of evil in our lives so that it works for the good of those who love Him. That is all we need! What more could we possibly want?

Now, as we walk, we walk with hope and we walk with confidence. We are not proud or haughty, or even self-assured, because we know our power and strength is not of our own making. It comes from above. Even in death, we have this confidence, whether it comes today, tomorrow, or long into the future, because in Jesus Christ victory over sin and death is ours.

> "Death has been swallowed up in victory. Where, O death, is your victory? Where, O death, is your sting?" The sting of death is sin, and the power of sin is the law. But thanks be to God! He gives us the victory through our Lord Jesus Christ. Therefore, my dear brothers, stand firm. Let nothing move you. Always give yourselves fully to the work of the Lord, because you know that your labor in the Lord is not in vain."
> - I Corinthians 15:54-58

This is triumph over evil, when in Christ, through faith, we triumph over sin and death! Then, everything that Satan and his forces of evil have ever tried to accomplish, is undone. The victory is ours! This is great reward, to have such a gift so graciously bestowed upon us from such a loving and merciful God.

This victory is one that has been known to many in our past. By faith, Joseph knew of it, as did the man born blind who was so miraculously healed. Peter knew this truth by faith as did the Apostle Paul when he came to faith. This is the faith God wants us all to have. It is a faith that sees what God has done and knows that in Jesus Christ the greatest victory of all is ours.

This is the faith that is needed in the wake of 9-11. For it is this faith, whose object is Christ, that perceives God's great triumph over evil. He has overturned death's curse, brought about by our sin. He has made death into the blessed gateway to eternal life.

We are comforted, because God has revealed to us that this is His nature. This is who He is. This is what He does. He works night and day in the most mysterious and profound ways to save us because He is the God of salvation—our salvation. In Him, this insight is wholly true:

> The ultimate triumph over evil is realized in every act of God where He exercises His almighty power and infinite wisdom to use, frustrate, or overturn the forces of evil at work in this world, so that finally, His saving purposes for mankind are accomplished.

- CHAPTER SEVEN -

INSIGHT #7

The ultimate triumph over evil is known
personally only through faith in Jesus
Christ, in whom we become victors with
God over every evil force at work in this
world, both within us and outside of us.

Truth Is Always Questioned
If you had not been in front of that television screen on September 11, to see everything with your own eyes, would you
have believed the report? Maybe you weren't. Maybe you first
heard about the attack on the Pentagon and the collapse of the
Twin Towers in New York from someone else. How did you respond? Was there at least a moment when you doubted the
report? Did you think, at first, that what you were told could
not possibly be true? I know that when I watched everything
as it transpired that morning, I still could hardly believe my
eyes. That's the way it sometimes is with the truth. Good or
bad, sometimes it is just too hard to believe. Sometimes we
wonder if what we hear is the truth.

As you've taken time, through this writing, to consider these
perspectives on 9-11 from a Christian viewpoint, the question

might still be raised, how do we know any of this is true? How do we know that Satan and his host is our greatest enemy? How do we even know for sure he is real? How do we know that the world and everything in it is under the watchful care of a loving, saving, providential God? How do we know that evil's primary goal is to challenge our faith and render us spiritually dead? How do we know that this gospel mission centering on Jesus Christ is truly, what God wants us to do? Many bad things happen in this life, how can we be sure that this God of our salvation is our greatest ally and friend? How do we know God's power and wisdom will overcome evil? How can we know any of this is true?

I recall sitting in a philosophy class in my first year of college at the University of Wisconsin. For the length of a semester, the instructor decided to "challenge our thinking and powers of reason" by having us struggle with the age-old question of the existence of God. Session after session was spent in back and forth banter, none of which proved to be profound and none of which proved to be the least bit edifying. As students, one after the other, day after day, did their best to major in minors and spout their most poignant points of peripheral piffle, the rest of us yawned. It was probably the most useless and meaningless course of instruction I have ever taken in my life. By the end of the semester this grand conclusion was reached: the only thing certain about the existence of God is that we are certain that no one can ever be certain that he, in all certainty, exists. What a waste.

It seems as though this is how it has always been, since the grand creation and the dawn of time. God makes Himself known to man and man makes God an unknown. God reveals truth and mankind lets Satan help him obscure the truth in lies.

God's truth has been questioned since the beginning of time and will be questioned until time comes to an end, when God, in His full glory, reveals Himself to a world of doubters. It will happen. As sure as September 11 happened, that day too will come. Until then, we are called upon by God to make these truths known to the world, to give answer to those questions when they arise, and try to remove unbelief and doubt as best we can. It is, in fact, the Holy Spirit working through us, but the Holy Spirit guides us too in this effort, to make this daunting task a work of joy and not just a work of unending frustration.

However, an interesting thing seems to happen when days of almost unfathomable evil befall our world and enter individual lives. For believers, though faith is challenged, it often grows stronger. For unbelievers and doubters, those challenges to God's truths are awakened and truth is questioned all over again, perhaps more aggressively than ever before. This should not surprise us, for believers know to turn to God and to His Word for strength and guidance at such times. Satan will use those times to challenge faith and make unbelief more firmly entrenched in the hearts of doubters everywhere.

When the greatest day of evil came upon the world, that is exactly what happened. God's truth was challenged. God spoke and unbelieving man spit back sarcasm and doubt. You too have heard of that day. It was the day Jesus, the Son of God, stood before his persecutor, Pontius Pilate. Do you remember their exchange?

> "Pilate then went back inside the palace, summoned
> Jesus and asked him, 'Are you the king of the Jews?'...
> Jesus said, 'My kingdom is not of this world. If it were,

my servants would fight to prevent my arrest by the
Jews. But now my kingdom is from another place.'
'You are a king, then!' said Pilate. Jesus answered,
'You are right in saying I am a king. In fact, for this
reason I was born, and for this I came into the world,
to testify to the truth. Everyone on the side of truth
listens to me.' 'What is truth?' Pilate asked.... Finally
Pilate handed him over to them to be crucified."
- John 18:33, 36-38; 19:16

You can almost hear Satan laughing still. This was his great
day! He had Pilate right where he wanted him and like a good
little monkey, he played his role perfectly, did exactly what
Satan wanted him to do, and spoke with such vile. Satan loved
it. Satan also thought he had Jesus right where he wanted
Him to be. Little did he realize that the God of all mercy and
grace had His Son exactly where He wanted Him that day as
well. God in wisdom and power was about to turn the tables on
sin and death. This was the greatest day of evil but God's great
day of triumph was only a hop (day 1), a skip (day 2), and a
jump (day 3) away.

GOD'S GREAT DAY OF TRIUMPH:
When Truth Was Made Sure

Yes, three days later, on Easter morning, the women went to
the tomb to complete the anointing of Jesus' body but the tomb
was empty. The disciples rushed to see for themselves after
hearing the report that was, to them, just too unbelievable to
be true. They found everything just as the women had told
them. The angels' proclamation was true! "HE IS RISEN!"

In that resurrection, not only Jesus' life was restored, but also the truth of God, made known through the ages. On that first Easter the truth of God was made known through the words of God's own Son who had been restored to life. In His resurrection, the Word of God, spoken by the Father and revealed further by His Son, was made certain and sure. Jesus' resurrection tells us that all His promises to us are fulfilled. It tells us that all His words to us are true!

That evening Jesus appeared to His disciples for the first time. This was God's great day of triumph. Through that appearance, God's truth was revealed to Jesus' disciples. Through it, God's truth was revealed to the world.

> "On the evening of the first day of the week, when the disciples were together, with the doors locked for fear of the Jews, Jesus came and stood among them and said, 'Peace be with you!' After he had said this, he showed them his hands and side. The disciples were overjoyed when they saw the Lord. Again Jesus said, 'Peace be with you! As the Father has sent me, I am sending you.'"
> - John 20:19-21

The bitter war to secure salvation for all mankind was over. Jesus had been sent by His Father on a saving mission. The day of evil was past and God's great day of triumph had burst forth. Now everything sprang to life.

Jesus' pronouncement of "peace" was so very appropriate. The day of evil was gone. There was no longer any reason for these first disciples to be afraid or to doubt. Was their three-year walk with Jesus worth it? Yes! He was standing, alive, before them! Were their sins forgiven, as Jesus had assured them? Undoubtedly, yes! Jesus was standing, alive, before them, having died for the sins of the world! Was eternal life theirs? Without a doubt, it was! Jesus was standing, alive, before them, never to die again. His life was their life!

One by one, they could go down the list of everything Jesus had taught them, every word of truth He had shared, and every promise He had extended to them, and they could now say YES to them all. What He taught was sure! Every word was true! Every promise for the present and for the future was as good as fulfilled! Their God and their resurrected Lord was standing before them and their God and their Lord does not lie!

I find it very interesting that when John, writing under inspiration of the Holy Spirit, records the disciples' response to Jesus' sudden presence in the room, he writes only, "The disciples were overjoyed." No other detail is added. No party-like celebration is pictured. No description is given of disciples joyfully jumping up and down, smiling broadly, laughing loudly, hugging Jesus, and hugging one another. It's almost anti-climactic. Yet, those things probably did happen because that's how humans respond at times of great, surprising joy and relief.

I remember a time when I was in first grade and I had just come home from school. My mother was practically ecstatic. She was on the phone, talking excitedly to someone. I couldn't figure out what was going on. She seemed to be flying around the house, unable to stop. Finally I asked my sister and was told, "Dad won a car!" I said, "Really! Wow! What color?" I tried to get mom's attention for a little more detail but couldn't. The best I could get was, "We won a new car," and then she was on the phone excitedly talking to someone else.

Well, I seem to remember going to my room or outside for a

while. When I came back just a short time later, there was no longer any excitement in the house at all. Mom even had kind of a strange, almost somber look on her face. So I asked her, "Mom did dad win a new car?" She said something like, "No, it's just some toy thing."

Well, what happened was this. While I had been out of the room, mom had finally reached dad at work to tell him the good news. She told him that the company where he had filled out a contest entry form to win a new car had called and said, "You're the big winner of a light-blue Cadillac!" Dad said, "I don't remember entering any contest to win a new car." She reminded him of the auto show that he gone to with us kids tailing along. Those were the people who had called. Then he remembered the contest he entered. He had to tell her, 'No, that wasn't a contest for a real Cadillac! That was a contest for one of those pedal cars for the kids! Did we really win?" Mom's bubble burst.

I don't think she ever even rode that car but it was just the right size for the rest of us kids and we all liked it. We used it for years—racing down the hill out in the country where we used to live. Of course, the point in time came when the pedals didn't work anymore but so what, we didn't need them—a good push and away we'd go! We had a great time but the only fun mom ever had with that car was thinking at first that it was a real automobile—sorry mom.

Overjoyed, that's what my mother was when she thought she had won that shiny new Cadillac, but she did one other important thing. She was so overjoyed that she couldn't wait to share the good news. In fact, she was telling everyone in the family and in the neighborhood before she even told dad! She was one happy camper.

That's also what the disciples were, overjoyed when the risen Christ appeared to them. I'm sure they did all those things too that people do when they just cannot sit still but have to leap for joy. Is there a reason God records none of their excitement? Perhaps there is, for the next words recorded are Jesus' words to them, "Peace be with you! As the Father has sent me, I am sending you." It is as though Jesus is saying, "If you're overjoyed, then show your joy by going out into the world and telling everyone the good news. Tell them that because I live, all people can live. I am sending you to bring this message of hope and joy to the world. Now go."

Jesus did not ignore their joy that first Easter night, he channeled it. What made Christianity spread like wildfire throughout the world? These were overjoyed disciples, whose lives had suddenly been altered by Jesus' resurrection. Just like my mother, who could not stop spreading the news when she thought she had won a new car, these were excited and motivated disciples, who expressed their joy by hiding no longer, but boldly stepping out into the world and sharing this good news over and over and over again.

MAN'S GREAT DAY OF TRIUMPH:
When The Truth of God Is Believed

There's a little something missing in this account of Jesus' appearance to His disciples that first Easter night. Thomas is missing. He wasn't there. We're not told where he was. We're just told he wasn't there and this is how he responded when the other disciples reported Jesus' appearance to him.

> "Now Thomas (called Didymus), one of the Twelve,
> was not with the disciples when Jesus came. When

the other disciples told him that they had seen the
Lord, he declared, 'Unless I see the nail marks in his
hands and put my finger where the nails were, and
put my hand into his side, I will not believe it.'"
- John 20:24, 25

We've all been there. "You must be kidding me. That could
not have happened. You have to be mistaken." That's what we
say when we hear something that is just too improbable to be
true. It's met with skepticism and unbelief.

"Prove it!" That's also what we might say. That is what Thomas said when they told him Jesus had appeared to all of them.
"I need proof. I want to see the marks in his hands and touch
the spear wound in His side. I want to pinch Him and see if it's
really Him and not just a ghost. Let me do that! Only then will
I believe."

Poor Thomas; there was no peace yet for him, no joy, no
assurance of salvation won and sins forgiven. He was still afraid,
still out of touch with reality, still lacking direction and hope.
He was still without faith. However, a week later Thomas was
at the right place at the right time, and his life too was forever
changed.

"A week later his disciples were in the house again,
and Thomas was with them. Though the doors were
locked, Jesus came and stood among them and said,
'Peace be with you!' Then he said to Thomas, 'Put
your finger here; see my hands. Reach out your hand
and put it into my side. Stop doubting and believe.'
Thomas said to him, 'My Lord and my God!' Then
Jesus told him, 'Because you have seen me, you have

believed; blessed are those who have not seen and
yet have believed."
- John 20:26-29

How would you like to be in Thomas' place, forever remembered as the disciple who doubted? As bad as that is, there's
something even far worse: never being a disciple because,
though you heard the truth, you would not believe it.

Doubting Thomas became believing Thomas. It is difficult
to imagine how ashamed Thomas must have felt as he stood
before His Lord. Jesus politely yielded to his demands and
reached out His hands to him. He turned to him His side so
that his doubting would be put to rest with physical proof.

Why, for Thomas, was it all so necessary? After all, he did
have the testimony of his companions. He knew them all well.
He saw that they were all changed men. What did he think,
that they would lie to him too? Yet, in his unbelief, he was calling all of them liars and saying Jesus was a liar too. Nonetheless, Jesus kindly acquiesced to his unbelieving heart. We have
a very patient and forgiving Savior. It was a week late but Thomas' day of triumph came that day when He uttered amazingly and apologetically, "My Lord and my God!" It was Thomas' personal day of triumph. Jesus' reply to that scientifically
developed confession of faith is for the ages to hear, "Blessed
are those who have not seen and yet have believed." Those words
are for you and me. We need to heed those words well.

It is no wonder then, that John ended this all-important
section of his Gospel with these words:

"Jesus did many other miraculous signs in the presence of his disciples which are not recorded in this

book. But these are written that you may believe that
Jesus is the Christ, and that by believing you may
have life in his name."
- John 20:30, 31

Everything we have studied thus far about Adam and Eve,
about Joseph, about David, about Saul; all of it, everything in
Holy Scripture is written to point us to Christ, so "that by believing" we might have life in His name. God's great day of
triumph came when His Son was raised from death to life. Man's
great day of triumph comes through faith in that risen Savior
Jesus Christ. Jesus said,

"I am the way, the truth and the life."
- John 14:6

It was no accident that the first century Christian movement was known as *The Way*. That designation represented
what they taught from the words of Christ Himself. The way,
to truth and to life, is only through faith in Him. He is truth
and He is life. His resurrection assures us of this eternal truth.

"To the Jews who had believed him, Jesus said, 'If
you hold to my teaching, you are really my disciples.
Then you will know the truth, and the truth will set
you free.'"
- John 8:31, 32

Today, educators and philosophers borrow these famous
words of Christ, as do politicians, religious leaders of different
persuasions, and people of all different kinds, to try to justify

or lend some degree of credence to what they are offering or teaching. As Christians, we need to keep proclaiming this message to the world so that these words are always remembered in their most important spiritual context: the context of freedom from sin and Satan, the context of Christ as the way, the truth, and the life, and the context of what constitutes true children of God. This spiritual freedom that can be ours, and this eternal truth we are to treasure above all else, comes to us only through faith in Jesus Christ. The great triumph over evil will be ours only through faith in Him as resurrected Lord and King.

> "This is the victory that has overcome the world, even
> our faith. Who is it that overcomes the world? Only
> he who believes that Jesus is the Son of God."
> - I John 5:4, 5

Quite a bold statement, wouldn't you say? There is a way to overcome the world with all its soul-destroying allurements. There is a way to overcome the evil that repeatedly manifests itself in this world to destroy us both physically and spiritually. John writes with confidence. If you have faith in Jesus Christ, you already are victorious over the world with all its ills. We come to our seventh insight.

INSIGHT #7

The ultimate triumph over evil is known personally only through faith in Jesus Christ, in whom we become victors with God over every evil force at work in this world, both within us and outside of us.

Victory's Beginning: REPENTANCE

Repentance is not a very popular word or concept these days. It clearly implies that an error has been made, a sin has been committed, and a wrong needs to be addressed. We need not shy away from it. We dare not. It is what is required at the beginning of the road to triumph over evil.

The greater part of John the Baptist's ministry was calling people to repentance as that first important step to receiving the "Lamb of God who takes away the sin of the world" (John 1:29). Therefore, Jesus too spoke often about the importance of repentance.

In the context of our study, the question is, what role does repentance play in relation to the events of 9-11? One might come up with many ways in which repentance applies and many reasons why repentance is called for after 9-11. Some of those calls for repentance may be justified and appropriate. Others may be entirely inappropriate and out of place. We need to be careful here. Again, we do not want to fall prey to Satan's trap and think that God is punishing sin on 9-11. Nonetheless, the call to repentance is justified today and we find that justification in the words of Christ Himself. Here is what He said in a context similar to ours. We can be thankful we have these words recorded for us in Luke's Gospel. They will help us understand how repentance applies for all of us after September 11.

> "Now there were some present at that time who told Jesus about the Galileans whose blood Pilate had mixed with their sacrifices. Jesus answered, 'Do you think that these Galileans were worse sinners than all the other Galileans because they suffered this way? I tell you, no! But unless you repent, you too

will all perish. Or those eighteen who died when the
tower in Siloam fell on them—do you think they were
more guilty than all the others living in Jerusalem?
I tell you, no! But unless you repent, you too will all
perish.'"

- Luke 13:1-5

Down through history there has been a tendency on the
part of people of all different faiths to equate a direct cause/
effect relationship between sin and suffering. Most of the book
of Job deals with that very flawed approach to the subject. In
these verses from Luke's Gospel, Jesus references two well-
known current events from His day to address this very issue
as well. He does not elaborate on the events themselves. There
is no need to. He is not interested in the details. It may also be
entirely appropriate to conclude that much may be inferred
from the fact that He doesn't elaborate on the details. He doesn't
go into a long detailed explanation as to why these events happened. He simply acknowledges that they did happen. He
doesn't go into long dissertations as to who was to blame for
these events. He shows us that we should be careful not to
conclude too much from these evil events, but just stresses one
or two important truths that we are to draw from them.

In a kind of eerie way, they may remind us of September
11. There are similarities. The first incident appears to have
been quite gruesome and violent in nature. Jesus was told of a
group of Galileans "whose blood Pilate had mixed with their
sacrifices." Nothing more is said, but we clearly gather that it
was a horrific event and news of it spread quickly.

In the second incident, Jesus refers to 18 people who lost
their lives in Siloam when a tower collapsed and fell down upon

them, crushing them to death. Eerily, we cannot help but think of the Twin Towers in New York.

In both cases, Jesus knew what the people of His day were thinking, "They must have been great sinners to have such tragedy fall upon them. God was punishing them for some great sin." Concerning the Galileans who died at the hand of Pilate, Jesus asked rhetorically, "Were they worse sinners because they suffered this way?" Regarding the 18 who died when the tower collapsed on them, Jesus asked, "Were they more guilty than anyone else?" He answered both questions very firmly and directly in the negative, "I tell you, no!" In other words, if that is what the people thought, they were completely missing the point. Then he told them, not once but twice for emphasis, "Unless you repent, you too will all perish."

Imagine if Jesus had uttered those words to us today. What would he have said about the events of 9-11? Let's paraphrase a little bit here. Perhaps this is how He might have responded:

> Now there were some reporters present at the time who told Jesus about the Americans in Washington D.C. whose blood certain terrorists had violently shed when the airplane they commandeered crashed into the Pentagon. Jesus answered, "Do you think these Pentagon employees were worse sinners than all the other people in the United States because their lives ended this way? I tell you, no! But unless you repent, you too will all perish. Or those hundreds upon hundreds who died when the Twin Towers in New York fell on them—do you think they were more guilty than all the others living in New York? I tell you, no! But unless you repent, you too will all perish.

This little paraphrase is not meant to belittle, mock, or treat insignificantly the events of 9-11 in any way. In fact, it is meant to help us place those events in the context in which Jesus would have us deal with them. That is critically important.

Were the people who died on 9-11 greater sinners than anyone else? Of course not! Did those people lose their lives because God was fed up with the sins of others in our nation? How ridiculous for us to think and talk like that!

What then are the truths to be gleaned from those events in the spiritual context in which Jesus would have us deal with them? There are two. The first is a call to action. Specifically, "Repent." The second is a call to be aware that our end can come at any time. We must be ready, therefore, at all times. We are ready when we are truly repentant over our own sins, which is the first step of faith. "Repent and believe," Jesus might say, "or you too will all perish." The time for faith is now, not tomorrow, because tomorrow might be too late.

September 11 should lead us to see how fleeting life can be. It can be like a vapor, here one day and then suddenly, unexplainably, it is gone. Jesus wants us to be ready for our end, whenever it might come. The first step in readiness is turning back toward God. That concept is what is known as repentance.

September is not about remembering specific sins that caused the tragic events of that day. If that is what we think, then we tragically miss the mark. September 11, however, is about evil. It is about the sins of men who chose to be guided by the powers of evil in this dark world to take innocent lives. It is about what sin produces in this world. It is about a spiritual depravity within man that remains to this day. September 11 should lead us to shake our heads and ask, "What kind of creature is man that such evil can come from him?"

God would have us look inward, after September 11, and see the evil that is within us too. He wants us to see that there is great reason why we so desperately need Jesus Christ and the salvation He has won for all. September 11 isn't only about terrorists, innocent people dying, and a nation now at war. Those are all the externals. That is obvious. In the deeper context in which Jesus would have us look, September 11 is about evil works in this world that are drawn from sin that lurks within every human being. Jesus wants us to each examine ourselves and make a change, so that when death comes, we do not forever perish from His presence.

Therefore, we need to see our own sins in order to make the way straight to receive Christ into our heart. All of us have sins that are known not only to us but also to God. We need to reflect upon them, confess them, and turn to Christ for the forgiveness He has ready and waiting for each of us.

Nor does it hurt for us to reflect upon evils that are so prevalent in our own nation today. This kind of self-examination will make us stronger. God can use these events to wake us up to the wrongs we need to correct in our own nation and in the communities where we live. These sins are not the cause of 9-11 but they are worth reflecting upon after 9-11 so that the evils that exist in our own lives are rooted out and replaced with the love and hope found in our Savior Jesus Christ.

We really do not have to look far. As we mourn the thousands who lost their lives on that dreadful day, and stand in shock over the 3,000 plus lives that were tragically ended on September 11, we would do well to reflect upon the fact that in our nation the lives of nearly 4,000 unborn children are snuffed out through abortion *every day*. It too is a national tragedy and very grievous to God who is the author and giver of life.

Child abuse, in ever-growing numbers, exists not only among the poor of our nation but even in the wealthiest segments of our society. MADD—Mothers Against Drunk Drivers—came into existence because of the plague of alcohol abuse that costs hundreds of lives on our nation's highways each year. The evils of drug abuse and the profiteering in drugs continue to plague our nation, resulting in the loss of lives for thousands yearly, and the further erosion of our culture. There appears no end in sight because so many are unwilling to turn from these evil ways.

There is more. There is always more. We could go on and on but what we need to see most of all is that Jesus' words are true. Becoming victors over evil, moving from terror to triumph, requires that first important step of turning from evil and back to God. That is what repentance is. That is what God calls upon each of us to do. The more each of us does that individually, the more it will hold true that we have repented as a nation. That is the only way it will happen.

Repentance, therefore, is so terribly important because it is that first step back to God for us as individuals and as a nation. It is a humble and contrite acknowledgement of the sin and evil within us, accompanied by trust in God's grace and His promise of total forgiveness in Christ. You see, God does not just leave us hanging when repentance flows from our hearts. He lifts us from our sorrow and remorse with the good news that in Christ all our sins are forgiven. Nevertheless, that spirit of humility must first be there if we hope to receive Christ aright. Without it, we will feel no need for Him.

"Pride goes before destruction, a haughty spirit before a fall."

- Proverbs 16:18

Sinful human pride does so much to get in the way of the
spiritual healing that is so necessary in becoming one with
God again. God, in His Word, tells us of someone who learned
this truth well but learned it the hard way. Who do you suppose wrote the following words?

> "Clothe yourselves with humility toward one another,
> because, 'God opposes the proud but gives grace to
> the humble.' Humble yourselves, therefore, under
> God's mighty hand, that he may lift you up in due
> time. Cast all your anxiety on him because he cares
> for you." - ?

Who do you suppose found the clothing of humility a most
necessary garment for covering the natural skin of sinful human pride? Who found the gift of God's grace most precious
after pride had ruled for too long in his life? Who was humbled
powerfully "under God's mighty hand" and who was "lifted up"
from the dark depths of despair when the day of sorrow came?
Who found great relief in casting the anxiety of sin and doubt
upon Christ?

If you guessed the disciple Peter, you guessed right. These
words were recorded in his first epistle, chapter 5:5-7. Peter
had learned the sad lessons of haughtiness and sinful pride
the hard way. Pride was always getting him into trouble and
Christ was always bailing him out. From his bold confessions
of faith to his utter despair in denying Jesus Christ, pride, along

with overconfidence in himself, was always launching him on
a roller coaster ride that finally left him lost, confused, and
living in fear. Easter changed all that for Peter. After Easter,
Jesus lifted him up again. His sin of denial was forgiven and
Peter's life was forever changed through Christ's resurrection.
Therefore, he also could write these words from knowledge that
came by experience, and from wisdom that came through faith.

> "Be self-controlled and alert. Your enemy the devil
> prowls around like a roaring lion looking for some-
> one to devour. Resist him, standing firm in the faith,
> because you know that your brothers throughout the
> world are undergoing the same kind of sufferings.
> And the God of all grace, who called you to his eter-
> nal glory in Christ, after you have suffered a little
> while, will himself restore you and make you strong,
> firm and steadfast. To him be the power forever and
> ever. Amen."
> - I Peter 5:8-11

Peter had seen the face of the enemy that night in the courtyard as Jesus' enemies stood all around him. He learned then
what it meant to "stand firm in the faith." He came to know
what it meant to suffer for the sake of Christ. It was hard. It
meant challenge, trial, and sacrifice. But he also learned what
it meant to be restored by the "God of all grace." Peter had
experienced Christ's undeserved love toward him first hand
and it was the most precious of all the gifts he had ever received in life. Through faith he remained "strong, firm and steadfast" until his last day when faith led him to make the final
sacrifice for the sake of the gospel of Jesus Christ. Now, eternal

life is his. It all began, Peter knew, with a humble, contrite, repentant heart.

The Blessings of Faith, JESUS' BEATITUDES

It doesn't take long for a repentant heart that is growing ever stronger in the true faith, to begin to perceive faith's many other blessings. You see, that's what's next. God does not leave us hungry for very long. His desire is to set the table fast, load it up, and let us eat to our heart's content. God wouldn't make a very good dietician. He enjoys, too much, watching us grow spiritually fat. He's always too busy filling everyone up with the gifts of His rich grace that overflows in abundance. But that's OK. That kind of spiritual abundance is the best food we could ever hope to have.

In what is probably the most magnificent description of the blessings of faith found anywhere in all of Scripture, Jesus started His Sermon on the Mount with what has come to be known as The Beatitudes. The word *beatitude*, though not found in Scripture, simply means, *supreme blessing*. Jesus showed in His sermon that God has not only one, but indeed many supreme blessings, or beatitudes, for us.

It is unfortunate that as the years have passed by, the Beatitudes have often been taken out of context to mean something quite different from what Jesus originally intended. Since that time, many people of different philosophies and religious persuasions have used them to produce almost a kind of "new law." "Be humble, be meek, be merciful, be pure, be a peacemaker, and you will live a life pleasing to God." That is not the meaning of the beatitudes. That concept even goes against the meaning of the word *beatitude* itself. These are not "supreme laws" of God to be followed, but *supreme blessings* of God to people of faith who know Christ as Lord.

The first clue to this truth is found in the words of introduction to the Sermon on the Mount drawn from Matthew's
Gospel. Take special note of what is written in this introduction.

> "Now when he saw the crowds, he went up on a
> mountainside and sat down. His disciples came to
> him, and he began to teach them, saying . . ."
> - Matthew 5:1, 2

As always, the crowds were following Jesus wherever He
went. So Jesus "went up," moving Himself a distance away from
the people, took a position, and sat down on the mountainside.
Now there was room for His disciples. They came to him and
"he began to teach them," that is, His disciples, those who believed in Him!

The Sermon on the Mount is directed primarily at believers! I'm sure there were many others who heard Jesus' words
that day, and on other occasions as well. Yet, we have a setting
here in which the disciples are in training by their Lord and
He is teaching them. They were in preparation for their great
mission into the world that was to come. This, you could say,
was their seminary training. In a way, it is unfortunate that
this section ever came to be known as the Sermon on the Mount.
It was not a sermon at all. It was a Bible class, if it was anything. Jesus was doing more teaching than preaching.

Our Lord had chosen a select group of disciples to follow
Him virtually everywhere He went, not for show, but for sub-
stance. As He trained them for their mission in the first century church, they did not learn haphazardly. Jesus was very

thorough, very repetitious, very direct, and very precise in His course of instruction for them. He taught *them,* in particular, and He often had to instruct them when the curious multitudes were around, because they were always flocking to Jesus. Yet, often, and it seems so here, His instruction was directed specifically at His chosen pupils, these select disciples.

There is great spiritual significance for us in understanding this setting. He teaches these truths to those who believe in Him, to those of faith. Faith perceives correctly these supreme blessings. It is a principle that is very similar to Jesus' habit of speaking in parables. Believers could perceive the spiritual nuggets of truth made known through the parables but unbelievers, specifically Jesus' enemies, would miss the point and, therefore, be unable to tread the truth of God underfoot. The disciples even asked Jesus one day why He spoke so often in parables. This is what He told them:

> "'The knowledge of the secrets of the kingdom of heaven has been given to you, but not to them.... This is why I speak to them in parables: 'Though seeing they do not see; though hearing, they do not understand.'... But blessed are your eyes because they see, and your ears because they hear. For I tell you the truth, many prophets and righteous men longed to see what you see but did not see it, and to hear what you hear but did not hear it.'"
> - Matthew 13:11, 13, 16, 17

As the parables were understood correctly through faith, so here, the Beatitudes, taught to the faithful, are understood correctly only through the eyes of faith.

When we examine these supreme blessings that God gives to those who place their faith in Him, we begin to see some interesting parallels develop to the words in Ephesians 6:14-17. There, Paul describes the various parts of the Christian's spiritual armor as God's great gifts to man. Faith protects everything God gives us. Both sections even end on the important note of sharing these blessings with the world now that we have received them. These parallels are worth noting as part of our study.

THE BEATITUDES
Matthew 5:3-10

"Blessed are the poor in spirit, for theirs is the kingdom of heaven."
– vs.3

Those who are "poor in spirit" are those who have been weighed down with the burden of sin. They represent those who are in need of spiritual renewal, have repented of their sins, and humbled themselves before God. They no longer trust in themselves, their own power, and their own might. For them, the way has been made straight for God to enter their hearts and lift them up. When the "shield of faith" (Ephesians 6:16) becomes theirs, as a gift of the Spirit, they are no longer poor but made rich. The kingdom of heaven becomes their inheritance, for they are children of God through faith.

"Blessed are those who mourn, for they shall be comforted."
– vs.4

Death came in some unbelievably heavy doses on September 11. We have many who mourn for loved ones. In Christ, there is the comforting sure hope of life, even in the face of death, for all who believe. Many are finding that comfort as they bear this "helmet of salvation" (Ephesians 6:17). Satan would have us believe that death is the end of things, but the gift of salvation, that we take hold of through faith, assures us that we are delivered from death's curse. Jesus lives and we too will live. In Christ, those who mourn find comfort and hope for the future.

> "Blessed are the meek, for they will inherit the earth."
> – vs. 5

This world has seen its powerful people from the Pharaohs to Alexander and from the Caesars to those who rule our modern world. September 11 is but another reminder to us that throughout history we find individuals who repeatedly try to gain control in the earth by exerting every means possible to wreak havoc in the world and gain greater power. Those who are so proud to think they have the earth under their dominion now, will not rule later. That gift will come to those who are meek and have yielded by faith to the truth that Jesus is the true King of all.

Once again, as God's children take up the "shield of faith" to protect themselves from Satan's powerful attacks, they look by faith to Christ as their protector. We are weak but He is strong. In the new heaven and the new earth, we will inherit the earth, for we will rule over everything with Him.

> "Blessed are those who hunger and thirst for right-
> eousness, for they will be filled."
> – vs.6

We are immediately reminded of the "breastplate of righteousness" (Ephesians 6:14) that Paul encourages to keep in
place at all times. Who are those who hunger and thirst for
righteousness but those who are eager to overcome sin and
enter a right relationship with God? In Jesus Christ that hunger is satisfied. He is the "bread of life" (John 6:48). In Him we
find eternal life and are perfectly restored in our relationship
with God.

Events like September 11 do not alarm us because our thirst
was never for this life anyway. While those of faith will also
treasure relationships with friends and family now, they recognize that these are gifts from God and that the greatest relationship they have is that of being restored in oneness with
their Creator through the agency of Jesus Christ. God is their
highest good and so they are ready to be taken from this world
to their eternal rest with God in Christ at any time.

> "Blessed are the merciful, for they will be shown
> mercy."
> – vs. 7

The "belt of truth" (Ephesians 6:14) that is to remain buck-
led around our waist to hold every other piece of armor in place,
teaches us the truth that everything we are in Christ, everything we have, everything we hope to receive, is a result of
God's mercy and grace. That truth, that God has been merciful
to us and has forgiven our sins for Jesus' sake, will lead us to

show mercy ourselves.

September 11 is not a call to hate; it is a call to arms. Even foot soldiers, while waging a war and fighting for a just cause, can act bravely, but also mercifully. After all, that is what Jesus did for us. He was surrounded by enemies, fought our battle for us, won a great victory, and all the while extended mercy even to those who were most opposed to Him. God asks us now, to take this spirit into every battle we fight in life. He calls upon us to be merciful as God in Christ has been merciful to us. Faith perceives this truth and our faith will reveal itself in the mercy we show to those who stand opposed to us.

"Blessed are the pure in heart, for they will see God."
– vs.8

I've always felt this supreme blessing of faith, seeing God, is best understood when we look at it in reverse. Who is it that can see God and recognize Him? Only those who are "pure in heart" can recognize God. God is seen through the gift of faith. We see in Jesus Christ the truth that He is the Son of God and Savior of the world. We perceive this truth only with hearts that have been made pure through faith. Only then, will we ever see God.

Again, those who wear this "belt of truth" know the true God, see Him, find in Him strength for their battle against the forces of evil, and thus, prevail to the end. We need to see God after September 11, as infinitely powerful and infinitely wise. Only then will we see the good that He is able to work through all of this. Those who see God in this way have pure hearts because they know the truth and believe it to be so. Eventually, they will stand before God and see Him face to face, in heavenly dwellings.

> "Blessed are the peacemakers, for they will be called
> sons of God."
> – vs.9

The Nobel Peace Prize is one of the greatest honors bestowed upon people in the world today. It is given only to those who have dedicated their lives to the pursuit of world peace and have made very real and significant contributions toward that end.

However, Christ was not speaking about that kind of peace. Trying to make the world a more peaceful place is an honorable task and there is nothing wrong with that, but we do not become "sons of God" by just promoting world peace.

It is not by chance that Paul refers to the Christian soldier's footwear as the "gospel of peace" (Ephesians 6:15). The message we bring to the world is a message of peace from God to man. As we proclaim the gospel, we are the kind of peacemakers God wants us to be. Our proclamation is one that tells the story that in Christ, our war with God is over, all sins are forgiven, God is our friend, and has become our salvation. The angels proclaimed this peace the night Jesus was born. It is God's good will to mankind through the gift of His Son. In Jesus, God's gift to the world, we have peace with God. Through faith in Christ, that gift of peace becomes our own, and we become sons of God and heirs of eternal life.

In the midst of all the evil of this world, we need not compound our misery by turning away from the one in whom we can find peace and rest. In times of trouble, it is a great comfort to know that no matter what this world might throw at us, we have peace with God, through Jesus Christ, who is our peace. We need such assurance as this after September 11.

> "Blessed are those who are persecuted because of righteousness, for theirs is the kingdom of heaven."
> – vs.10

We are not given the "sword of the Spirit, which is the Word of God" (Ephesians 6:17) to wield it low. When the day of evil comes and faith in Christ is challenged in a host of ways by Satan's army, we are to raise it high to defend ourselves. That is one reason God has blessed us with His Word. If we stand our ground and do not give up the fight, the kingdom of heaven will be our supreme blessing. It is ours now, as long as we fight the good fight of faith, and by God's strength, remain firm to the end.

We have seen that when the day of evil comes, Satan will take everything in his arsenal to convince us that God is weak, that God does not love us as much as He tells us, that God holds back from us, and that God does not have our best interests at heart. Since September 11, Satan has been working overtime to convince us that our hope is in a God that is not there for us. Faith takes the sword of the Spirit, the Word of God and fights that attack with God's truth. We have God's promise that the kingdom of heaven will be ours. We will be freed from this struggle at last and forever with the Lord, a *supreme blessing* indeed.

The Victorious Blessings of Faith

When the day of evil comes, as loved ones are suddenly taken from us, and our world seems to be crumbling all around us, we can still find hope for the future. We can still find joy and peace. We can find them through faith in Jesus Christ.

> "Therefore since we have been justified by faith, we have peace with God through our Lord Jesus Christ..."
> – Romans 5:1

> "May the God of hope fill you with joy and peace as you trust in him, so that you may overflow with hope by the power of the Holy Spirit."
> – Romans 15:13

Day after day, we hope for many things in life. We might hope that as we travel we are kept safe from anything that might harm us. We might hope that a new business undertaking is successful. We might hope that the neighbor's dog would stop its incessant barking. We are not filled with joy when we hope for such things. There is no peace because what we hope for is not yet realized.

However, through faith, we have peace and joy right now because every spiritual blessing we hope for is certain, sure, and complete in our Savior.

We hope we will get to heaven when we die. We know that through faith in Christ we will. This gives us peace. This fills us with joy.

We hope that God will not hold our sins against us. He does not, for in Christ they are all forgiven. This gives us peace.

This knowledge fills us with great joy.

We hope our loved ones who have parted from this life, as friends with Christ on earth, will live with Him also as friends in heaven. We know that through faith in Christ they rest with Him there. This gives us peace. This certainty fills us with unending joy.

One by one, list them all. List all your spiritual hopes. They are all certain in Christ. We do not hope as the world hopes. We hope in complete accord with the many blessings God showers down upon us every day. All our hopes, made through faith, continue to bring us repeated peace and joy, for in Christ they are all certain and sure.

The enemies Paul describes in Ephesians 6 are formidable. "Our struggle is not against flesh and blood, but against the rulers, against the authorities, against the powers of this dark world and against the spiritual forces of evil in the heavenly realms" (Ephesians 6:12). Yet, we go forward. We might be apprehensive because of the uncertainty over how our enemy might attack but we need not be afraid. We are not afraid because in faith we stand with God at our side. We boldly stand courageous and without fear.

> "When you go to war against your enemies and see horses and chariots and an army greater than yours, do not be afraid of them, because the Lord your God, who brought you up out of Egypt, will be with you."
> – Deuteronomy 20:1

> "Be strong and courageous. Do not be terrified; do not be discouraged, for the Lord your God will be with

you wherever you go."
– Joshua 1:9

I have seen that Christians can be strong and they can even be quite courageous at times. I have also often seen that Christians can become discouraged, and sometimes it happens very easily. Most of the time discouragement comes when we exhibit weakness of faith. It happens when we are depending more than we should upon ourselves and less than we should upon God.

The next time you find yourself discouraged for any reason, simply take the time to ask yourself this one important question, "Where am I focused?" If your answer is upon anyone or anything other than God, which it will be, then pray, "Lord, for this task, help me to focus my eyes on you." Wait and see what comes. It will not take long. Your confidence will dramatically increase. You will find courage to overcome obstacles that you first thought were insurmountable. Finally, you will find direction and clearness of vision for the appointed task.

God does that for us. It is one of the great blessings of faith. Use the power of God's presence in your life. It is there for that very purpose. Use it after 9-11 and in every other day of evil. Focus upon Him and His certain promise to be with you always in your journey through life.

In this way, faith also gives us great confidence when we pray.

"For the eyes of the Lord are on the righteous and his ears are attentive to their prayer . . ."
- I Peter 3:12

"This is the assurance we have in approaching God:
that if we ask anything according to his will, he hears
us."
- I John 5:14

"Ask and it will be given to you; seek and you will
find; knock and the door will be opened to you. For
everyone who asks receives; he who seeks finds; and
to him who knocks, the door will be opened."
- Matthew 7:7, 8

Every Christian knows that we need to pray. Furthermore,
we know that God encourages us to pray frequently. However,
many children of God sometimes overlook the confidence with
which God wants us to pray. God will listen to a wet noodle but
He prefers a straight stick. So stand before Him, Christian, as
He would have you stand!

In your heart, in your mind, and in your spirit approach
God that way, standing straight and tall, with gladness of heart
that you are able to come before the Ruler of the universe, with
confidence and with firmness of conviction. You come before
your King but you also come before your greatest friend, the
one who loves you more than anyone else. He is listening. He
wants what is best for you. He wants so much to hear your
request for it expresses faith and trust in Him—and He is simply delighted when you turn to Him in prayer. Faith gives us
confidence that He listens, that He understands our request,
and that He will answer in ways that best suit our present and
future welfare.

Perhaps one of the reasons God allows days of evil to enter
our lives—days of trouble and days of hardship—is because

those are the times in which we are most inclined to turn to Him. I do not even wonder if this is true, I know it is true.

We are too often lazy Christians, not just in our mission life but also in our prayer life. We become too easily entangled in Satan's traps of self-confidence and self-reliance. Then something happens and we are reminded how much in life is out of our control. It is then, when we are most vulnerable and most confused, that God knocks on our heart's door. Faith, which seemed for a while to be hibernating, inactive, and dormant, awakes. God is there and at the opening of that door, He speaks to us tenderly, "I am here to help you. I am here to deliver. I am here to care for you."

At that moment, when we surrender our lives to him anew— or even if it is for the very first time—a peace fills us and a rest calms us, like nothing we have ever known before. This too is one of the great blessings of faith. This we need to have after 9-11. We need this blessing of faith whenever the day of evil comes.

"You are my hiding place; you will protect me from trouble and surround me with songs of deliverance."
- Psalm 32:7

"Because the Sovereign Lord helps me, I will not be disgraced. Therefore I set my face like flint, and I know I will not be put to shame."
- Isaiah 50:7

"So we say with confidence, 'The Lord is my helper; I will not be afraid. What can man do to me?"
- Hebrews 13:6

Today our nation faces a great crisis. We are challenged. We are put to the test. We need help for this task. God is there for us. Yet, in the midst of this great national struggle, there exists an even greater spiritual struggle. Satan will use these events to drive a wedge between God and us. The devil does not want us to know Him as our helper. Do not let Satan do that. Take up the shield of faith and look to your Creator as your great Deliverer in this time of need. We need to be like flint, hard like rocks, unmoved in our confidence and in our reliance upon Him. He will not let us down. He is there for us. Faith looks to Him for help and deliverance. We need this blessing of faith after 9-11. We need God's help whenever the day of evil comes.

Faith not only enables us to clearly focus upon God to find courage in the tasks and challenges of life that lie before us, but it also enables us to clearly focus on the present and on our future. Paul was the great missionary he was because his faith blessed him with a vision of the present and the future that was so very spiritually illuminating.

> "But we have this treasure in jars of clay to show
> that this all surpassing power is from God and not
> from us. We are hard pressed on every side, but not
> crushed; perplexed, but not in despair; persecuted,
> but not abandoned; struck down, but not destroyed.
> We always carry around in our body the death of Je-
> sus, so that the life of Jesus may also be revealed in
> our body.... It is written: 'I believed; therefore I have
> spoken.' With the same spirit of faith we also believe
> and therefore speak, because we know that the one

who raised the Lord Jesus from the dead will also
raise us with Jesus and present us with you in his
presence."
- II Corinthians 4:7-10, 13, 14

Hard pressed, perplexed, persecuted, struck down—but not
crushed, not in despair, not abandoned, and certainly not destroyed. This was Paul's life as a missionary spreading the gospel of Jesus Christ. He was always under duress but never
defeated because his power and strength were from God, not
man.

In the first century, they spoke valiantly, this message of
life and salvation in Christ. They did so against tremendous
opposition, because by faith they knew that for the present,
this saving message needed to be heard by everyone. For the
future they trusted, by faith, that even if death should come to
them, just as Jesus rose from death, they would be raised to be
with Him. This is the focus faith brings to the present and the
future. It all centers on Jesus Christ. The true story that follows, beautifully illustrates this truth.

One night as I was leaving my office, a little later than
usual, I happened upon the nightly janitor who was beginning
his rounds. Some time earlier, we had come to share our mutual faith in Christ and I had learned from him of the struggles he was facing with lymphatic cancer. The cancer had flared
up again and his glands were swollen considerably. New rounds
of chemotherapy were beginning.

We talked. We talked about the cancer and we talked about
Christ. We talked about the comfort and hope He gives to us
whenever the day of evil comes. Then he began to talk even
more about his life and he began to share some things with me

he had never shared before.

He told me that a good part of his life had been lost to sin, specifically drug abuse and addiction. It had mastered him for a time—a long time. He reasoned that many of his health problems today, could easily be attributed to his drug abuse from years ago. However, the point in time came when God opened his eyes to the life he was living and how it was not only destroying him in every way, both physically and spiritually, but destroying his family as well. God opened his heart to turn around, to repent, to turn back to God, and change his life. At that time, the effects of his addiction were threatening his very life. He prayed God with one request, that he might just live long enough to see his children grow up and old enough to care for one another after he had passed away.

Years have past and God has nearly granted his request. In only a year or two, the last of his children will graduate from high school but he continues to wonder if he will indeed make it. He has placed everything in God's hands trusting that His will for him and his family will be best. Sometimes however, it gets hard.

He told me that just a few months ago he had suffered another setback. It was so serious that he wondered if he would really live long enough to see his youngest through high school. He became somewhat discouraged over this prospect and worried over how much time was left for him on this earth to care for his family. About the same time, other members in his family lost a little child at birth. They had been hoping for so long to be blessed with the gift of a child. They thought the time had come. It was not to be. Sadly and unexpectedly, he found himself not only in ill health but also attending the funeral of this dear infant child.

When the day of the funeral came, He was still distraught over the uncertainties of his own condition. He arrived at the cemetery grounds. While there, he couldn't help but notice that all the tombstones identified infants who had died only days from birth. This section of the cemetery was for infants only. There were many buried here. He began to count them all but there were too many to continue. Then he began to study them more closely. He went from one to the next. As he did so, he started to count again, not the tombstones this time, but the days of life they told. He began to add them up one by one. One day old—two days old—one week—three days—seven—ten—four—eighteen—eleven—two—and then on they went, one after another. Then it dawned on him, what God was opening his eyes to see. It was remarkable and very illuminating, what was there before him.

With the blessing of faith, that has now enabled him to focus clearly upon the uncertainty of the present and the certainty of his future with Christ, he confessed to me, "Suddenly I realized, that if I were to walk through the cemetery and add up all the days that all these children lived on this earth, one after another, that I would still have lived longer than all of them combined." Instantly he realized that his times were in God's hands and God had already blessed him with life, with days, and with years that were far more than he ever deserved in the first place. He thanked God for the truth he learned that day, for the spiritual renewal that became his, and he has been thanking God every day since.

This is one of the great blessings of faith. It gives true meaning to our lives. It enables us to stop worrying. It enables us to focus clearly upon our present situation and the clear future we have in Christ. Faith enables us to keep it all in proper perspective. That also, is what we need faith to do for us after 9-11. That is a blessing we need from faith whenever the day of evil comes.

The Apostle Paul had such a clear focus on the present that even in weakness he could find strength. He came to look upon all kinds of suffering, misfortune, and evil in life, not from a negative standpoint but from a very positive standpoint. He could do this because God had blessed him to see this truth through the eyes of faith.

"To keep me from becoming conceited because of these surpassingly great revelations, there was given me a thorn in my flesh, a messenger of Satan, to torment me. Three times I pleaded with the Lord to take it away from me. But he said to me, 'My grace is sufficient for you, for my strength is made perfect in weakness.' Therefore I will boast all the more gladly about my weaknesses, so that Christ's power may rest on me. That is why, for Christ's sake, I delight in weaknesses, in insults, in hardships, in persecutions, in difficulties. For when I am weak, then I am strong."
- II Corinthians 12:7-10

Down through the centuries Christians have speculated about Paul's *thorn in the flesh*. We do not know exactly what this affliction was. Whatever it was, it tormented Paul on a regular basis. It was painful. It appears he suffered this ailment until his life in this world ended.

However, what we do know is how Paul dealt with this affliction. First, he didn't blame God for it. By faith, he understood that such misery and suffering does not come from God.

He saw evil as the source of this misery. Specifically, "a messenger of Satan" had been sent to torment him. This is the first
truth faith enabled him to perceive, that evil and suffering in
this world is of Satan, not of God.

Secondly, faith moved him to turn to God in prayer for relief. He pleaded with God three times that it be taken from
him. God's answer to him was no. "My grace is sufficient for
you," God revealed to him.

Sometimes God deals with us that way. He may allow suffering and misfortune to come, and He may allow it to continue without any immediate relief. Faith is able to perceive
that God, in His wisdom, may allow suffering to come for a
time. Through faith, Paul was able to recognize this.

Through faith, he also understood this important truth: suffering can serve a very useful purpose in our lives. In this case,
Paul came to understand that his affliction was allowed by God
to keep him from becoming "conceited because of these surpassingly great revelations."

God had chosen Paul for a very special purpose as His
spokesman to the Gentiles. The early church grew dramatically under the most difficult and challenging conditions. Paul
was the gospel's chief ambassador in those early years. Under
inspiration of the Holy Spirit, he had written some of the most
remarkable books of the entire Bible and his letters make up a
substantial portion of the New Testament. His leadership in
the first century church was challenged at times, but, nonetheless, Paul was certainly respected for his work and his zeal.

How easy it would have been for Paul to let all this go to his
head. How easy it would have been for him to think more highly
of himself than he ought. How easy it would have been for him
to begin boasting in himself. He didn't though. Paul attributes
this, not to his own strength of character, but to this "thorn in

the flesh" which God had allowed to torment him. He was able to see that it served a noble purpose in keeping him humble and focused upon God as the real reason for his accomplishments.

God's grace was sufficient for him and so he stopped petitioning God to take this affliction away from him. God's undeserved love toward him continued to produce the richest of spiritual blessings in his life and it was enough. In fact, his sufferings served to make him look to God more and more as time went on. Therefore, though sufferings were increasing, Paul was growing stronger, not weaker. God's strength was becoming perfected in him! Through faith, Paul understood this, and so much so that as sufferings increased, he came to rejoice in them. Weaknesses, insults, hardships, persecutions, and difficulties of all kinds did not deter him. They only forced him to look ever more firmly to God for strength. He was never left wanting. So he wrote, "When I am weak, then I am strong."

Doesn't it seem like a contradiction in terms? How can we be the strongest when we are at our weakest? Yet, it really does work that way. When we are at our most vulnerable, most fatigued, and most inclined to fail, that is when the Christian's faith will kick in. That is when we are forced to turn to God for help and strength. God knows this about us. He would prefer that we not wait so long before turning to Him, but He knows us better than we know ourselves. So, he allows suffering and evil to come. Then we turn to Him. Then we rise victorious, as His strength is made perfect in us.

We need to have Christ's power rest on us when the day of evil comes. We need that power after 9-11. We need to exhibit that kind of faith today that reaches out to God as our great source of strength. Then His strength will become ours.

September 11 has reminded all of us that in this world we can experience great loss quickly, violently, and tragically. This world and everything in it is fleeting. Nothing is permanent, except God's great love for us in Christ. It captures our hearts here, fortifies us throughout life, and lifts us to the gates of heaven when we leave this world. It is always with us. It is a love that has secured for us a permanent place with God. It is a love that has won for us a righteousness from God that enables us to stand before Him as dear beloved children, forgiven and made pure through the blood of the Lamb, Jesus Christ.

This gift of life and salvation in Christ is the one lasting, eternal treasure we have. Gain this and you have so much more. Gain this, through faith in Christ, and all other attachments in this world may be lost, but we still have great gain. This is true for you. It is true for me. It is true for everyone. It was very true for the Apostle Paul.

"I consider everything loss compared to the surpassing greatness of knowing Christ Jesus my Lord, for whose sake I have lost all things. I consider them rubbish, that I may gain Christ and be found in him, not having a righteousness of my own that comes from the law, but that which is through faith in Christ—the righteousness that comes from God and is by faith. I want to know Christ and the power of his resurrection and the fellowship of sharing in his sufferings, becoming like him in death, and so, somehow, to attain to the resurrection of the dead."
- Philippians 3:8-11

It is clear. In life, God desperately wants us to take a view of the world that keeps Christ as Lord, our most treasured possession. What does this mean? It means the God of our salvation comes first, above anyone or anything else. Why is this so important? For many reasons, but in the context in which we are addressing this issue now, it is because nothing in this world will last. Death comes. Loneliness sets in. Hopelessness, fear, depression, anger, bitterness, and/or resentment can easily take the place of what is lost in life, after it has been so richly treasured. God does not want this to happen to you or to me. He wants for us "surpassing greatness," that comes from knowing Christ Jesus as our living Lord.

The world we live in today makes a great deal out of loving one another, so much so, that we are told if we simply love one another, all other problems will be solved. "All you need is love." Isn't that what the Beatles sang? I liked the song too. Unfortunately, it's not true. It's a nice thought, but it is not true. This is why.

You may love your spouse with all your heart. Your children may be your heart's great delight and you will do anything for them. You may honor your mother and father in ways that are unmatched by anyone else. Whoever it might be, you may love them with every part of your being, and show it in an unending multitude of ways, but it is not all you need, and it is not all they need. Your love will not keep suffering from entering their door. Your love will not keep Satan from trying to devour them. Your love will not prevent cancer from growing inside of them. Finally, your love will not keep them from dying.

September 11 has come and gone. On that day alone hundreds of people who were loved, parted from this life and from others who loved them. Love did not save them from the disas-

ter that befell them. That evil day came and the love of so many
could not prevent it. Yet, the great truth that Christian faith
perceives is that the surpassing greatness of Christ's love does
save. When Jesus is our treasure, in loss we find great gain.

God does not want us to love anyone above Him, in part,
because He does not want us to experience the hurt and pain
of losing our greatest love. If Jesus is our greatest treasure, the
"surpassing greatness of knowing Christ Jesus" as Lord, assures us that we can never lose our greatest love! That pain
will never be felt! Jesus lives! He lives to bring us home to be
with Him. There we will live with Him eternally!

Furthermore, we may not be able to save others just by
loving them, but Jesus can. If Jesus is our greatest treasure,
we will share Him, and who would not share such a treasure
as Jesus, especially with the people whom we love? Faith comes
by hearing the message that Jesus saves. Righteousness, life,
and salvation come through faith in Him. The "surpassing greatness of knowing Christ Jesus" is realized every time we share
Christ and faith is born anew in someone else. For then, even
though death comes, loved ones who believe are delivered and
saved. On the last day, they are raised up from death to life. We
are raised up from death to life. We are all raised up from death
to life. We are together again! That is great gain. It happens
only when we consider everything else as secondary to knowing Christ Jesus as Lord. This is great gain, for apart from
Christ everything is lost. With Christ, everything is gained!

The ultimate triumph over evil is known
personally only through faith in Jesus
Christ, in whom we become victors with

God over every evil force at work in this
world, both within us and outside of us.

Faith in Christ as Lord will forever be the ultimate message of Christianity, for it alone is that which secures the total
victory when the day of evil comes. Therefore the terror of sin
and death is no more, for through faith in Jesus Christ we are
triumphant and, even now, live with Him on into eternity.

- CHAPTER EIGHT -

INSIGHT #8

The ultimate triumph over evil is repeated daily, from faith to faith, as God's
children remain true to their mission and
proclaim to the world the triumphant
victory that is ours in Christ.

Faith in Mission

Chapter 7 ended on the important truth that great gain is realized for us, and for our loved ones, as we share the saving
message of Jesus Christ with one another. RECEIVING the
great blessings of faith carries with it a responsibility. We are
to SHARE the faith! Jesus said,

> "You are the salt of the earth. But if the salt loses its
> saltiness, how can it be made salty again? It is no
> longer good for anything, except to be thrown out and
> trampled by men. You are the light of the world. A
> city on a hill cannot be hidden. Neither do people
> light a lamp and put it under a bowl. Instead they
> put it on its stand, and it gives light to everyone in
> the house. In the same way, let your light shine be-
> fore men, that they may see your good deeds and

praise your Father in heaven."

- Matthew 5:13-16

You may have noticed that this familiar section of Scripture is also part of Jesus' Sermon on the Mount. In fact, interestingly enough, it comes immediately after the Beatitudes. That is significant. Having received all of these *supreme blessings* through faith, now we are to go out and share these blessings with others. We can do nothing other than that. We cannot keep quiet with this good news. We will feel compelled to tell.

Jesus likens us to salt. This is the most basic flavoring for food known to people across the globe. Yet it also has other useful qualities. It may be used as a preservative or for sterilization and the killing of germs and other bacteria. But what good is salt if it has just been sitting around for so long that it loses its saltiness? "It is no longer good for anything, except to be thrown out," Jesus said.

Time passes and we Christians become very comfortable in our faith, so much so, that we can become something like spiritual couch potatoes. We sit around enjoying all the blessings of faith and bothered little by the fact that many others know nothing of these rich gifts in Christ that are also for them. If we are complacent to the spiritual needs of others, we are what Jesus is describing here. We have become salt that has lost its saltiness. What good are we? What spiritual good are we to anyone else? Then comes the day of evil—a day like 9-11. It should wake us up to see the importance of sharing Christ with anyone who will listen because there may not be a tomorrow. Today is the day of salvation!

If we truly are lights in this dark and evil world, then, as

Jesus tells us, we will not be able to hide this light of truth that is ours. How could we? Why would we even want to? If faith lives within us, the light is also there, and we will not be able to hide it. God not only wants his saving message to be heard, he wants others to see through us the hope, joy, and love that faith brings. We also testify to Christ by the way we live as children of God. The Christians of the early church were known this way. It was said of them, "See how they love one another." We testify of Christ not only by what we say but also by what we do.

If you were like most Americans after 9-11, you were pretty much glued to your television set night after night, keeping abreast of all the latest news regarding the terrorist attacks and the war effort. It was impossible to miss the reports about the Christian foreign aid workers who had been taken captive by the Taliban while in Afghanistan, thrown into prison and charged with spreading Christianity, a crime punishable by death. Two of those Christians being held were Americans. Their names were Dayna Curry and Heather Mercer.

About the time they were to go on trial, the bombing began in Afghanistan by allied forces. They had arrived at a prison in the city of Ghazni and within an hour, after their arrival, the city was in turmoil. As they looked out the window of their prison cell, they could see the Taliban fleeing in every direction. Then there came an eerie quiet. A short time later, after about thirty minutes, they heard soldiers loudly bang down the prison door. Northern Alliance mujahideen commanders and soldiers rushed in and started yelling, "You're free! You're free!" That evening they were lifted out of harm's way when American special operations helicopters arrived to rescue them, and amazingly, they have now returned home to their families.

Things could have ended very differently for these two young women. What would have happened to them if 9-11 had never happened? Would there ever have been a war in Afghanistan that would have led to a rescue? Would the Taliban have executed them? Would we have ever even heard about them? All those questions are immaterial now. God had a plan for them. God had a plan and a reason for placing them in Afghanistan in the first place. He had a plan of rescue in store for them as well. Maybe He also has a plan for them to return someday. They have said they would like to.

There are many stories of heartache and tragedy from 9-11. This, however, is a story of great victory and hope. The story of these two women intrigued me from the very beginning and the more their story unfolded, the more amazed I became at them, and over how God was using them and watching over them. At a very dark hour, they shined like beacons of light for everyone to see. Their testimony, their courage, and their calm trust in God through their whole ordeal, was one of the most refreshing and uplifting stories in the weeks that followed the September 11 tragedy. It's what we needed. It is what God wanted us to hear. In these two marvelous children of God, we see what God wants us to be, salt and light.

They had gone to Afghanistan as Christian aid workers, "to serve the poor of the earth." God had led them there and once there God continued to guide them. In Afghanistan, they had opportunity to help build homes for refugees, assist with food distributions, and carry out their own personal ministry. They came not just as aid workers, they came as *Christian* aid workers, and they did nothing to hide that fact. That, finally, is what led to their arrest.

They were accused of spreading Christianity and were arrested. After their rescue and return to the United States, they were interviewed by Katie Couric of NBC's Today Show. In that interview they were asked if this was indeed the reason why they were over there, to spread the Christian faith. This is how Heather Mercer responded.

> "Well, we went out as Christian aid workers. I think one thing that's been on Dayna's and my heart for a long time is to serve the poor of the earth.... (We are) Christians and people who want to follow Jesus. It becomes a natural overflow of our lives. And in the context of Afghan culture, religion is a number one topic of discussion. So you discuss—almost daily people discuss God. They discuss their faith because that's who they are. And so often we'd find ourselves in conversations where our friends would share about their faith and in turn they'd ask us about ours. So it was just, really, a natural overflow of our lives and who we are."
> - Heather Mercer (Christian Aid worker in Afghanistan)

Jesus said, "You are the salt of the earth." Jesus said, "You are the light of the world." Jesus said, "In the same way, let your light shine before men, that they may see your good deeds and praise your Father in heaven." When Jesus spoke those words, He was describing people like Dayna Curry and Heather Mercer. What a spiritually refreshing pair they are. What a wonderful example of faith in mission they have set for us all.

When asked if they had indeed distributed Christian literature and shown videos about Christ to Afghan families, they acknowledged that they had been accused of these two things and these charges against them were true. They had shown a Jesus film and given out a children's storybook about Jesus that was written in the Afghan language. They made no apologies.

In the same interview, when they were asked if they had indeed known how dangerous this situation was for them, they simply acknowledged that, yes, they knew. Dayna Curry also explained,

> "We were just sharing about what we believed and they were interested to know who Jesus was. I think, sure, we knew there was a risk. But the family is willing to take the risk, so if they wanted to see it (the Jesus film), then how can you say no?"
> - Dayna Curry (Christian Aid worker in Afghanistan)

I am still amazed at the courage and spiritual integrity of these two women. We stand in wonderment over how they were able to share their faith with such boldness even under the threat of execution by the Taliban. We are astonished over how they willingly endured so much for the sake of the gospel and can still smile about all of it while they share their story. Apparently, Dayna and Heather, through faith, knew what the Apostle Paul knew.

> "I can do everything through him who gives me strength."
> - Philippians 4:13

Thank you Dayna and thank you Heather, for the strength of your convictions in Christ, for the example that you have set for all of us, and for uplifting our spirits at a moment in our nation's history when we needed just that. God placed you there for a very special purpose. You have lifted the banner of Christ high and let your light shine. It is still shining bright for all of us to see. I do not know what God has in store for you, but I have little doubt the spiritual implications will be great. Thank you for your fine example of Christian service.

The story of Dayna and Heather has been repeated many times in the history of God's people. Satan has often tried to use force and brutality to close the mouths of Christ's faithful servants, but always, those efforts ultimately end in failure. God's Word will advance. It is God's plan for the world and it will happen. The blessed privilege is that God calls us into this service. Dayna's and Heather's situation may remind us of another time in the early years of the church when the faithful were commanded not to speak.

> "Then they called them in again and commanded them not to speak or teach at all in the name of Jesus. But Peter and John replied, 'Judge for yourselves whether it is right in God's sight to obey you rather than God. For we cannot help speaking about what we have seen and heard.'"
> - Acts 4:18-20

Yes, that is it. We cannot help but speak. We have to be salt. We have to be light. It is just as Jesus said and that brings us to our eighth and last important insight.

INSIGHT #8

The ultimate triumph over evil is repeated daily, from faith to faith, as God's children remain true to their mission and proclaim to the world the triumphant victory that is ours in Christ.

This Was Paul's Great Mission

If ever there was a man who was dedicated to this task, it was the Apostle Paul. From the day Christ confronted him on that road to Damascus, to the final breath he took, sharing the saving gospel of Jesus Christ was his foremost task in life. The resurrected Christ had completely changed him. Proclaiming the gospel had become his great mission in life.

"First, I thank my God through Jesus Christ for all of you, because your faith is being reported all over the world. God, whom I serve with my whole heart in preaching the gospel of his Son, is my witness how I constantly remember you in my prayers at all times; and I pray that now at last by God's will the way may be opened for me to come to you. I long to see you so that I may impart some spiritual gift to make you strong—that is, that you and I may be mutually encouraged by each other's faith. I do not want you to be unaware, brothers, that I planned many times to come to you (but have been prevented from doing so until now) in order that I might have a harvest among you, just as I have had among other Gentiles. I am obligated both to Greeks and non-Greeks, both to the wise and the foolish. That is why I am so eager to preach the gospel also to you who are at Rome."

– Romans 1:8-15

Victory over sin, over Satan, over death, over every evil was being realized throughout the world, already in Paul's day, because the saving gospel of Jesus Christ was being shared. Paul found ample reason to thank God, but especially for all the faithful. From one believer to the next, the gift of faith in Jesus Christ was "being reported all over the world."

We need to understand how remarkable all this was. In the span of approximately 30 years, the Christian church had gone from a small band of eleven frightened and discouraged disciples, to a worldwide movement of hundreds of courageous Christian men and women who were willing to face death rather than deny Christ and relinquish their faith. How did this happen? Primarily, there were two reasons for this remarkable transformation.

The first is the reality and power of Jesus' resurrection. The tomb was empty and the only explanation for it, that the opposition could come up with, was that a frightened group of weakling disciples had made it past the Roman guard and stolen Jesus body away. That lie never fit and everyone knew it then, as we know it today. Roman soldiers were not so inept, and these men were not so foolish as to be willing to suffer death for something they knew was a lie. The resurrected Jesus had appeared not only to a select few disciples but also "to over five hundred brothers at the same time" (I Corinthians 15:6). That resurrection changed lives and it is still changing lives today.

Secondly, the gospel was being shared in dramatic fashion. No one could keep quiet! The news just had to be shared. From faith to faith the proclamation of the gospel was changing lives so that by the time Paul wrote his letter to the Christians in Rome he could thank God that Christian faith was being reported all over the world!

For Paul, however, this still was not enough. In his opening remarks to these Christians at Rome, we see how locked and focused he was on this mission. He wrote in terms of serving God through "preaching the gospel." His mission was a mission of constant prayer for the saints. He prayed that his journeys might take him to places where he had not yet preached so that he might "impart some spiritual gift," even to those in Rome. His mission was to share his faith and he prayed that others would wholeheartedly share their faith as well. This would result in mutual edification and encouragement. He wanted this in order that a "harvest" might be realized for God. Faith repeatedly springs to life whenever and wherever the gospel is shared. "That is why," he wrote, "I am so eager to preach the gospel." That is why the church grew so rapidly. Paul and others like him found great desire and urgency to cast out their gospel nets. They had indeed become *fishers of men*.

This Is Our Mission: Prayer

Jesus Christ, the object of saving faith, defines our mission for us, just as He defined Paul's mission for him.

> "Go into all the world and preach the good news to all creation."
> - Mark 16:15

".... you will be my witnesses... to the ends of the
earth."
- Acts 1:8

For three years, Jesus prepared his disciples for this task.
He prepares us for this same task through the gift of His Word,
through Baptism, the Lord's Supper, and through faithful parents and teachers who share with us these life-giving truths.
We are given them not just for our own benefit but also for the
benefit of others so that many more might share the victory of
faith with us. This mission has been confirmed by the Apostles.

"But you are a chosen people, a royal priesthood, a
holy nation, a people belonging to God, that you may
declare the praises of him who called you out of darkness into his wonderful light. Once you were not a
people, but now you are the people of God; once you
had not received mercy, but now you have received
mercy."
- I Peter 2:9, 10

If God has chosen us, it is for a special purpose. If God calls
us priests, He has a special service for us to perform. If He has
made us a holy nation, it is to be set apart from the world by
offering something the rest of the world cannot give. God has
made us His own through faith and now He defines our mission for us, which is this: "declare the praises of him who called
you out of darkness into his wonderful light."

Our mission is carried out in a variety of ways. First, it is
often a mission of prayer. After September 11, the prayers of

the faithful went up in force. There is always a need for prayer but there was a great need for prayer on September 11 and in the days that have followed. There is the continuing need to turn to God and ask Him to care for all who are in want. God desires this from us. He warmly invites us,

> "Call upon me in the day of trouble; I will deliver you and you will honor me."
> - Psalm 50:15

We need to keep praying that God will heal the wounded, not only in body but also in spirit since September 11. We need to pray for families that have been devastated with sorrow by the loss of life. We need to pray that people come to know God in truth, through Jesus Christ, so that they too learn to whom they can pray. For God assures us that as we turn to Him in prayer, help and deliverance will come. As we watch Him respond to our many needs, we will find ample reason to thank Him and honor Him.

We need to pray for everyone, for rulers in our nation, and for peace in this world from one continent to the next.

> "I urge, then, first of all, that requests, prayers, intercession and thanksgiving be made for everyone—for kings and all those in authority, that we may live peaceful and quiet lives in all gentleness and holiness. This is good and pleases God our Savior, who wants all men to be saved and come to a knowledge of the truth."
> - I Timothy 2:1-4

Our mission as Christians is to pray for our President and Vice-President, their wives and families, and for all those who lead our nation. We need to pray that God will give them wisdom, courage, perseverance in the midst of this great struggle, and good health, so that as God's representatives, they are able to bring us safely out of this conflict. We need to pray the same for leaders of nations throughout the world so that by the efforts of all, peace might prevail over evil and hatred.

Prayer plays a very significant role in the Christian's mission. It is a constant and sometimes even silent, yet very powerful method of bringing to this world what it needs the most. We are reminded often in God's Word, that when we pray, we always need to pray that God's will be done. This can sometimes be hard, because it means yielding to God's answers to our prayers. Those answers are not always what we expect or even what we want. Yet, godly prayer trusts that His ways are best for us. Godly prayer relies on His infinite wisdom, when what He allows makes no sense to us at all. We see issues in this world dimly and with glasses that are tainted by sin. God is able to view the complete picture in its every intricate detail. Therefore, God reminds us that the faithful always pray according to God's will. This is, after all, the way Jesus taught us to pray.

"... your will be done on earth as it is in heaven."
- Matthew 6:10

"This is the assurance we have in approaching God: that if we ask anything according to his will, he hears us."
- I John 5:14

Does this mean that if we ask God for something that is contrary to His will, He does not hear us? No, He still hears but He is not attentive to our request. After all, why would He attend to something that He knows will only harm us, in the final analysis? Would any parent be attentive to the request of a child when they know that fulfilling the request would harm their child? Of course not. If we do not act that way with our own children, then why should we expect God to deal any differently with us? Parents find great delight in children who are not troublesome and argumentative, but trustingly submit to their parents' will for them. God delights when, in prayer, we willingly submit to His will for us. It is always for the best.

To this end, we need to pray for one another, that everyone would submit to God's will and trust that His ways will work a blessed purpose even through the most horrific acts of evil. We need to pray for healing, physically and spiritually.

> "Therefore confess your sins to each other and pray
> for each other so that you may be healed. The prayer
> of a righteous man is powerful and effective."
> - James 5:16

We have seen many ways in which Satan and his host will try to pull us away from God and entice us to turn away from Him. Since September 11, there is a need for healing among many. For many people, Satan is challenging faith in ways they have never experienced before. People are in need of our prayers so that healing will come and faith in God will be preserved and strengthened. This too is part of our Christian mission. We have God's assurance that the prayers of the righteous in Christ are "powerful and effective." We need to exercise the power that

God grants us through prayer.

We are taught in Holy Scripture that faith comes through hearing the message, so we need also to pray for the gospel, that this good news in Christ spreads. Even if, in the past, individuals responded to that message with resistance and unbelief, perhaps now, having been heard anew, it might awaken insights to God that were never known before. This can be a great blessing in the aftermath of the disaster on September 11.

> "Finally, brothers, pray for us that the message of the Lord may spread rapidly and be honored, just as it was with you."
> - II Thessalonians 3:1

> "Devote yourselves to prayer, being watchful and thankful. And pray for us too, that God may open a door for our message, so that we may proclaim the mystery of Christ, for which I am in chains. Pray that I may proclaim it clearly, as I should."
> - Colossians 3:2-4

I just read an article in the newspaper this morning about a man who had survived the WTC collapse and had been in Jerusalem over the last few days. While there, a suicide bomber had set off an explosive killing himself, another elderly individual, and injuring about a dozen others. This man, who had survived the WTC disaster, escaped death for a second time in only a few months. Now hospitalized in Jerusalem, he said that these events are giving him reason to pause and ponder why, on these occasions, he was spared, and what meaning this has for his life.

These kinds of stories and real life events are going to begin to materialize more and more as we move beyond 9-11. We need to pray that as people see these blessings materialize, they see the hand of God in their lives, and open their hearts more and more to Christ's great love for them. These are God-given doors of opportunity for us. Paul encourages us to be ever "watchful and thankful" so that when these opportunities come, we recognize them for what they are, answers to prayer. They are answers to what is to be an ongoing and special prayer on our part that God may open doors in people's lives where the precious gospel might be proclaimed and gladly received. Preservation of life, protection from physical disasters and from man's terrorist acts, times of need and times of want, periods of suffering and periods of unexpected joy—all of these, and many more like them, can be doors of opportunity that God places before us to share the saving gospel with others. We need to pray that more and more these doors might open in people's lives. We then need to be ready and willing to respond, with Christ's message of hope and joy, when they do.

This, after all, is why we pray, so that in every way possible, all people everywhere will be delivered from every form of evil, whether it is the evil within us or the evil that is so often very powerfully at work outside of us.

> "And pray that we may be delivered from wicked and evil men, for not everyone has faith. But the Lord is faithful, and he will strengthen and protect you from the evil one."
> - II Thessalonians 3:2, 3

As a nation and as individual citizens, we have been placed on a high state of alert to the ever-present danger of more terrorist attacks. There remain "wicked and evil men" out there who are bent on our destruction. This alone provides ample reason for us to pray. We need to pray for the preservation of life and the preservation of faith. We need to pray for the protection of individual people from further evil attacks and the protection of our nation as a whole.

Paul wrote, "Not everyone has faith." Not everyone will be guided by Christ's principles of love, mercy, and forbearance in the way that they deal with mankind. Evil remains in the world as a constant threat to faith and as a constant threat to life itself. However, this underscores not only why we should expect evil events to occur again, but also why we need to keep praying. The faithful need to pray because "not everyone has faith" and, therefore, not everyone will be praying! Therefore, we must! If we are not found praying powerful and effective prayers to the King of kings, then who will? God reminds us that the prayers of the righteous in Christ are critically important in addressing the spiritual and physical well being of people everywhere.

As we become active in this mission of prayer, we must not forget to be thankful to God for His many blessings and for the many ways in which He gives answer to our prayers, even in times of great suffering.

"Be joyful always; pray continually; give thanks in all circumstances, for this is God's will for you in Christ Jesus."
- I Thessalonians 5:16-18

When we look at the events of September 11, as horrifically evil as they are, some might find it difficult to remain joyful and some might find it difficult to give thanks to God. Yet, as has been noted earlier, there are many ways in which God's grace and His arm of protection was prevalent on September 11 and beyond. From firefighters and police officers to volunteers of all kinds, from brave citizens to leaders of our nation and those who serve in our armed forces, from disasters thwarted—some of which are known only to God Himself—to military battles won and faith strengthened, in all of these ways and many more like them, we find reason to give God thanks. He continues to serve, preserve, and protect us, and our nation, in a multitude of ways. He does so whenever days of evil come. He will continue to do so. Therefore, we always have reason to give thanks to Him.

It might also be helpful to understand that there is a difference between happiness and joy. We may not always be happy when the day of evil comes. Remember, even Jesus wept at the death of His dear friend Lazarus. Yet, we always have joy. In death, we find joy in Christ's promise of eternal life. In suffering, we find joy in Christ's promise that He is always with us to strengthen and to heal. Even in sorrow, we find joy and confidence in Christ's assuring word to us that He is able to work all things for our good. In everything, we may not find happiness, but we can find joy. Christ's many promises to us make it so. Faith will look to find that joy in Christ in every circumstance in life. Faith will find it, because God is always there at work in our lives. Our ever-present joy is found in the blessing of His constant presence.

This Is Our Mission: Sanctified Living

Possessing this kind of a thankful spirit, at all times and in all circumstances, is a special gift of God and not everyone has it. For those in Christ who live their lives in this way, there is not only great peace that is individually received, but a light is shining brightly for many others to see. This spirit of optimism and confidence in God, which is expressed in an unfailing spirit of thanksgiving, will be seen by the world. This too is part of our mission as Christians. Ours is a mission of **sanctified living**. We are to be visible in this way to the world. We are again reminded of Christ's words to us to be salt and light.

"In the same way, let your light shine before men, that they may see your good deeds and praise your Father in heaven."
- Matthew 5:16

Dayna Curry and Heather Mercer could have lived much safer lives while in Afghanistan. They could have gone as Christian aid workers but still lived only as "closet" Christians while they were there. Or could they? Of course they couldn't. Their love for the poor and needy, and their desire to help them, sprang from Christ's love for them. People naturally saw their good deeds and began asking what motivated them. People wanted to know what drove them to such fine service as this. They could not hide the news. They had to share what they knew to be true.

The Christian's mission in life is fulfilled in a very natural visibility to the world that is not so much purposeful as it is unavoidable. We need always to be mindful of this, for there are two very simple facts that will be forever true about how

319

people view Christians. First, people will often take special notice of Christians when they sin, but secondly, and what we often forget, is that they also will take special notice of them when they do well. That is true because when Christians do well, they usually do exceptionally well and that is noticed. This should not surprise us, especially when we realize that these works are not our own but God's works done through us.

When Christians sin, much is made of their transgressions. We might not like being more severely criticized for our shortcomings than others are for theirs. Yet, for us, whether this is right or wrong is not the issue. It is simply a fact that we must recognize as followers of Christ. Christ makes us visible when we come to faith. Expect sin in your life to be magnified when it happens. It is the cost of being visible and being a disciple.

However, when Christians excel in sanctified living, people will also sit up and take notice. I have seen it happen often and you have too. When Christ's undeserved love spills into, then over, and then out of our lives, people notice. Sometimes it manifests itself in a tremendous work of love, expression of mercy, or forgiveness toward someone. Sometimes it manifests itself in an especially high level of patience or perhaps constancy and perseverance in times of extreme duress. Sometimes it manifests itself in understanding, wisdom, or caring instruction and empathy. Sometimes it manifests itself in the highest level of service toward others in need, or as an especially high regard to our sense of duty toward mankind that translates into repeated acts of kindness. Christians are often very different people. They talk differently. They act differently. They may, under numerous circumstances, dress differently, and overall, just present themselves differently to the world in both body and spirit. They do this humbly, not to boast, not for show, and not to draw attention to themselves, but because this is simply who they are. They are different, just as Christ was different and therefore was noticed by this world when He lived here with us.

If we are firmly grounded in Christ by faith, He will be clearly seen in us by others around us, and we will appear as different people in this world. It is natural and it is what God wants to happen. For when we are visible and at our best, the light of Christ's love is visible through us. We have tremendous opportunities to let our light shine in a variety of ways throughout the course of our lives. September 11 is another of those opportunities and today, more than ever, people need the light of Christ's love to shine into their hearts. Let it happen through you.

Through faith in Christ, God has made us His children to be expressions of His love to the world. This is our mission. There is enough sin in the world. God wants there to be more of His love made known through us.

> "Above all, love each other deeply, because love covers over a multitude of sins. Offer hospitality to one another without grumbling. Each one should use whatever gift he has received to serve others, faithfully administering God's grace in its various forms."
> - I Peter 4:8-10

Love is able to "cover over a multitude of sins" in our lives because, for one, it prevents the harsh realities of sinful tendencies and attitudes within us from erupting into full-blown acts of evil and violent behavior. Even when sins are committed, Christ's love, shown through us, can be like a soothing ointment to take away the hurt and the sting.

September 11 has especially underscored the need for Christ's love in a world struggling with the ongoing presence of evil. People are hurting and in sorrow. They can find, in Christ's love, peace, hope, and rest. This violent expression of evil upon our nation has also threatened to evoke sinful expressions of hate, anger, and prejudice from us, against other people who are just as innocent as the victims of 9-11 are. If Christ's love is within us, it will even cover these potential sins and prevent such violent expressions of prejudice or anger from growing within us. Hospitality and service are the marks of Christ, not revenge, distrust, and hatred. We need Christ's love expressed through us today more than ever. Our mission of sanctified living in Christ is meant to be a blessing of helpfulness to anyone in need.

> "For the grace of God that brings salvation has appeared to all men. It teaches us to say, 'No' to ungodliness and worldly passions, and to live self-controlled, upright and godly lives in this present age, while we wait for the blessed hope—the glorious appearing of our great God and Savior, Jesus Christ, who gave himself for us to redeem us from all wickedness and to purify for himself a people that are his very own, eager to do what is good."
> - Titus 2:11-14

It was hard to control some emotions on September 11. It is still hard at times. Yet, God wants us to trust His wisdom and power so firmly that through all of this, we can be "self-controlled" in our response to everything that has happened.

I was struck by something God revealed to me the other day, as I was reading from the 10ᵗʰ chapter of Luke's Gospel. There, in verses 32 through 34, Jesus again predicted his suffering and death. He boldly announced to His disciples that they were heading up to Jerusalem where all these things would take place. The disciples, we are told, were "astonished" and others who followed were "afraid." Yet, knowing the great evil that was on the horizon, they went, "with Jesus leading the way." That is self-control in the face of evil.

God wants to develop that kind of self-control in us. Then we will be able to be of help to others. Jesus wants us to be the kind of people who, even in the face of great evil, are able to remain self-controlled and "eager to do what is good." He doesn't want us to compound the problem of evil in the world, but be part of the solution to the problem. Therefore, we are called upon to be kind in our dealings with one another.

> "Rejoice in the Lord always. I will say it again: Rejoice! Let your gentleness be evident to all. The Lord is near... whatever is true, whatever is noble, whatever is right, whatever is pure, whatever is lovely, whatever is admirable—if anything is excellent or praiseworthy—think about such things. Whatever you have learned or received or heard from me, or seen in me—put into practice."
> - Philippians 4:4-5, 8, 9

> "... live a life worthy of the calling you have received. Be completely humble and gentle; be patient, bearing with one another in love."
> - Ephesians 4:1, 2

Quite a task, isn't it? We are to take everything that is true, everything that is noble, everything that is right, pure, lovely, admirable, excellent, and praiseworthy; then take humility, gentleness, patience, and forbearance, and combine it all into one neat, beautiful package in us. That seems impossible, doesn't it? These traits may seem more like the opposite of what we are. Yet, combined, they are Jesus Christ. These traits are what He is.

These traits represent what we can be, when Christ lives in us and through us. When this happens, will it make a difference in people's lives today, after 9-11? Make it your mission to live such a sanctified life of kindness in Christ to others and watch the changes that come. God will work those changes in you and in others, through you.

This Is Our Mission: Proclamation

A mission that is of prayer and sanctified living is a great deal to try to accomplish in one's life. However, there is one more. Our mission is also one of proclamation. We are called by Christ to proclaim the truth of God's saving Word.

> "Preach the Word; be prepared in season and out of season, correct, rebuke and encourage—with great patience and careful instruction.... But you, keep your head in all situations, endure hardship, do the work of an evangelist, discharge all the duties of your ministry."
> - II Timothy 4:2, 5

Today, in the aftermath of September 11, we have the opportunity to proclaim God's Word "out of season." These events came upon us quite unexpectedly. Now, God wants us to speak out with the truth.

In the face of what is being said about God that is not true, He wants us to "correct" and set the record straight. In the face of what is spoken against God that would lead people to turn away from Him, He wants us to "rebuke" and declare as false. In the face of what is today, tremendous sorrow and loss, He wants us to use His Word to extend encouragement and hope, drawn from His truths. He wants us to do it carefully and patiently, knowing that in trying times like these, souls are bruised and tender. He does not want us to be rough in our presentation of the gospel, but blow as a gentle whisper the truth of Christ's love, so that weak faith is not snuffed out but softly flamed more brightly to life. Where there is unbelief and with it, hostility, anger, and resentment toward God for allowing these days to come, He wants us to carefully instruct and encourage with His truths, but all the while knowing that we may have to endure some hardships, rejection, and insults as we work.

This is but part of the faithful discharge of the duties of our ministry as Christ's ambassadors. It is what Christ endured in His ministry, with a kind, understanding, and forgiving heart. Jesus asks us to carry this same spirit into our ministry of proclamation today. We must "keep our heads" when the day of evil comes and speak not only the truth of Christ, but also speak with the spirit of Christ. Our mission is to bring hope from the dark, gloomy dungeons of despair and doubt.

"Always be prepared to give an answer to everyone who asks you to give the reason for the hope that you have. But do this with gentleness and respect."

- I Peter 3:15, 16

The events of September 11 continue to evoke the question, "Why?' We need to be ready to give answer. "Always be prepared," Peter encourages us here. That will be hard at times. To some things, there are no easy answers. However, note what God is telling us through the pen of this bold disciple. He is not telling us that we need to explain everything in life. We cannot. Some events remain locked in God's mysterious plan of salvation for the world and are known only to Him. However, what He does ask us to do is "to give the reason for the hope that you have," a hope that is still alive and well even though the events of September 11 confuse so many.

We too may be perplexed but we are not lost. We too may be saddened but we are not in despair. Our hope remains in Christ. He is our hope because He is our life in death, our salvation from sin, and our great deliverer from every snare of the evil one. This is good news that all of us can share, and do so gently and respectfully, even though we might be inclined to do otherwise when our faith is being questioned or challenged. We will remember Christ. We will give answer with His gentleness and His tender love. We will do it this way, because we know that we proclaim this gospel to bring the blessing of faith into the lives of others who need desperately to believe.

> "For I am not ashamed of the gospel, because it is the power of God for the salvation of everyone who believes: first for the Jew, then for the Gentile. For in the gospel a righteousness from God is revealed, a righteousness that is by faith from first to last, just

as it is written: 'The righteous will live by faith.'"
- Romans 1:16, 17

Faith—it is that one great gift of God that makes every other blessing from God our own. It is the shield that protects everything else.

Just think of it. You have the blessed privilege to work with God and to share in the salvation of everyone who believes, through the gospel message you proclaim. It does not end even in your lifetime. You can have an eternally important role to play in the victorious saving faith of people for years to come, and to the end of time, as others share what you first shared with them! This is a blessed honor and privilege from God, to be enlisted by Him in this mission of proclamation.

The triumphant victory over evil marches on through the ages, from one person's faith to the next. Are we too ashamed to speak this saving and victorious message? Never! It is "the power of God for the salvation of everyone who believes." After the terror of September 11, this is news that everyone needs to hear. When the day of evil comes, this is the message of triumph that must be shared!

> The ultimate triumph over evil is repeated daily, from faith to faith, as God's children remain true to their mission and proclaim to the world the triumphant victory that is ours in Christ.

The End of the Struggle: VICTORY!

There is a blessed end for the faithful in their struggle against evil's dark forces. The Apostle Paul wrote of it and eloquently, under inspiration of the Holy Spirit. He wrote these words near the end of his struggles with evil. We see his battle scars reflected in these words but even more powerfully, we see the shining glory of God's grace toward him in crowning him with victory at the end of his great struggle. By these words, we must live now, in the wake of September 11. By these words, we will live through eternity, for in them is told the story of the victory over evil that is ours through faith.

> "I have fought the good fight, I have finished the race, I have kept the faith. Now there is in store for me the crown of righteousness, which the Lord, the righteous Judge, will award to me on that day—and not only to me, but also to all who have longed for his appearing."
> - II Timothy 4:7, 8

Will there be another September 11? Faithful to our mission, we fervently pray that there will never be another day like that. Yet, only God knows for sure. Jesus has warned us that with the increasing passage of time, our days will grow darker.

Whatever comes to us in the near future or in the distant future, this much we know to be true: on the last day, evil's ugly attempt at conquest of this world will end. Through faith in Christ, all God's children will be brought into the eternal mansions Christ has prepared for them and there will be a new heaven and a new earth. This will be the home of God's elect. "The wolf will live with the lamb, the leopard will lie down with the goat, the calf and the lion and the yearling together; and a little child will lead them" (Isaiah 11:6). Then,

He will make all things new and "He will wipe every tear from their eyes. There will be no more death or mourning or crying or pain, for the old order of things has passed away" (Revelation 21:4).

We have this victory now, as much as faith has entered our lives and Christ has entered our hearts. The greater your faith, the more successful you will be in your daily struggle with evil when it comes.

Come it will, in all its fury. The God of our salvation is stronger than them all. So let Satan and his host come. We fear no evil. In Christ, the victory, through faith, is ours.

To God, In Christ, Be The Glory!

ISBN 155369890-8

9 781553 698906